MENSWEAR
BUSINESS TO STYLE

MICHAEL P. LONDRIGAN

LIM, THE COLLEGE FOR
THE BUSINESS OF FASHION

FAIRCHILD BOOKS, INC.
NEW YORK

Director of Sales and Acquisitions: Dana Meltzer-Berkowitz
Executive Editor: Olga T. Kontzias
Senior Development Editor: Jennifer Crane
Development Editor: Joseph Miranda
Assistant Development Editor: Blake Royer
Art Director: Adam B. Bohannon
Production Director: Ginger Hillman
Senior Production Editor: Elizabeth Marotta
Associate Production Editor: Andrew Fargnoli
Associate Art Director: Erin Fitzsimmons
Project Manager: Ron Edwards,
    Focus Strategic Communications
Development Editors: Linda Aspen-Baxter, Ron Edwards
Photo Research and Permissions: Ellen Barrett Dudley,
    Matthew J. Dudley
Copyeditor: Susan McNish
Cover Design: Erin Fitzsimmons
Cover Art: Veer
Text Design: Tom Helleberg

Library of Congress Catalog Card Number: 2007942716
ISBN: 978-1-56367-559-1
GST R 133004424

Printed in the United States of America

CH13, TP09

CONTENTS

EXTENDED CONTENTS

2. CUSTOMER DEMOGRAPHICS

3. DESIGN

10. SPORTSWEAR

11. TRENDS IN THE MENSWEAR MARKET

12. SUPPORTING CAST

PREFACE

Think fashion, and menswear is probably not the first thought that comes to mind. More often than not your first thought will most likely be about women's wear, as this dominates the fashion scene. That is why many courses taught on our campuses across the country focus on the women's market. This text was developed to introduce the fashion student to a vibrant and exciting menswear market.

The menswear industry has undergone tremendous change in the past several decades. We have witnessed changes in fashion as well as the buying habits of consumers. New designers and private-label programs have invigorated the menswear business, giving birth to color direction and style changes rivaling women's wear.

Menswear: Business to Style introduces the reader to the menswear business, looking at history, demographics, design, manufacturing, retailing, the media, trends, and key organizations that support the industry—all interacting to create an interesting, challenging, and profitable business model.

Chapter 1 begins with a brief history of menswear, looking at garments from as far back as ancient Greece and linking them to current styles. The chapter also looks at how events in history have helped to shape what we wear, and it investigates popular culture and its effect on trends.

Chapter 2 opens with a discussion of demographics as they relate to the menswear industry. We also introduce the topic of psychographics, which I liken to the "why men buy what they buy" aspect of the business, and attempt to shed some light on this complex subject. We then focus on age as a key determinant in the demographic profile, explaining why men wear what they do at various stages in their lives.

Chapter 3 discusses the role of the designer—where designers get their inspirations and how they go about planning a line. While looking at the design process, students are introduced to fibers and textiles that are important to the menswear market. In addition, the topic of licensing as a marketing tool for the menswear market is introduced and discussed, as well as reasons for entering into a licensing agreement.

Chapter 4 takes the reader into the world of manufacturing, looking at the various sourcing options open to a company that produces menswear. Quality control and the use of technology are introduced as well as research techniques employed by designers and product developers.

Chapter 5 starts us on the path to understanding the importance of the retail community, from its origins to its current state. The various retail outlets available to sell and market menswear are explored, and the importance of each is discussed. In this chapter we also look at the use of technology at the retail level.

Chapter 6 focuses on the important role the media plays in creating an interesting and exciting platform for menswear companies to express themselves. The different forms of media are reviewed, and we look at differences between public relations and advertising as they are used to market and sell menswear products.

In **Chapter 7**, we start to get more product-specific, looking at the various classifications of tailored clothing. Once these classifications are identified, the text examines specific design features while discussing differences between tailored clothing and tailored outerwear.

Chapter 8 introduces the reader to the men's furnishings department by discussing the various products that make up this area. Merchandising techniques unique to the furnishings market are investigated, and specific design features are revealed.

Chapter 9 takes the reader into the world of formal wear, starting with a look at the origins of the tuxedo. From there, the text discusses specific design features while explaining differences in the formal wear market.

Chapter 10 brings the student into the world of sportswear by looking at the elements that make up this category and by discussing the various classifications within it. In addition, key silhouettes are studied and changes in style reviewed.

Chapter 11 is all about trends. The text introduces the idea of what a trend is by illustrating some of the current trends in the market. The text is but a snapshot in time, and so these trends are presented strictly as examples to show the student what is considered a trend, and the importance of trends to the market. As the chapter points out, by the time this text is printed, the fickle consumer will quite possibly have moved on to the next big trend.

The final chapter, **Chapter 12**, highlights some of the supporting cast that makes up the menswear industry. This is by no means a definitive list, but is made up of many of the associations and organizations that I have had the good fortune to be involved in on some level. I have listed these "supporting" organizations because of their contribution to the richness of the menswear market and because they are excellent sources of information for anyone interested in expanding their knowledge of menswear.

In introducing this dynamic, multi-faceted business we call menswear, the book incorporates real-life examples and experiences of the author to help students gain a better understanding of how the menswear market operates and how they can become a part of this business if they choose. I have included personal anecdotes in the form of sidebars to convey my own experiences, sharing some of the things that I enjoyed and showing the humorous side of the business.

ACKNOWLEDGMENTS

I would like to dedicate this textbook to my Mom and Dad; I know they would be very proud if they were here today.

To my loving wife, Marie; none of this would be possible if she had not encouraged, guided, and been there for me on our life journey together. To my son, Paul, and daughter, Leah, for their love and support, and to all those who have helped in the process along the way—I couldn't have done it without you!

Olga Kontzias, Jennifer Crane, Joseph Miranda, all with Fairchild Publications; Ron and Adrianna Edwards, Matthew and Ellen Dudley, Linda Aspen-Baxter, and Susan McNish, all with Focus Strategic Communications; Professor Guy Adamo and to all my colleagues at Berkeley College whom I have had the good fortune to work with in the past; and to all those many people who have crossed my path in my menswear career here in the United States and around the globe, I thank you.

ONE

MENSWEAR—THE PAST

IN THIS CHAPTER, YOU WILL LEARN
THE FOLLOWING:

- how men's fashions of the past influence men's
  fashions of the present
- how various events in history helped shape men's
  fashions
- the ways in which popular culture influences men's
  fashions

The title of this chapter is "Menswear—The Past." The question is posed, where did it all begin? "At first, men created clothing that proclaimed their rank, occupation, warrior status, or leadership role. They also dressed to look sexually attractive and to achieve personal gratification. The modern era brought new considerations to bear on the image of masculinity, along with a more subdued, conventional approach to apparel and a ceding of fashion supremacy to women" (New York Public Library, p. 1). Let us look to the past for clues to our current fashions.

We can trace the history of menswear back to the Greeks, Romans, Saxons, and Normans, up through medieval times and right into the twenty-first century. Volumes have been written on this subject. However, for our purposes and to provide a glimpse into the past, we will take a historical tour highlighting key elements from various periods that have had major influences on menswear. Our tour will concentrate

Figure 1.1 *The figure on the left is wearing a short chiton; a round fibulae on the wearers' right shoulder holds the garment closed. A himation is worn by the figure on the right.*

on the styles of the twentieth and twenty-first centuries. Clearly, the most intriguing and influential time period was the twentieth century, and it continues to affect the way we dress today.

In our journey through time, we will identify individual garments that became the building blocks of fashion. In one form or another, these garments have lasted throughout the ages. As we begin our tour, remember that there were no name-brand designers, no retailers, and no manufacturers until technology took hold during the nineteenth and twentieth centuries. Before that, all garments were hand sewn.

ANCIENT GREEKS, FIFTH CENTURY BC

Our fashion tour through history starts with the ancient Greeks. The dress of the day was a linen tunic known as a **chiton**. This garment was usually long with pleats, and it sometimes had braids at the neckline and seams. A garment called the **himation** was worn over the chiton. The himation, also known as a cloak, was joined at the shoulder by a pin called a **fibulae** (see Figure 1.1).

ANCIENT ROMANS, FIRST TO FIFTH CENTURIES

One does not have to be a student of history to recognize the Roman **toga**. This article of clothing, popularized by actor John Belushi in the 1978 movie *Animal House,* remains a fraternity/sorority favorite on many college campuses today.

What was the toga of the ancient Romans? It started out as many yards of fabric that draped around the body in folds. It formed a short sleeve on the right arm, which remained uncovered, while it covered the left arm to the wrist. There was even enough fabric to form a hood, if the need arose. Was this the first "hoodie"?

SAXONS AND NORMANS, FIFTH TO FOURTEENTH CENTURIES

Little changed from the time of the ancient Romans to the Saxons and Normans. Dress remained quite simple, with linen still the fabric of choice for the upper class and wool for the masses. The wool and linen used to make these garments was gathered by hand and homespun. Remember, this was well before any equipment was used to spin wool and linen; production of textiles remained a home industry for many centuries, and garments were hand sewn. The linen was derived from the stalk of the flax plant, and the wool came from the local herd of sheep.

Short tunics were worn with large neck openings and side slits to allow for movement. The edges were decorated with embroidery. The tunic was sometimes worn with a girdle. The narrow belt-like girdle around the waist was not just for fashion; it also served a practical purpose. It was used to support a pouch wallet or, if the wearer was a member of the nobility, perhaps a sword or dagger. For special ceremonial events, the tunic was longer, approximately ankle length, and was called an over-tunic. The over-tunic usually had no sleeves.

By the Middle Ages, the **super-tunic** was introduced which generally came to the knees.

Figure 1.2 Soldiers and the masses wore tunics as their sole garment. Sleeveless tunics were called **dalmatica.** Both the toga and the tunic were usually made from wool and were decorated with edge stitching to indicate the wearer's profession.

Figure 1.3 By the Middle Ages, the loose-fitting toga had given way to the tunic, which was worn closer to the body.

This garment was shorter than tunics prior to the Middle Ages and worn over another tunic. It had sleeves that ended in a bell shape with a turned-back cuff.

Cloaks and **mantles** were added during the Middle Ages. These garments were often embroidered and fastened at the right shoulder with a clasp or brooch. Cloaks and mantles were generally square or rectangular, and they varied in length. The large circular cape had a hole in the center for the head and was caught at the side by a long ribbon, which was then attached to clasps placed on either side of the front of the garment, allowing the garment to fall in folds. Braes or breeches were also introduced during this period. These garments were made of linen, wool, or cotton and were tied at the ankle and bound to the thighs.

MEDIEVAL, TWELFTH TO FIFTEENTH CENTURIES

Fashion changed little between the twelfth and fifteenth centuries. Tunics became slightly closer fitting, while skirts, which were worn by men as the lower part of the tunic, were shorter and slit to the thigh (see Figure 1.4). The skirts were joined below the waistline to the top of the tunic. Only men and women of the upper classes were allowed to wear them. They were generally made of costly silks and embroidered with gold thread and decorated with precious stones.

The super-tunic was lined with fur in colder climates. The basic tunic, although relatively unchanged, became known as the **cote**, and the super-tunic was called the **surcote**. This style

Figure 1.4 The later Middle Ages saw the development of closer-fitting tunics with short skirts, often slit to the thigh.

became less popular when the **tabard** came into favor. A tabard had no sleeves and reached the calves. It was open at the sides and fastened at the waist by clasps.

With the coming of the fourteenth century, garments became shapelier to better reveal the leg wear. Around the fourteenth century, a **doublet** or **gipon** replaced the tunic. The doublet was a man's snug-fitting full-buttoned front jacket. It was worn over the undershirt and cut to fit the body closely and was closed down the front with laces or buttons.

Other garments that evolved during this period are described in Table 1.1.

Figure 1.5 *A surcote (or surcoat) was a long tunic often worn over armor.*

	TABLE 1.1. GARMENTS OF TWELFTH TO THE FIFTEENTH CENTURIES	

GARMENT	DESCRIPTION
Cote-hardie	Close-fitting, knee-length overgarment buttoned down the front; elbow-length sleeves with a long extension consisting of fabric hanging down the back as a short tongue or flap
Jacket	Short body garment; an outer garment worn after 1450; replaced the cote-hardie
Jerkin	Worn over a doublet, sometimes with huge funnel-shaped hanging sleeves; replaced the cote hardie
Houpplelande	Introduced around 1380; a flowing gown falling in folds from shoulder to the ground with very wide sleeves; in 1450, the term *houpplelande* was discarded in favor of the term *gown*
Cloak and mantle	With hood attached, used as outerwear during this period; generally worn for warmth and while traveling

As is evident from the garments mentioned above, we are starting to get to a stage where the garments worn by men had some bearing on today's fashions. Let us continue our journey through time.

Around the time of Henry VIII of England (1491–1547), fashion continued to change, but at a slow pace. The doublet remained close fitting, and, overall, men's garments became shorter. One addition to the doublet was the **stomacher,** which was a front chest piece covering a low-fronted garment. The stomacher was the forerunner of something that is still used today on most woven dress shirts and sport shirts—that is, the **placket,** or **plackard,** as it was also known. Plackets run down the front of the shirt where the buttons are placed.

The style of the doublet started to undergo changes due to military influence. Examples of these changes included the following:

- o   detachable sleeves
- o   rolls of fabric at the armhole
- o   padded sleeves
- o   sleeves fixed with wire or bone, known as **farthingale sleeves**

Petticoats for men also came into fashion. The petticoat was a short, waist-length, coat-like garment worn between the doublet and shirt. Its main purpose was to provide warmth; it later evolved into the

Figure 1.6 *The double-breasted frock coat was common by the nineteenth century. These outer garments had buttons and pockets.*

waistcoat. Gowns continued to be worn over doublets.

Our tour cannot neglect accessories, or furnishings, as they would formally be called later in history. Some important styles, such as hose, hats, collar ruffs, cravats, and gloves, were introduced in the sixteenth century. Men began wearing hose in various shapes and forms, starting in medieval times. The wearing of hose continued into the seventeenth century, with the addition of the garter, which was worn to keep the hose in place.

EIGHTEENTH CENTURY

The beginning stages of industrialization brought about several changes in how garments were made. These changes included the following:

- the standardization of sizes
- more efficient methods of making clothes
- fabrics that were easier to weave as a result of new equipment and improved yarn-spinning techniques

The double-breasted coat was worn by the common folk, while a person of higher social stature wore a suit consisting of a frock or coat, waistcoat, and breeches. Coats varied in length; the big advancement was buttons. Pockets were added at this time, with or without flaps.

Frock coats were loose fitting with turned-down collars. Apparel began to serve more utilitarian purposes. The working class took to wearing frocks to protect their clothes from dirt, while members of the upper class wore them for riding. The frock was quite similar to the coat, but it was cut bigger to allow more room for movement. In the late eighteenth century, the double-breasted version of the frock coat was introduced and remained popular well into the next century.

Waistcoats, precursors to the modern vest, were close fitting and reached above the knee. Originally, they had three-quarter length sleeves; later, they had no sleeves. Waistcoats could be single breasted or double breasted.

Figure 1.7 *Waistcoats were originally close-fitting garments that reached above the knee in either single- or double-breasted styles. They were the precursor to the modern vest.*

NINETEENTH CENTURY

In the nineteenth century, a clearer picture of menswear started to emerge. Several different types of coats dominated the landscape. **Skirted coats** had tails at the back divided by a vent and pleated tops with buttons on the hips (see Figure 1.8). These coats were made in single- and double-breasted models.

The frock coat was single breasted and buttoned from the neck down to the waist. The **tailcoat** or **morning coat** was usually double breasted, although for evening wear, some of the styles were single breasted. The collar was high in the back and low in the front to form a V shape, while the waistcoat was short with wide tails. An extra buttonhole was included at the top of the lapel on the wearer's left side, which was used to hold a flower.

In the late nineteenth century the term *loungewear* was introduced. Loungewear at that time was very formal compared to what we would call loungewear today. It consisted

Figure 1.8 *Skirted coats had tails at the back divided by a vent and pleated tops with buttons on the hips.*

of a jacket with matching trousers; this was the forerunner of the nested suit (jacket and pants sold together on the same hanger), which will be discussed in Chapter 7. The fit became more focused on the body contours, and side seams and darts were incorporated into sewing techniques.

Also in the nineteenth century, the "tweed side" lounge jacket was introduced from Scotland. The styling of this jacket consisted of a single-breasted model with a small collar, short lapels, and patch pockets. Around the middle of the century, a double-breasted style of the lounge jacket was developed, which became known as the reefer or pea coat. Today we still refer to "reefers" and "pea coats"; however, now they refer not to loungewear but tailored outerwear.

Several other versions of the lounge jacket appeared on the scene with names like the Prince of Wales and the Norfolk. Each were slight variations on the original. By the end of the nineteenth century, the lounge jacket had become the most popular style.

The one item with which men could readily express their fashion sense was the waistcoat,

Figure 1.9 *The Norfolk jacket, like those worn by the figures in the foreground, is a belted garment with pleats in the front and rear. It is one of the most popular types of lounge jackets.*

which could be highly decorative. Waistcoats were generally made out of richly embroidered fabrics; the embroidery was all hand stitched at that time. Like the waistcoats of the previous century, these could be found in both single- and double-breasted models; they could have notched or rolled lapels and two pockets, sometimes on the same side—one chest pocket and one waist pocket. Lapels will be more fully discussed in Chapter 7.

In the nineteenth century, terms such as *formal wear, sportswear, outdoor wear,* and *leg wear* came into use, and menswear started to move into categories that are still used in fashion today. Embroidered velvet jackets were the look in formal wear. Traditional styles gave way to a single-breasted jacket with no tails, tight black trousers, and a satin waistcoat. This look coincided with the naming of the **tuxedo**. The birthplace of the tuxedo was, in fact, Tuxedo Park, New York. There, it was first worn by Griswold Lorillard (son of wealthy tobacco magnate Pierre Lorillard), in 1886—although some people credit James Brown Potter of Tuxedo Park as the inventor. Formal wear, including the tuxedo, will be covered in greater depth in Chapter 9.

Sportswear included smoking jackets, which were fairly short and usually made of velvet or a quilted material.

Hunting coats resembled short frock coats with deep, flapped pockets. The hunting coat was usually worn with knickerbockers, knee-length trousers that sometimes fastened at the knee. Football outfits consisted of striped

(a)

(b)

Figure 1.10 The tuxedo is the most popular form of formal wear. It consists of a jacket (single or double breasted) and matching pants, often with satin lapels and matching satin stripes down the outer seams of the pant legs. A vintage tuxedo is shown in *(a)* and a modern example in *(b)*.

jerseys, knickerbockers, and stockings. These outfits were not so dissimilar to what can be seen on any weekend all around the country during football season.

During the nineteenth century, the development of waterproof fabrics supported the development of **outdoor wear,** or what we call outerwear today. These styles consisted of a **greatcoat** or **overcoat,** which reached the knee or ankle. It was single breasted with a button front and flapped pockets. Waterproof fabrics gave rise to several styles of outerwear, including the **Taglioni,** the **Petersham,** and the more popular **chesterfield coat.** The signature feature of the chesterfield was the fly front. The **ulster** was another popular model; it had a detachable hood and it was buttoned. The chesterfield coat will be discussed further in Chapter 7.

Figure 1.11 Smoking jackets were fairly short and usually made of velvet or a quilted material.

Up to this point, we have glimpsed menswear through history from ancient Greece to the nineteenth century and looked at articles of clothing that set the stage for what was to come. In subsequent chapters, we will examine the twentieth century up to our own time in greater depth.

The twentieth century was a time of enormous change and innovation, including in menswear. To organize the material, we have arbitrarily designated two time periods: 1900 to 1949 and 1950 to the present, moving from the twentieth century and into the twenty-first century.

(a)

(b)

Figure 1.12 *The original greatcoat was a garment made of waterproof fabric that usually reached the knee or ankle. It was single breasted with a button front and flapped pockets;* **(a)** *shows a chesterfield coat;* **(b)** *shows an ulster greatcoat.*

TWENTIETH CENTURY

EARLY TO MID-TWENTIETH CENTURY (1900–1949)

The defining style of the first half of the twentieth century is the suit, which was adopted by the middle class. Worn in the early twentieth century as everyday wear, this style became the uniform of the day for office workers in the later part of the century. Today's business suit is a clear outgrowth of the early suit and is still a must-have item in any man's wardrobe. Styles included single-breasted and double-breasted models, and they could be found in checks, tweeds, stripes, and solids. Regardless of a man's ethnic background or financial status, the central item in his wardrobe was a suit. Remember, casual clothes as we know them today were not common, and men wore suits for leisure as well as work. Whether one grew up in the United States or immigrated here, the easiest way to gain respect in society was to wear a suit.

MID-TWENTIETH CENTURY TO TURN OF THE CENTURY (1950–PRESENT)

The second period, from 1950 until today, can be categorized as the **casual years**. After World War II, Americans started to enjoy a period of revitalization, and men found themselves with more leisure time. Influences on menswear included the following:

- Military styling inspired many of the fashions of the times, and men began to wear items such as berets, duffel coats, bomber jackets, chinos, and cargo pants.
- Music influenced the fashion scene as well, with Elvis Presley leading the way. Elvis borrowed looks from various places and was well known for his tight-fitting pants coupled with jackets and ties.
- Movies also started to energize fashion. For example, in 1954's *The Wild One*, Marlon Brando's character wore a black leather biker jacket, white T-shirt, and oversized cap. Fans immediately began to copy Brando, creating a demand for the styles he wore in the movie.
- René Lacoste first created his famous **polo shirt** in 1933, but it was not until 1952 that it went on sale in the United States. Lacoste was a famous French tennis player and businessman who was nicknamed "the crocodile" or "the alligator" for his tenacious style of play on the court. Today,

Figure 1.13 (a) Elvis Presley, a musical icon of the 1950s, wearing his trademark tight pants and single-breasted sport coat. (b) Marlon Brando's "bad-boy" image inspired a generation with his leather biker jacket and cuffed denim jeans.

(a)

(b)

(a)

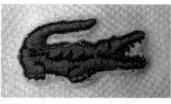

(b)

Figure 1.14 René Lacoste (right) after winning a tennis match *(a)*. His nickname, "the alligator," became the logo and trademark for the Lacoste brand *(b)*.

his namesake knit polo shirts are still popular and retail for about $80 each—a far cry from the humble beginnings of the early Lacoste polo shirt that retailed for under $10.

The Mod movement of the 1960s was yet another source of fashion inspiration. "The **Mods** (a term derived from the word *modernist*) were an essentially urban movement, and were rivals to the generally more rural biker gangs known as 'rockers.' Mod music was drawn from rhythm and blues and from Black culture" (Harris & Brown, 2003, p. 28). Mod fashion was strongest in London, which was considered the international center of men's fashions in the 1960s. This was a time for experimentation in fashion, and new designers were drawn to the London scene. The styles being created for men were considered new and innovative. Nothing was off limits. Designers such as Pierre Cardin and Nino Cerruti came of age in the 1960s.

Music and styles were also influenced by artists such as the Beatles and Bob Dylan. The Beatles made it cool to wear longer hair and clothing that went against the so-called establishment, such as Nehru jackets and wild-colored shirts. The Beatles also gave rise to a whole generation of men wearing Sergeant Pepper outfits. As for Bob Dylan, his casual laid-back look of jeans and denim jacket was the epitome of style during the 1960s.

How can we forget the hippie movement of the 1960s? The Vietnam War was unpopular, and it spawned an entire generation who used fashion as well as their voices to convey their messages. Second-hand clothes, military surplus, and, of course, denim jeans and T-shirts became the prominent fashion statement of the times.

In tailored clothing, suits remained somewhat conservative. The only noticeable change occurred in the lapels of suits, which got very wide. Ties widened as well. A high point of the hippie movement took place in 1969, with the Woodstock music festival. The documentary film *Woodstock* is worth viewing as it shows a mass of humanity in the fashion of the day.

The 1970s was the counterculture decade, notable for its sexual freedom, music, and new fashions for men. This was a time of exaggeration. Lapels on jackets were extremely wide. Men wore platform shoes, which were sometimes several inches high. Bell bottom pants were greatly exaggerated; some called them "elephant bells." The unisex styling that had started in the 1960s continued into the 1970s. It was a time of confusion with no real trends emerging. Punk rock, disco, and alternative rock were all competing on the

Figure 1.15 *The late 1960s was a time for men to experiment with fashion. The rules of style went out the window, and long hair, torn jeans, and T-shirts were the uniform of the day.*

same stage, each with their own distinct fashions. The punk rockers were into wild hair and even wilder clothes with ripped jackets and tight-fitting pants and no color story to speak of. The disco guys were all dolled up in jackets and ties with a black and white color story dominating the scene, punctuated by woven polyester printed shirts, while the alternative rock groups were somewhere in between disco and punk rock.

Designer jeans created by the likes of Ralph Lauren, Giorgio Armani, and Calvin Klein became a status symbol for men. Knitted tops became popular during 1970s and '80s in various styles, such as crew necks, boat necks, collar and placket models, and tank tops, and, of course, the ever-popular turtleneck. Knit tops could be worn as stand-alone pieces, or they could be used as layering pieces.

Jeans and T-shirts still dominated, although the sweat suit began to make a strong move in fashion. The sweat suit was typically knitted from fleece, but it was also available in terry and velour. It became a common sight among youth, and it also became so popular with older adults that the garments were nicknamed "mall walkers." Athletic shoes manufactured by companies such as Nike, Reebok, adidas Group, New Balance, Saucony, and Converse became the footwear of choice. (Chuck Taylor, one of the great basketball players of the 1920s, was the first person to ever enter into a formal licensing agreement, and Converse, which is now owned by Nike, still bears his name.)

In the 1980s the term *yuppie* was coined to describe "upwardly mobile young professionals." Spending on fashion was on the rise. Torn jeans became a fashion statement, although they were different from the ripped jeans that came into fashion again in the 2000s. The holes in the jeans in the 1980s were self-created; the mass-produced jeans available in the 2000s are manufactured with holes already in them. There is a saying that fashion repeats itself; ripped jeans are a classic example of a popular fashion from the 1980s that came back in 2005. The only difference is that, later, thousands of workers in factories all over the world were actually paid to put holes in the jeans.

During this decade designers Perry Ellis, Donna Karan, Ron Chereskin, Gianni Versace, and Tommy Hilfiger entered the fashion scene. Each of these designers brought something

THE BARNEY'S EXPERIENCE

I remember 1976 in particular. I had just gotten married wearing a beige tuxedo with brown platform shoes. Color was finding its way into menswear and was starting to show up in many different aspects, from formal wear to casual wear. It was the same year that I had graduated college and I was confronted with the specter of having to buy a new suit to wear while looking for a job. Not knowing much about fashion back then, especially about tailored clothing, I asked around and was told that Barney's in Manhattan was the place to go. So, off I went to Barney's, where I picked out a killer beige double-breasted signature Pierre Cardin suit, wide lapels and all. I paid $250 for the suit, which was big bucks back then. I proudly wore the suit to the interview and I got the job. I kept that suit for the next 25 years. Not that I wore it for all that time, mind you, but
(continued)

different to fashion. Versace brought high-priced sportswear. Perry Ellis presented more mainstream, moderately priced looks. Ron Chereskin is known for his comfortable men's cotton briefs. Donna Karan created dressy sportswear with a department store distribution. Tommy Hilfiger ran the gamut from street and urban wear to tailored clothing.

World events over the last 20 years of the twentieth century also helped to shape fashion. These events include the following:

- the collapse of the Soviet Union
- the Gulf War
- the establishment of the **North American Free Trade Agreement (NAFTA)**
- the Uruguay Round of the **General Agreement on Tariffs and Trade (GATT)**, announcing the end of quotas

These are just a few examples of events around the globe that had an effect on fashion. For example, GATT and NAFTA helped open trade among countries, and the new access to cheaper labor brought about by such agreements enabled designers and manufacturers to create products that consumers might have regarded as too expensive in the past. Events such as the Gulf War and the collapse of the Soviet Union also created opportunities for designers to draw on influences that were not readily available in the past. The Gulf War brought a new color scheme to the military fatigue look—desert sand versus the olive drab green that was so popular earlier. The fall of the Soviet Union gave the industry access to styles and designs that had been

it was such a beautiful suit; it had Pierre's name stitched in gold lettering inside the jacket. I could not stand to part with it until 1993.

Should you ever get to the museum at the Fashion Institute of Technology, you will find my suit hanging there with other famous designer clothes that have been donated over the years. Successfully donating to this museum is no easy feat as you have to submit the article of clothing to a committee and they vote on whether to accept the garment or not. I think it was the story about the job interview that sealed the deal. (See Figure 1.16.)

Figure 1.16 Double-breasted worsted wool Pierre Cardin signature suit purchased by the author in 1976 from Barney's New York. It now hangs in the museum at the Fashion Institute of Technology.

hidden from the West for decades, and it also opened up opportunities for manufacturing. GATT and NAFTA will be discussed further in Chapter 4.

I first encountered the leisure suit while working for JCPenney as a catalog inventory control specialist. I had just been transferred into subdivision 526, which I guess was a precursor to a men's sportswear department, as it seemed that any apparel product that did not fit into a neat category such as suits, sport shirts, etc. wound up there.

The leisure suit had taken the country by storm. Men of all ages adopted the style as it gave them a fashion freedom not known before. The leisure suit was made out of 100 percent double knit polyester and came in colors that were new to the men's market, such as maize, powder blue, and mint green. But as quickly as the fashion started, the bottom fell out of the stock market. The textile mills and the apparel manufacturers loved the suits because the fabric ran easily on the machines, the

(continued)

garments were easy to construct and, of course, all were made in the United States back then.

As an inventory specialist it was my responsibility to advise the buyer on reorder issues and I had a bad feeling about the last order the buyer wanted to place, an additional 100,000 suits for immediate delivery. I cautioned that I thought the trend was changing, and, sure enough, as soon as those suits showed up in our catalog distribution centers the demand dropped to nothing and we had to liquidate every last piece. Given the nature of the polyester from the 1970s, those suits are still around. You can still find some older gentlemen, usually in Las Vegas or Atlantic City, wearing one of the now infamous leisure suits. If you are curious you can probably purchase one on eBay!

Other events that helped shape fashion include the following:

- the O. J. Simpson trial
- the scandal involving President Clinton and Monica Lewinsky
- the return of Hong Kong to China
- Federated Department Stores' purchase of Macy's after it went into bankruptcy

Each of these events in some way had a direct or indirect effect on fashion. The trial of O. J. Simpson saw a boost in Bruno Magli shoes and leather gloves. When Monica Lewinsky was on the nightly news, the beret was repopularized. The turnover of Hong Kong to China led to a flood of cheaper imports. Federated's purchase of Macy's changed the landscape of the department stores and breathed new life into designer collections and labels that were sold in those stores.

More specifically, fashion for men saw the grunge look, flannel shirts and jeans, Dr. Martens, the hip-hop style characterized by baggy jeans, oversized shirts, and Timberland boots. All of these styles were seen not only in the big cities but throughout the country, thanks in part to mass media. Sellers of used and vintage clothing, such as Goodwill, the Salvation Army, and consignment shops, saw an upswing in business as styles headed for the retro look.

Casual Fridays took hold in a major way during the 1990s, and soon expanded to the rest of the week, with button-down dress shirts and sport shirts, khakis, and loafers becoming the uniform of the day. There was still a strong tailored clothing business, but there was a fundamental shift in the way men were dressing, resulting in many new business opportunities for manufacturing and retailing companies.

For many men, this was the first time they actually had to think about getting dressed in the morning to go to work. Imagine a man who had been wearing a suit every workday for 20 years suddenly needing a casual outfit to wear to work. As a suit wearer, he probably had five or more suits. He wore a different one each weekday and varied them with accessories. He knew which tie went with which suit and which shirt to wear. Suddenly, he had choices. What color khakis should he choose? Which dress shirt or sport shirt should he wear? Which shoes should he wear with the khakis and dress shirt or sport shirt? Should they be knit or woven? He even had to choose his socks. What color should they be?

Designer influences included Richard Tyler, Joseph Abboud, Isaac Mizrahi, Todd Oldham, John Galliano, Jill Sander, and Hugo Boss, along with the names mentioned previously that still had thriving businesses. These designers brought new looks to menswear. Each had their own signature style and all were in the moderate to upper price points. Their fashions were available in the better department stores and fine specialty stores around the country, and it was a sign of style and taste to wear one of their garments. The looks that these designers created had a European flair with a body-conscious fit and used color to create unique looks. As a group, they were not afraid to explore style possibilities that would compliment the male figure nor were they afraid to use colors that were not normally available from the mainstream retailers.

The year 2000 brought a new century, a new war, world terrorists, and George Bush Jr. as president. Technology was changing rapidly—from the Internet to high-definition TV and radio to cell phones that could do almost anything. In response, designers started to create garments to serve specific purposes, such as carrying cell phones and iPods. One company, PopXpress, has even developed a product called the iBoxer, which comes in different models designed to hold the various sizes of iPods.

The casualization of America continued at a strong pace. More and more companies went casual. JCPenney appointed a new chief executive officer from outside the company for the first time. Mike Ullman decided that everyone should "dress like Mike," and that, of course, was casual. This directive is quite a departure for the company when you consider that, not all that long ago, it regarded sport jacket and slacks combinations as too casual for their employees!

Ripped jeans were still strong, and designers and retailers were trying different nuances, such as paint splatters and distressed denim. The term *premium denim* came into use in the industry. Of course, that meant higher prices—but what were consumers really paying for? For the most part, the higher price tag was based on the unique finish applied to the jeans and the brand name that was on the label.

Khakis, button-downs, knits, jeans, and T-shirts were still very much a mainstay in the wardrobe, but there were new finishes, new fabrics, and a push for sustainable fibers. Sustainable fibers are those made from renewable materials such as corn, soy, seaweed, bamboo, and coconut husks, in addition to old standbys such as cotton, hemp, linen, and wool. Sustainable fibers are natural fibers that are grown, as opposed to synthetic or man-made fibers that require petro-chemicals in the processing and development stages.

Despite the continued casualization of America, there has been a bit of a backlash, with some companies requiring that the dress-down look not be too casual. There has been a resurgence in what the industry calls "dress casual," which is a trend toward dressier looks and, in some cases, back to full suits. For some time, employers allowed their associates to dress casually, and often they did not even have a formal dress code that defined casual wear. But many companies, particularly those in which employees deal with the public, decided that the degree of casualness had gone too far, and that ripped jeans and T-shirts were not appropriate for places of business.

What else is going on in the 2000s? Today's students will be the ones to explore what men's fashions will be in the future. As we move out of this decade, we wait to see what the next decade will bring. Who knows where the fashion trends will lead us!

of us went straight to the local burger and brew and had a nice lunch. It was only after the lunch that we were told about these two rules—about men having to wear a full suit, and about that no-drinking thing.

Luckily we were not due to report to our respective departments until Monday, which gave several of us, myself included, time to go and purchase some new suits. My Pierre Cardin special had already seen better days, and the beige color with those wide lapels would not go over too well with my new employer.

CONCLUDING THOUGHTS

The goals of this chapter were to help you learn the following:

o   how men's fashions of the past influence men's fashions of the present
o   how various events in history helped shape men's fashions

o   the ways in which popular culture influences men's fashions

You took a brief tour of the history of menswear beginning with the Greeks and continuing up to modern times. Along the way, you learned about historical events that helped capture the fashions of the times and that illustrated how culture influenced what men wore.

In the next chapter, you will turn your attention to the subjects of demographics and psychographics. The discussion of demographics will focus on age as a defining characteristic in determining fashions for men.

KEY TERMS

casual years

chesterfield coat

chiton

cloak

cote

cote-hardie

dalmatica

doublet

farthingale sleeve

fibulae

frock coat

General Agreement on Tariffs and Trade (GATT)

gipon

greatcoat

himation

houpplelande

jacket

jerkin

mantle

Mods

morning coat

North American Free Trade Agreement (NAFTA)

outdoor wear

overcoat

Petersham coat

petticoat

plackard

placket

polo shirt

skirted coat

sportswear

stomacher

super-tunic

surcote

tabard

Taglioni coat

tailcoat

toga

tuxedo

ulster

waistcoat

DISCUSSION QUESTIONS

1. Review the different historical garments that were discussed in this chapter.

   a) Identify features on five of the garments from the past that you can identify in today's menswear styles. List the features and discuss why you believe they have lasted through the ages.

   b) Develop five new styles using features from the past. You can sketch your own styles, or select pictures from magazines or the Internet to represent the styles that you wish to develop.

2. Identify which period in the twentieth century you believe had the greatest impact on contemporary menswear. Why did you select this period? What styles do you think will endure? Can you see future generations wearing similar styles?

REFERENCES

Boston, L. (1998). *Men of Color Fashion History, Fundamentals*. New York: Artisan.

Harris, C., and Brown, M. (2003). *Twentieth-Century Developments in Fashion & Costume: Men's Costume*. Broomall, PA.: Mason Crest Publishers.

New York Public Library, Humanities and Social Sciences Library. (2006). *A Rakish History of Menswear*. New York: Author.

Sichel, M. (1984). *The History of Men's Costume*. New York: Chelsea House Publishers.

TWO

CUSTOMER DEMOGRAPHICS

- how demographics provide important information to the menswear industry
- how psychographics applies to product design and marketing in the menswear industry
- how age is a key indicator in the male consumer's buying decisions

WHAT ARE DEMOGRAPHICS?

Throughout your studies of the fashion industry, you will hear the terms *demographics* and *psychographics*. "**Demographics** offers information about consumers that focuses on understanding characteristics of consumer groups such as age, sex, marital status, income, occupation, ethnicity, and geographic location" (Burns & Bryant, 2002, p. 568). The demographic landscape is of interest to those in the menswear industry because it involves people, who, by extension, make up the very markets in which the menswear industry wishes to operate. In 2007, the total population in the United States was slightly over 300 million. Males comprised approximately 49 percent, or 147 million, of that total. That represents a sizable market.

Age is a primary factor in the buying decisions of males. Demographers, those who study and report on trends and changes in demographics, have created the following categories based on age:

o   Baby boomers, those born between 1946 and 1964, account for approximately 84 million of the total U.S. population and, as a group, earn about $1 trillion annually.

o   Generation X, those born between 1965 and 1976, totals around 49 million individuals and represents close to $1.4 trillion in annual purchasing power.

o   Generation Y, those born between 1977 and 1994, accounts for 72 million individuals; this group is not far behind the baby boomer population in terms of number of individuals. Generation Y has an average disposable income of $91 per week and spends $169 billion per year while influencing another $30 billion in family spending.

These are neat categories that the demographers have devised. However, in this chapter, the author has chosen to develop different age categories based on real and perceived buying patterns. Before exploring these age categories in detail, take a look at some of the other demographic characteristics.

SEX

As this is a menswear text, the focus is on the male sex. This text assumes that males make their own buying decisions when it comes to shopping for apparel, although such decisions are often influenced by females. As discussed later in this chapter, the common practice of having a female in the family make most or all of the purchasing decisions is changing, as more and more males become increasingly comfortable shopping for basic or fashion apparel on their own.

MARITAL STATUS/INCOME

Along with marital status, some marketers also look at variables that affect family size and family life as influences on purchasing decisions. The family life cycle takes into account whether a male is married or not and the stage he is at in his life. It includes the following categories:

o   married with young children
o   divorced with young children or no children
o   married with children in college, or an empty nester
o   married with grown children not living in the same house

Age, a primary factor in the purchasing decisions of men today, cuts across all segments of the life cycle. Age and income together have a direct bearing on what, where, and how men spend their money. If a man has young children and both he and his partner work, he might have limited disposable income to spend on clothes for himself. On the other hand, if a man's children are grown and out of the house, he might have more than enough disposable income to do and buy what he pleases.

People's occupations have a direct effect on their ability to buy products for themselves and their families. Occupation is linked to income and, therefore, to buying power. This text places greater emphasis on a man's occupation than a general marketing text would, as an individual's occupation will determine his apparel needs. Does the occupation call for manual labor and, therefore, rugged work clothes? Is the occupation in an office setting, and if so, is casual clothing or tailored clothing the norm? If a man is a single Wall Street executive making a six-figure income, it is safe to assume that he can afford to buy nice suits. On the other hand, an executive who is supporting a wife and six children, five of them in college, may also require tailored clothing, but his purchase choices will likely be far different from those of the single executive. Occupation plays a part in determining the wardrobe, but it is just one variable that comes into play.

ETHNICITY

Marketers can also use race and ethnicity as variables for segmenting markets. Two of the fastest-growing segments of the U.S. population are Asian and Hispanic. The growth of these segments creates unique challenges for the menswear industry, not only in terms of fashion, but also in terms of size specifications. In the past 20 years, the size of men's garments has increased because the typical male American has grown larger. This increase in size proportions, coupled with the idea that a looser-fitting garment is more comfortable, poses issues of fit in the Asian and Hispanic markets. The men in these markets tend to be more fit and smaller in stature than the average American male, thereby requiring different size specifications.

In addition, there has been a large increase in the urban market of menswear, which has traditionally been targeted toward the young black consumer. Marketers have become more aware of these ethnic groups and continue to look for ways to increase their business among these groups.

GEOGRAPHIC LOCATION

Geographic location plays an important part in the marketing of menswear. The United States is a country with a variety of climates—for example, in December it can be hot in Florida and freezing in the Northeast. Regional variations in temperature account for the main differences in men's fashions on a geographic basis today. Urban versus rural location is another geographic consideration, although it is less important now than it once was. In the past, an interest in fashion would be concentrated in major cities; it might eventually have filtered to smaller cities and then into the rural landscape. However, with electronic communication today, everyone is tuned in to what is happening instantaneously and can be part of the fashion scene. The proliferation of retailers throughout the United States and the ability of anyone, anywhere, to buy online have further reduced the significance of geographic factors other than variations in climate.

"**Psychographics** refers to information gathered about a target group's buying habits, attitudes, values, motives, preferences, personality, and leisure activity" (Burns & Bryant, 2002, p. 576). Demographics and psychographics measure very different aspects of the consumer. Demographics are quantifiable; they are measures of concrete facts that describe the consumer. Psychographics are much more difficult to measure as they deal with the question of *why* consumers buy what they buy, and they are based on more abstract variables such as personality characteristics, motives, and lifestyles. "It is hard to measure personality traits accurately, especially since most personality tests were developed for clinical use, not for segmentation purposes" (Pride & Ferrell, 2003, p. 180).

Although difficult to measure, psychographics are interesting to study and can often give the apparel designer an indication of what to produce based on observing personalities, motives, and lifestyles. To further understand psychographics, one needs to look at the categories that marketers have established to separate people. Psychographic segmentation divides buyers into three categories based on the following:

o   social class
o   personality traits
o   lifestyle

People who share a particular demographic category may have very different psychographic makeups.

"Social classes are society's relatively permanent and ordered divisions whose members share similar values, interests, and behaviors" (Armstrong & Kotler, 2007, p. 132). Social class is not determined by any single factor but is made up of the following factors:

- occupation
- income
- education
- wealth

In some societies, the social order is fixed, and one cannot move from one class to another. However, in the United States, social class structure is less rigid, and if one possesses the necessary tools, which would generally be associated with income and wealth, then it is possible to change social class. This change can cut both ways in terms of movement; by acquiring wealth, one can assume a higher social status and, conversely, with the loss of one's fortunes, one's social status can decline.

As far as menswear is concerned, social class can influence purchasing decisions based on wealth as the primary factor. In the case of those males in the lower and middle classes, choices will be limited based on disposable income and by the very nature of their class status. A male in the upper crust of society will be assumed to be able to purchase whatever he desires, or whatever the social situation demands. An example that comes to mind is the sport of polo, which is played in only the higher social circles. There is a manner in which one is expected to dress while playing the sport and while watching from the stands.

PERSONALITY

"Each person's distinct personality influences his or her buying behavior. Personality refers to the unique psychological characteristics that lead to relatively consistent and lasting responses to one's environment" (Armstrong & Kotler, 2007, p. 137). Personality is often described in terms of traits such as extroversion, introversion, dominance, self-confidence, and aggressiveness. Marketers seek to understand aspects of brand loyalty, and they try to link behavior patterns with brand choices. In terms of menswear marketing, shaping a marketing campaign based on personality can be tricky. Suppose a company is trying to attract a young, hip, fashion-conscious customer to purchase its products. Loud music and movement might be used to create excitement about the product. In this case, the underlying thinking is that the ultimate consumer is an extrovert and, therefore, loud music and excitement will appeal to people with those traits.

LIFESTYLE

The final psychographic trait that is identified by marketers is lifestyle. Lifestyle is defined as a person's pattern of living and encompasses the following:

o   activities (e.g., hobbies, work, shopping, and sports)
o   interests (e.g., cooking, gardening, and reading)

- opinions (e.g., what one thinks of oneself, politics, and social issues such as the environment)

Lifestyle is also defined by how people spend their time and what activities they pursue. As mentioned earlier, these characteristics are difficult to measure. Marketers for menswear attempt to focus on several of these characteristics, emphasizing some over others depending on the product and target market in question.

CHANGES IN CONSUMER DEMOGRAPHICS

Dr. Alfred V. Sloan Jr. is a professor of fashion marketing at the Fashion Institute of Technology, located in Manhattan's fashion district. He is a resident expert in demographics, although he would argue that "there are no experts in demographics as the numbers constantly change" (Dr. Alfred V. Sloan in discussion with the author, October 14, 2006). After serving in Europe during World War II, and then completing his graduate degree at New York University, Dr. Sloan entered the world of fashion. His retail career spanned 11 years, first with the Strawbridge and Clothier department store chain (now part of Macy's) in Philadelphia, and then with Associated Merchandising Corporation (AMC), which is now owned by Target.

From there, Dr. Sloan went into education, teaching at the State University of New York's Orange County Community College in upstate New York for a couple of years. In 1959, he began teaching at the Fashion Institute of Technology. His knowledge and years of industry experience

Figure 2.1 Dr. Alfred V. Sloan Jr. is a professor of fashion marketing at the Fashion Institute of Technology in New York City; the school is seen here from Seventh (Fashion) Avenue.

have made him an expert in retail mathematics and consumer motivation, which deals primarily with consumer demographics.

Dr. Sloan's observations about the changes that have occurred in consumer demographics over the past 50-plus years include the following:

o In 1962, the U.S. population was approximately 200 million. In 2006, the population had grown to 300 million. The growth in 44 years is nearly equivalent to twice the population of Great Britain. This growth has opened new markets that did not exist before. The time span between 1962 and 2006 encompasses most of Generation X and all of Generation Y. During this time frame, many young men's apparel companies opened, and there was strong growth in the emergence of designer labels in the United States.

o The median age during that 44-year time span grew from 33 years to 38 years, and this median age continues to inch upward.

This change reflects an aging population whose life expectancies have increased due to advances in health care. The increase in median age also reflects the aging of the largest segment of the population, the baby boomers. This increase in the average age signifies the potential for new markets catering to an aging population and could represent further marketing opportunities.

o   The U.S. population is growing at a rate of 1 percent, or approximately three million people, per year. Two-thirds of that increase is from births within the United States, and one-third is due to immigration. As the population increases, new fashion markets will open up, and existing ones will continue to grow.

CHANGES IN ETHNIC DEMOGRAPHICS

The male population in the United States can be quantified into four main ethnic markets:

Figure 2.2 In the United States, the four main ethnic groups of males are white, Hispanic, black, and Asian.

white, Hispanic, black, and Asian. The following percentages can be attributed to each group:

- white: 68 percent
- Hispanic: 14 percent
- black: 12 percent
- Asian: 4 percent
- other: 2 percent

The Hispanic market in the fastest-growing one in terms of percentage increase in the United States, and that trend is likely to continue well into the future. The Asian population represents the next fastest-growing market.

The increases in the size of these two groups can be attributed to both immigration and native births (Dr. Alfred V. Sloan in discussion with the author, October, 14, 2006).

Why would this information be important to the fashion industry? The fact that these two groups are the fastest growing can mean new market opportunities for apparel companies and retailers that can recognize population trends and prepare to fill a potential need. By way of example, Perry Ellis International (PEI), a well-known men's apparel company with headquarters in Miami, Florida, recently launched a new brand called Cubavera. This brand was a direct result of PEI's understanding the trends and looking to capitalize on a new market. "Cubavera's modern tropical-inspired collection translates the joy of Hispanic culture into fashionable apparel" (Perry Ellis International, 2007).

Figure 2.3 Asian males comprise one of the fastest-growing ethnic markets.

In addition to brands targeted to the Hispanic market, many new companies have emerged that cater to the young urban black consumer. One of these is the Sean John clothing line established by hip-hop artist Sean Combs. Diddy, as he is called by the media, started out in the street wear business and has moved into tailored clothing and cologne. There are many more examples of minority-owned companies that have launched successful

Figure 2.4 Hispanic men comprise the second-largest ethnic market for menswear (white men comprise the largest market), and this group will continue to grow rapidly.

businesses in the men's fashion industry, such as FUBU, South Pole, and Phat Farm, to name a few.

MALE AGE DEMOGRAPHICS

By themselves, the numbers and information provided by Dr. Sloan do not mean much, but when they are viewed as a whole, one starts to get a picture of who the male consumer is and from which groups the growth in the market is coming. Table 2.1 shows that the census data breaks males into six main categories by age: 0–4 years, 5–19 years, 20–44 years, 45–64 years, 65–84 years, and 85+ years.

Analyzing the population growth in each of the age categories, one can see how the male population is aging. Given this information, companies that operate in the menswear market can better prepare to respond to these changes. For instance, men are living longer, and if the trend holds true, men's fashion needs will continue into later years than they do today. What will men wear? Who will provide the clothing for this market?

Taking into consideration the author's industry experience, the census data, and Dr. Sloan's insights, the author has chosen to break down the male population into four age groups, rather than the six used by the U.S. Census Bureau. The author feels that these four age groups are representative of male consumer buying patterns and habits by age clusters, and that, in general terms, they would be valid for all male consumers. Note that these categories are not based on formal research, and some will argue that there should be more categories, or that the ages within each range should be expanded. However, these categories suit the purposes of this text and illustrate the author's points. The groups are as follows:

o   12–18 years
o   19–25 years
o   26–35 years
o   35 years plus

POPULATION OR PERCENT, SEX, AND AGE	2000	2010	2020	2030	2040	2050
POPULATION TOTAL						
TOTAL	282,125	308,936	335,805	363,584	391,946	419,854
0–4	19,218	21,426	22,932	24,272	26,299	28,080
5–19	61,331	61,810	65,955	70,832	75,326	81,067
20–44	104,075	104,444	108,632	114,747	121,659	130,897
45–64	62,440	81,012	83,653	82,280	88,611	93,104
65–84	30,794	34,120	47,363	61,850	64,640	65,844
85+	4,267	6,123	7,269	9,603	15,409	20,861
MALE						
TOTAL	138,411	151,815	165,093	178,563	192,405	206,477
0–4	9,831	10,947	11,716	12,399	13,437	14,348
5–19	31,454	31,622	33,704	36,199	38,496	41,435
20–44	52,294	52,732	54,966	58,000	61,450	66,152
45–64	30,381	39,502	40,966	40,622	43,961	46,214
65–84	13,212	15,069	21,337	28,003	29,488	30,579
85+	1,240	1,942	2,403	3,340	5,573	7,749
FEMALE						
TOTAL	143,713	157,121	170,711	185,022	199,540	213,377
0–4	9,387	10,479	11,216	11,873	12,863	13,732
5–19	29,877	30,187	32,251	34,633	36,831	39,632
20–44	51,781	51,711	53,666	56,747	60,209	64,745
45–64	32,059	41,510	42,687	41,658	44,650	46,891
65–84	17,582	19,051	26,026	33,848	35,152	35,265
85+	3,028	4,182	4,866	6,263	9,836	13,112

(continued)

Some will argue that the last category, 35 years plus, is much too broad, especially with males living well into their 80s. However, the reality today is that males, whether they are 35 or 85, still want to dress well and wear fashionable clothes, and they want to appear hip and younger. Men who would have been considered "old" a few years ago are dressing today with an eye for what is fashionable. By way of example one only needs to look at how the media portray

TABLE 2.1. (CONTINUED)

POPULATION OR PERCENT, SEX, AND AGE	2000	2010	2020	2030	2040	2050
PERCENT OF TOTAL						
TOTAL	100.0	100.0	100.0	100.0	100.0	100.0
0–4	6.8	6.9	6.8	6.7	6.7	6.7
5–19	21.7	20.0	19.6	19.5	19.2	19.3
20–44	36.9	33.8	32.3	31.6	31.0	31.2
45–64	22.1	26.2	24.9	22.6	22.6	22.2
65–84	10.9	11.0	14.1	17.0	16.5	15.7
85+	1.5	2.0	2.2	2.6	3.9	5.0
MALE						
TOTAL	100.0	100.0	100.0	100.0	100.0	100.0
0–4	7.1	7.2	7.1	6.9	7.0	6.9
5–19	22.7	20.8	20.4	20.3	20.0	20.1
20–44	37.8	34.7	33.3	32.5	31.9	32.0
45–64	21.9	26.0	24.8	22.7	22.8	22.4
65–84	9.5	9.9	12.9	15.7	15.3	14.8
85+	0.9	1.3	1.5	1.9	2.9	3.8
FEMALE						
TOTAL	100.0	100.0	100.0	100.0	100.0	100.0
0–4	6.5	6.7	6.6	6.4	6.4	6.4
5–19	20.8	19.2	18.9	18.7	18.5	18.6
20–44	36.0	32.9	31.4	30.7	30.2	30.3
45–64	22.3	26.4	25.0	22.5	22.4	22.0
65–84	12.2	12.1	15.2	18.3	17.6	16.5
85+	2.1	2.7	2.9	3.4	4.9	6.1

This table shows the projected trends of the male population. Notice how many older males will be in the general population over the next several decades. As someone working in the menswear industry, how would you see these changes affecting your business? What inferences can you draw from this information?

Source: U.S. Census Bureau, 2004, "U.S. Interim Projections by Age, Sex, Race, and Hispanic Origin," http://www.census.gov/ipc/www/usinterimproj/

Internet Release Date: March 18, 2004

Mick Jagger, who recently turned 65. He certainly does not act or dress like a senior citizen. He is not changing his fashion style because of his age, and he is not alone. There are numerous examples of senior males not "acting their age" and who are dressing and acting fashionably younger than their years.

Figure 2.5 *Senior citizens like Mick Jagger refuse to "act their age," and continue to dress and act fashionably.*

THE 12- TO 18-YEAR-OLD MALE

Let us look at the 12- to 18-year-old male. He is likely in school, be it middle school, high school, or just entering college. He has a fair amount of disposable income from family sources or summer/part-time jobs and no debts to speak of. Fitting in and looking good are important; peer pressure is a major influence. Undeniably, there are males younger than 12 who purchase apparel on their own, without their mothers' help, and this demographic age continues to move down. However, the general feeling is that 12 is the age when males begin to choose for themselves what to buy and where to make their purchases. Whether black, white, Hispanic, or Asian, young men of all ages develop their own sense of style and draw upon family, friends, and the media for fashion direction.

The 12- to 18-year-old shows a strong interest in shopping and uses the occasion as a way

Figure 2.6 Males begin to choose their own clothes at about age 12.

to connect with friends. The mall is a social institution, and the revival of downtown areas in some cities also attracts this age group, not only for fashion, but for other entertainment opportunities such as arcades, restaurants, and movie theatres. The natural extension of these activities is shopping. The mall also provides a practical place for the male to "hang out," as many in this age category lack mobility in the form of a driver's license. For this group, shopping can also be a "dating" activity. With the increased interest in fashion, young men often seek the approval of their female friends when shopping.

From a fashion standpoint, the main category of apparel is sportswear, with jeans and T-shirts as the main purchases. However, some in this group will discover tailored clothing. Generally, this demographic does not need a lot of tailored clothing at school, work, or when socializing, but they do purchase suits, sport coats, and dress slacks for special occasions. Young men attend weddings, funerals, proms, and bar mitzvahs,

Figure 2.7 Teens often go shopping as a dating activity.

and functions such as these require something more formal than T-shirts and jeans.

This information is important to understand because it influences not only consumers' buying decisions but what products are offered to them at the retail level. For example, the back-to-school selling season is still important to retailers, and in order to capitalize on it, they have to have the right merchandise. One way to choose the right products to carry is to be in tune with the trends and needs of this group.

Males in the 12- to 18-year-old group have a strong fashion sense, and they buy clothes that they think will make them look good. In addition, this group can also set trends to which retailers must pay attention. In the past, fashion trends started from the top down, set by high-end designers or movies and music. Today, fashion trends are often set by males on the street (e.g., the baggy-jeans look started by the skater movement, or the long white T-shirt worn by 12- to 18-year-old urban youths).

Figure 2.8 *The back-to-school sale season is still very important to menswear retailers.*

THE 19- TO 25-YEAR-OLD MALE

The next demographic group includes 19- to 25-year-old males. This group comprises several subgroups, including the following:

o college students
o college graduates
o workers, who might have entered the workforce right out of high school.
o military personnel

Some males in this age group are still living at home. Others are living on campus or just starting out in a first home or apartment. Fashion is still high on the scale of needs, but these needs have changed somewhat from those of the 12- to 18-year-old male. This group is less subject to peer pressure and more influenced by the stage of the life cycle they are in and what is going on around them. Many males in this age group begin to move away from sportswear and are introduced to tailored clothing, some for the second time. This group has a need for tailored clothing that is

Figure 2.9 *Upscale and hip fashion retailers like Abercrombie & Fitch cater to the minority who can afford luxury.*

much different from what they wore when they were younger. Now, many of them have jobs that require dressing up.

Disposable income may still be limited. Postsecondary education is expensive, and many males in this age group incur large student loans that they need to start paying off upon graduation from college. The amount of debt has an impact on disposable income, which in turn influences how much these men can comfortably afford to spend on fashion and where they shop. Although sometimes challenged by financial constraints, men in this group still want to look good and will spend what it takes. The fashion industry needs to be mindful of this and develop products that are fashion-forward but also affordable.

As in all age categories, a certain percentage of individuals in this group will be able to afford luxury items. This information can be used by the fashion industry to help develop their products and stay abreast of the trends that this group will experience. Although the group comprises a narrow band as far as age goes, companies that cater to it do well in the market. One example is Abercrombie & Fitch, a mall-based retailer that uses music and merchandising techniques such as low lighting to create a mood to attract this demographic. Men in this age category are willing to experiment with fashion, which presents opportunities for designers—both established and newcomers—to develop new and exciting products targeted toward them.

THE 26- TO 35-YEAR-OLD MALE

Most males in the 26- to 35-year-old group are out of school, although some may be pursuing a graduate or professional degree. Most are working and trying to find the right career fit. Males in this age group are not too dissimilar to the previous age group, but they are generally more settled. Disposable income rises after school loans are paid off and meaningful employment is gained. Clothing choices become more refined, and by the time they reach this age category, most males have perfected their own style, for better or for worse. Their purchasing habits show a marked increase in tailored clothing, and they continue to spend on casual sportswear to round out their wardrobes. They generally purchase sportswear for casual dressing, although some may also wear it at work.

The shift toward tailored clothing for this group is mainly due to employment needs, although, with the **casualization** of America, many employers no longer demand tailored clothing. As more companies have begun to espouse the philosophy of corporate casual, there have been huge changes in the dynamics of the fashion marketplace. As one example,

JCPenney has gone totally casual, a drastic change for a company that not so long ago required men to wear hats and formal suits—not sport coats and dress pants, but full suits. How times have changed!

CHANGES IN MALE SHOPPING PATTERNS

The way men from all three of these age groups (12–18, 19–25, and 26–35) shop has changed dramatically. Shopping patterns have changed, as has the way people buy clothes, with new technologies allowing them to shop from home. Internet shopping is on the rise across all age categories.

Societal changes have also had an impact on male shopping patterns. Over the past several decades, many males in American households have been raised by single mothers. With nearly half of all U.S. marriages ending in divorce, family roles for males have changed. Growing up in homes where the mother is the primary earner and head of the household, these males may be more inclined to adopt practices that were once associated mainly with females. According to one retail researcher, "Men under 35 shop more like their sisters than did their fathers and grandfathers. They shop the same kind of places. They are not just in and out fast, but are people who like to browse, using shopping as a community experience" (Byrnes, 2006, p. 4).

This change in shopping patterns suggests that retailers need to pay more attention to visual merchandising as well as store layout to attract and keep these customers in the stores longer. Increased customer service is another avenue

Figure 2.10 Males who grow up in female-headed families tend to adopt more "female" shopping traits.

to look at as a way to create repeat business, as the more time the male consumer stays in the store, the more money he will spend. Excellent customer service will go a long way toward improving sales, while poor customer service can turn off any shopper.

The smart retailers are noticing this trend and using visual merchandising techniques to attract male customers into their stores. Through the use of lighting, store layout, and music, retailers are creating an inviting atmosphere to shop in. Bergdorf Goodman in New York, for example, recently added a full floor of men's shoes, which in and of itself is not earth-shattering news. However, the ambiance that greets you when you arrive is extraordinary. Apart from displays of hundreds of designer shoes, the space boasts an inviting decor with the most comfortable chairs, and shoppers can sip martinis if they so desire. Now, that is effective marketing!

A recent study commissioned by *GQ* magazine (Byrnes, 2006, p. 5) found that, in 2006, 84 percent of men said they purchased their own clothes compared with 65 percent in 1996. Of the retailers surveyed, 52 percent said their typical male customer shopped at a store at least once a month. This figure was up by 10 percentage points over 2001. These statistics show a change in both the demographics and the psychographics; they indicate the "why"(psychographics) and not just who and at what age (demographics). In this instance, the *GQ* survey points to the fact that the male consumer is not only shopping more, but buying more on his own. This signifies a change in one of the psychographic traits, lifestyle, indicating that more males are shopping for their own clothes instead of having their wives, girlfriends, mothers, sisters, or significant others purchase clothes for them.

Although *why* men shop continues to be an elusive question to answer, one can look at the media coverage of men's fashions as a potential answer. Between 1996 and 2006, the number of television shows dedicated to men's fashions increased, and a lifestyle that includes shopping became more universally accepted in the male culture. This is a fundamental change that has started and will not abate in the near future. The makeup of the household will remain relatively static, with more and more males learning to enjoy shopping as much as their female counterparts do. For years it has been noted that women love to shop more than men, and that women have used the shopping experience not only to purchase products but as a social activity. Check out the local malls and you will find groups of males window shopping and sharing the shopping experience just as the females are doing.

Individuals 35 years and older comprise the largest segment of the market. Table 2.1 shows the numbers clearly. Why is this demographic not broken down into smaller markets, say 35–49 years, 50–60 years, and so on? In today's society, it seems the older males get, the younger and more vibrant they want to feel. One of the best ways to accomplish this is through fashion. Of course, someone in his 70s or 80s today might not keep up with the latest fashion trends, but that does not mean he cannot dress fashionably or that he has lost interest in clothes.

Based on industry estimates from 2006, adults in the United States over the age of 40 will spend $80 billion per year on products to help keep them looking younger. This dollar figure is the total for both males and females, but as evidenced by the number of cosmetics companies adding products geared toward the male consumer, the number of men using these products is on the rise. Companies such as L'Oréal, a division of

Figure 2.11 Older males still want to look younger, and their fashion purchases reflect this desire.

Figure 2.12 *Jeans and T-shirts were the fashion statement that defined the baby boomer generation.*

Procter & Gamble, Shiseido, and NARS, to name a few, are actively courting male consumers and developing products specifically for men. "Seven out of 10 men use some product meant for the opposite sex as part of their grooming ritual," according to the Grooming Lounge Web site (www.groominglounge.com) (Prabhakar, 2007, p. 1).

Casual clothes have become a lifestyle choice, and even as the baby boomers age, jeans and T-shirts will continue to be popular among them. In fact, any retailer today will tell you that fashion is all about "lifestyle branding," or creating a look around what people do, as opposed to just selling clothes for them to wear. No other fashion statement defines a generation like the jeans and

T-shirts of the baby boomers. This has created many opportunities for the fashion industry, and these opportunities apply to men of all ages.

The 35-plus age group still has a strong interest in tailored clothing, but once again, the tone for this category of merchandise depends on the individual and his employer's requirements. For many men, the tailored suit is the centerpiece of their working wardrobe. The formal suit is usually the last thing males wear as they leave this world. Maybe this, too, will change with time, and jeans and T-shirts will replace the burial suit. A recent article (Oleck, 2006) told the story of boomers choosing to celebrate their lives in death by creating funerals that personalized their very existence. Some celebrated through music; one couple loved to tango, so tango music was played during the funeral. Another boomer loved cars, and so was buried in a casket resembling a 1958 Corvette. A person's ashes can be made into a diamond or sealed into a concrete beehive sculpture and dropped in the ocean to make an artificial reef. With boomers dying at increasing rates, the funeral business is changing. One casket company recently entered into a licensing agreement with Major League Baseball to market caskets emblazoned with favorite team logos. Talk about dying for a championship!

Who influences the purchasing decisions of males aged 35 and over? As is the case of the previous group, the media and significant others are the prime forces behind what males wear. Generally, disposable income increases as men age. Fashion writer Stan Gellers (2006) noted that the 35-plus male, the son of the aging baby boomer, is being "rediscovered" as

real way to do so. Perhaps, if I really tried, I could count all the males going by on a particular day wearing cargo shorts or Hawaiian print shirts and try to guess their age, but the idea is to use this to get a feel for a trend.

Trends will be discussed in Chapter 11; companies are paying big bucks for this type of information and have developed a position called "trend spotter." The trend spotter's job is to collect information on trends, which is reported based on general themes (e.g., "trend spotter noticed a number of males wearing tighter-fitting jeans").

The best result of people watching and identifying trends is to go with your gut feeling. Like answering true and false questions, always go with your first choice! Next or are in search of that next time you have nothing to do big trend, take a few hours and wander the street or sit down in a high-traffic area. You never know what you will find.

Figure 2.13 *Speaking of loving music, if you are so inclined you can even get buried in the instrument of your choice.*

the next big thing—as one who loves clothes and spends money on them. According to Alan Burks at fashion designer Henry Jacobson, the real point is that "men over 40 will have more disposable income in the next 20 years. And they've grown up in the last few decades and have come to understand that how they look is important to who they are" (Gellers, 2006, p. 14). Andrew Mallor, who owns Andrew Davis, a specialty store in Fort Wayne, Indiana, was also interviewed by Gellers (2006), and he stated, "Our customers range [in age] from 20 to 30, but the bulk [are] 40 to 60. The latter group is more interested in fashion and

Figure 2.14 Compare the fashions of yesteryear **(a)** to those of today **(b)** to understand the powerful changes that have occurred over the years.

they're getting to the point where they have more disposable income than they had 10 years ago." He also observed that they are spending more on their clothes, adding, "They're not only concerned about their physical appearance—they want to look more contemporary" (Gellers, 2006, p. 14).

On the manufacturers' side, one of the recent entries into the marketplace is John Kenyon Cory of Kenyon Ridge. His target customers are in their late 20s to 40-plus. He describes his typical customer as follows: "He's the guy who cares about the way he looks. He wants to stand out quietly. He's a bit of a low-key dandy" (Gellers, 2006, p. 15).

SUMMARY

This chapter presented a capsule version of demographics, focusing on age as a defining element in the purchasing habits of the male customer. Although many issues affect men's buying decisions, age is one common factor—all men pass through the various stages that have been discussed in this chapter. Pull out the family photo album to see how the different generations of males dressed. As you look at the photos, you can get a real sense of the dynamic changes that have occurred over the years in men's fashions.

CONCLUDING THOUGHTS

The goals of this chapter were to help you learn the following:

- how demographics provide important information to the menswear industry
- how psychographics applies to product design and marketing in the menswear industry
- how age is a key indicator in the male consumer's buying decisions

Through the use of interviews and government census data, patterns for male buying habits have been established. This same information has been used to develop specific age categories to separate male consumers into target markets. These age segments were established based on the author's understanding of the menswear market and are open to debate. The main objective of setting these age categories is to open a dialogue within the menswear community establishing that age does matter in buying decisions.

In Chapter 3, the focus will move away from the consumer and turn to the design process. The design process covers several key aspects of the industry. As you explore this subject, you will gain an understanding of what it means to be a designer in the menswear industry.

KEY TERMS

casualization
demographics

psychographics

1. Use the latest available U.S. census data via the Internet to develop demographics for your own town/city. What is the median household income? What is the average age? How many males are there compared to the number of females? What is the racial composition of the population in your area? What inferences can you make about the typical menswear customer based on these characteristics? If you were to start a menswear business in your town/city based on the demographics alone, what would be your target market?

2. Search the Internet and library for magazines and other resources showing fashions from earlier decades. Note how men's fashions have changed over the years. What are some key differences from one decade or generation to the next? Consider overall demographics, as well. Are demographic changes over the years visible in the photos?

REFERENCES

Armstrong, G., and Kotler, P. (2007). *Marketing: An Introduction*. Upper Saddle River, NJ: Pearson Prentice Hall.

Burns, L.D., and Bryant, N.O. (2002). *The Business of Fashion: Designing, Manufacturing, and Marketing* (2nd ed.). New York: Fairchild Publications.

Byrnes, Nanette. (September 4, 2006). Marketers have been missing half the male population. They're finally paying attention. [online]. Available: http://money.aol.com/bw/general/canvas3/_a/revealed-secrets-of-the-male-shopper/200608 [August 28, 2006].

Gellers, Stan. (2006, October). Are we forgetting someone? *DNR*, pp. 14–15.

Oleck, Joan. (2006, August 20). Baby boomers liven up their funerals. *The Journal News*, p. 6E.

Perry Ellis International. (2007). Perry Ellis International [online]. Available: http://www.pery.com/brands/cubavera.htm [August 9, 2007].

Prabhakar, Hitha. (September 6, 2007). Women's beauty products men love. [online]. Available: http://www.forbes.com/2007/07/13/style-products-men-forbeslife-cx [September 6, 2007].

Pride, P., and Ferrell, O.C. (2003). *Marketing: Concepts and Strategies* (12th ed.). New York: Houghton Mifflin Company.

THREE

DESIGN

○ the steps in the design process

○ how changes in fiber and fabric development affect the textiles designers ability to create their lines of apparel

○ how developments in technology affect the design process

○ the potential and business ramifications of entering into licensing agreements

The previous chapters presented a brief history of men's fashions and a portrait of the customer, primarily through a discussion of demographics as they relate to age. It is time to switch gears and take a closer look at the design process. The menswear industry comprises several distinct segments, including tailored clothing, formal wear, furnishings, and sportswear. In this chapter, you will look at the role of the **designer** and the various techniques designers use to develop products for their specific target markets.

DESIGNERS

Consider all the different menswear products that are sold today, from socks for less than $1 a pair to custom-made suits that retail for $5,000.

Think about the size and scope of the market and keep in mind that a designer—whether

Figure 3.1 *Custom-made suits like this one often sell for $5,000 or more.*

famous or not—had a hand in designing all those products. In order to understand what a designer does, consider the following definition of *design*: "to delineate by drawing the outline of; to form an idea; to plan; to propose; to mean. As a noun, a representation of a thing by an outline; first ideas represented by lines; a plan drawn out in the mind; purpose; aim; project" (Patterson & Litt, 1993, p. 86). Note the part of the definition that states "first ideas represented by lines." In essence, this is what designers do; they put their thoughts on paper in the form of lines to create garments for the industry. These lines are drawings that are created by the designers to represent new garment ideas or updates to existing garments. The drawings can be rough or detailed, depending on the designer's sketching ability. Not every great designer is a great sketch artist, but all designers can take the sketches they do make and transform them into the fabrics and garments of their choosing.

In the past, it was not unusual for a menswear designer to walk around with a sketch pad

Figure 3.2 *Even today, some designers begin creating with sketches on paper, which they refine later.*

and pencil to record ideas and inspirations. These initial sketches were often very basic, and they would be refined later, when the designer returned to his or her office or work space. The more detailed sketches would then form the basis of the garments in the designer's lines. Today, some designers still use pen and paper, but many use computers to assist them in creating designs, as well.

How many menswear designers can you name off the top of your head? Do only a handful of names come to mind? Menswear designers include Ralph Lauren, Giorgio Armani, Sean Combs (Sean John), Kenneth Cole, Canali, Jhane Barnes, Emanuel Ungaro, Andrew Fezza, Ben Sherman, Calvin Klein, Ron Chereskin, Versace, Hugo Boss, Joseph Abboud, Gianfranco Ferré, Ermenegildo Zegna, and Zanetti.

The U.S. fashion industry generates over $180 billion in retail sales annually. Design makes up a significant part of the fashion industry, working on many different levels.

o Designers' creations are seen on fashion-show runways all over the world, as well as on the "red carpet" at such events as the Academy Awards.
o Designers can work for manufacturers, producing their own lines of merchandise or private-label brands for retailers. In this capacity the designer is employed by a manufacturing company and is responsible for providing design ideas and creating products for various retailers. Once the designer has developed the idea/product, the responsibility shifts to the sales team,

Figure 3.3 Many menswear designers, such as Ralph Lauren, are household names.

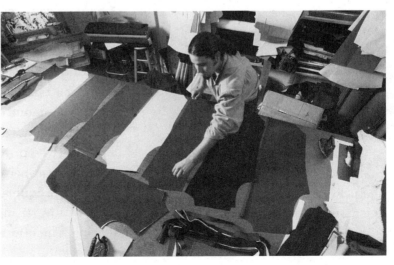

Figure 3.4 Fashion designers can function at a number of levels, from haute couture runway design to products for retailers.

whose challenge then becomes setting up appointments with the various retailers to make presentations with the hope of securing orders. This concept is explained in greater detail in Chapter 5.

- Designers can be employed by retailers, such as Macy's, designing products specifically for the retailers' own stores.
- Designers can be self-employed, developing collections for specific markets. For example, a designer might create a line of woven sport shirts with the objective of selling them at retail. Two things needed by this type of designer are financing and a strong idea. The designer does not have to establish a formal design house but can simply open a showroom and have samples made of his or her ideas. Many design companies start out this way. Ralph Lauren designed wide ties in the 1970s and started his business based on the above business model. In fact, he did not even have a showroom when he first started.
- Designers can create garments for individual clients. Many of the celebrities seen at various red-carpet events have one-of-a-kind designs created for them, as they do not want to be caught wearing the same outfit as someone else. Giorgio Armani and Oscar de la Renta are just two of the many designers who provide this service. In return for creating a special garment, the designer receives the equivalent of millions of dollars worth of advertising every time the person wearing it mentions it during the broadcast of the event.

Thus, the term *designer* can mean different things depending on the aspect of the industry in which the designer works.

In some instances, the person responsible for the design functions at a retail level is called a **product developer**. Product developers are not true designers in that they are not responsible for creating original designs. The job of the product developer is to develop and create products for the retailer by copying merchandise that already exists in the market and adapting it to fit the retailer's customers. Private-label merchandise and product development will be discussed in more detail in Chapter 5.

SOURCES OF INSPIRATION

Who are designers, and where do they get their inspirations? **Inspiration** is defined as "the art of inspiring; the drawing of breath; the Divine influence by which the sacred writers were instructed; influence emanating from any object; the state of being inspired; something conveyed to the mind when under extraordinary influence" (Patterson & Litt, 1993, p. 180). The part of the definition that captures the essence of what a designer really does is creating products by finding "influence emanating from any object." The influence can be anything from food to nature to a scrap of paper on the sidewalk.

PAUL PHILLIPS, DESIGN DIRECTOR
WITH TOMMY HILFIGER

Mr. Paul Phillips was a design director with Tommy Hilfiger. Paul says he finds his design inspirations "everywhere" and focuses on the sights and sounds around him 24 hours a day,

I remember one season in particular when he reinterpreted the design direction he was given and came up with designs that were well off the mark for Sears' target customer. However, he thought they were great! The sales team and I knew otherwise, and he had to redo every last one of them. That generally would not be a problem, but the presentation was in two days. The end result was that I found myself driving to the designer's apartment in Jersey City at 3:00 a.m. on the morning of the presentation to pick up the revised designs. Then, I had to catch a 6:00 a.m. flight out of Newark to Chicago. Thankfully, the reworked concept boards were right on the mark, and we got the order.

(As for the designer—the sales and design staff held a meeting later, at which it was agreed that he would be more attentive to the direction set down by the sales team, particularly with regard to my accounts!)

seven days a week. Anything might spark a new idea. As is true with many creative minds, the inspiration for a new idea can come from any direction at any time. It might be a billboard, a street scene, a store window, or even a dream—the possibilities go on and on.

Paul always focuses on one key element: the target market. He starts by asking, "Who is the customer?" For Tommy Hilfiger, the answer is any male from the age of 6 to 80. Of course, using such a wide age range is not practical, so Hilfiger breaks it down into manageable groupings, each with a theme. These themes change every season based on what is happening in the world of men's fashions.

Today, the market for Hilfiger is traditional, and the designer is returning to the preppy look he helped make popular in the late 1980s and early 1990s. By the end of the 1990s, the Hilfiger label had developed a large following among hip-hop artists, which had begun when Tommy's brother Andy started dressing rap stars in Hilfiger. That marketing move opened up a whole new market for the company across the country. It not only attracted customers in the large urban centers, but customers were drawn to the Hilfiger label from across middle America.

Today, Tommy Hilfiger is considered a luxury brand in Europe, and the company is working to translate that cachet to its products here in the United States. In the lingo of the industry, Hilfiger is trying to "trade up" his brand. In May 2006, Tommy Hilfiger sold the company to Apax Partners' Fund and, subsequently, moved the company headquarters from New York to Amsterdam, the Netherlands. For the first time

Figure 3.5 *For designers, inspiration can come from anywhere, even a gum wrapper.*

lo and behold, she looked down and spied a Wrigley's Spearmint gum wrapper in the litter underfoot. Without missing a step, she bent down to pick it up and smiled. I asked her what was up, and she announced that she had found the green that was missing in her color story! As you can see, inspiration can truly come from anywhere; you just have to be looking!

in the company's history, Hilfiger has signed an agreement with a sports figure to be their international brand ambassador for their formal wear and underwear. Hilfiger has also announced that the agreement will include the design and production of a limited-edition capsule collection which will be designed by Tommy Hilfiger and inspired by Thierry Henry's signature style. Thierry Henry is a soccer icon in Europe with a huge following, and Hilfiger will use his name and style to sell everything from $40 boxer shorts to $850 suits. Up until this signing, the success of the company had been

Figure 3.6 *Tommy Hilfiger is a world-renowned menswear designer.*

Figure 3.7 *Soccer icon Thierry Henry was the first sports figure signed by Tommy Hilfiger to represent his apparel line.*

all about Tommy Hilfiger. With the signing of Thierry Henry, the company has expanded its reach in the market; teaming up with an athlete who is readily recognizable in the European market will help move it to the next level. Although $850 for a suit may not seem outrageous to everyone, it is well above any price points that Hilfiger commands here in the United States.

Paul Phillips draws the analogy of fashion to food: "Every good restaurant offers a chicken Caesar salad, but what makes one different from the next is the dressing. That is what I look for in designing; everyone runs a polo shirt, but what special dressing can I add to my polo to make it different, something special that will still be attractive to my target market?" (Paul Phillips in discussion with the author, April 5, 2006).

Paul goes on to say that retailers are also like restaurants in the following ways:

○ Just as there are different levels of restaurants, from fast food outlets to five-star establishments specializing in haute cuisine, retailers have different levels, from discounters to boutiques.
○ Just as restaurants present their featured items on menus, each retailer has its own "menu" of apparel offerings.
○ The design inspiration shapes the look of both the menu of the restaurant and the floor of the retailer.

Paul has a unique view of the industry and draws on many sources for his ideas and designs in order to develop the right product at the right price for his target customer. The best advice that any designer can offer is to always focus on the end consumer. Who are you designing for? What are their likes and dislikes? What can they afford? If you can answer these questions and you have a fair sense of design, then you can be a successful designer.

RON CHERESKIN, FASHION DESIGNER

Ron Chereskin has been in the men's fashion business for over 30 years. However, he did not start out to be a world-renowned fashion designer; his artistic talent led him in that direction.

Figure 3.8 Ron Chereskin, a leading menswear designer, began his career as an illustrator.

He began his career as an illustrator, his work appearing in *Esquire, Ladies' Home Journal, TV Guide,* and many other consumer publications. One day, back in 1975, someone who worked for a leading tie manufacturer was flipping through a stack of magazines in a doctor's office. When he came upon Ron's illustrations, he was instantly struck by the idea that this artwork would be perfect for a necktie. As they say in the industry, "a deal was done," and Ron entered the fashion business.

Since the 1970s, Ron has focused on menswear, with the goal of developing a style that epitomizes comfort. His pastel cotton sweaters have become nationwide best-sellers. He takes his inspiration from the energy of New York City. It is no wonder he is the recipient of both the Coty and Cutty Sark awards for understanding sportswear design.

Today, Ron oversees a company that can be categorized as a marketing and licensing organization. The Ron Chereskin name is licensed to a host of manufacturers of products ranging from men's underwear to home furnishings. Ron designs products for each of the categories; he also receives input from the manufacturers that license his name. As Ron Chereskin is the brand, he retains final approval over the products that bear his name. As the head of a design and marketing company, Ron leaves the production issues to the manufacturers that carry the licenses.

LICENSING

Licensing involves making a formal agreement between two parties to produce and market merchandise under a particular name, typically a highly recognizable name such as that of a designer or celebrity. One party grants the other permission to use a name, trademark, or symbol. For example, Ron Chereskin has signed a licensing agreement with a company to manufacture, market, and sell men's underwear bearing his name. Ron designs the underwear, and the company that produces the underwear carries out the manufacturing, marketing, and sales efforts. Ron receives a percentage of the sales in the form of royalties for his designs and the use of his name. The actual percentage will vary by company and the type of agreement signed; the owner of the name or trademark typically receives anywhere from 4 to 10 percent of gross sales. Can you think of any companies, sports figures, entertainers, or designers that enter into licensing agreements?

The licensing agreement yields positive results for all parties in the following ways:

o   the person or company who is licensing the name
   o   enters new markets
   o   makes money
   o   creates greater exposure for the brand

Figure 3.9 *Companies, entertainers, sports figures, and designers enter into licensing agreements. Pictured is Derek Jeter of the New York Yankees.*

- o the retailer that carries these products
  - o gains greater access to a potentially new group of consumers
  - o increases sales opportunities on the licensed products
- o the manufacturer
  - o gains new avenues of distribution
  - o increases sales volume leading to greater profitability

Why do designers, retailers, and manufacturers enter into licensing agreements? Why do they not just do everything themselves? The general premise behind such agreements is that each party plays to its strengths and allows others to do the same. Each party does what it does best and gets others to do what they cannot do.

Ron Chereskin has a very successful men's underwear business. His products can be found in major department stores and over 1,000 specialty stores in the United States. Although Ron can design the underwear, he does not have,

Figure 3.10 *Name designers such as Ron Chereskin frequently have several lines of menswear and other products under license.*

nor does he likely want to acquire, the manufacturing facilities to produce it. Thus, he turns to experts in the field. He signs a licensing agreement; he designs the product, and the licensor manufactures, markets, sells, and distributes the underwear under Ron's watchful eye.

Recently, Ron saw an opportunity to enter into the tabletop business, designing table cloths, napkins, dishes, and flatware. Once again, Ron had the idea for the design, but he did not have the expertise to make any of the products. What did he do? He entered into several licensing agreements.

RON'S INSPIRATION

Ron is a successful designer with multiple products in several categories. Where does he get his design inspirations? He says, "My background as an artist continues to inspire and influence me. My goal is now what it always has been—to apply art to the everyday" (Ron Chereskin in discussion with the author, March 31, 2006). Ron relies on his own background in art to help inspire his creations from season to season. He explains, "It might start from a color or a swatch of fabric, a picture or billboard. From there, I use my art background to develop the thought into a complete theme, then into a design. These inspirations can happen at any time but, of course, become more focused with a deadline looming for a new collection" (Ron Chereskin in discussion with the author, March 31, 2006).

INDUSTRY CHANGES

Having been in the business for over 30 years, Ron has witnessed significant changes in the fashion industry. "By far the most significant change, and the one that has gained momentum in the past several years, is the consolidation at the retail level. There are fewer and fewer retailers to call on. Twenty years ago, if one retailer decided not to buy your collection, you literally walked across the street and sold it to someone else. Today, the street is disappearing. In addition to the retail consolidation, we have seen a consolidation at the manufacturing level" (Ron Chereskin in discussion with the author, March 31, 2006).

Ron raised an important point when he singled out the consolidation of manufacturers as well as retailers. With fewer companies to work with, choices for fabrics, trims, and production become more focused.

In his example about retailers, Ron mentioned that if a designer did not get an order from one retailer, he or she could just walk across the street to another retailer and, hopefully, get an order there. A similar situation is occurring with manufacturers. In the past, if your manufacturing partner could not make what you needed, you simply found another manufacturer who could. Generally, the alternate was in the same neighborhood. The reality today is that if one manufacturer cannot make what you need, you can still find another one to do it, but chances are it will not be in your neighborhood, and probably not even in your country. This aspect adds to the stresses and costs of doing business. Stress can be generated by having to worry about production taking place so far away, and the additional costs can come in the form of increased transportation expenses and the need to hire personnel to run an import division of the business.

As the fashion industry continues to grow and change, Ron wants to keep designing. "I will continue to design and do what I do best: create clothes with comfort and style that men cannot only wear but live in" (Ron Chereskin in discussion with the author, March 31, 2006).

TEXTILES

An understanding of textiles is essential to fully comprehend the design aspect of the menswear industry. What fabric makes a great tie? What fabric works best for an expensive suit? A successful designer needs to understand textile production from the field to the fiber to the fabric in order to design garments. Good designers understand how fiber properties contribute to the finished product and, therefore, which fabrics are best suited for each garment. The fiber is spun into the yarn that makes up the fabric, which will eventually be transformed into the garment.

Figure 3.11 *A knowledge of textiles is essential for any designer in the menswear industry.*

Which fabrics work best for different menswear garments? Silk is often the choice for ties. Various fabrics are used for dress shirts. For example, a designer may choose a 100 percent cotton fabric or a blend. If a blend is chosen, the designer then needs to consider which weave will work best, such as oxford, pinpoint oxford, or broadcloth. The choice depends on the designer's target market and what the consumer is willing to pay. Generally speaking, a pinpoint oxford dress shirt will be the most expensive; the fabric costs are higher than for broadcloth and the plain oxford as more yarns are used in constructing the pinpoint oxford fabric. The plain oxford could cost more than the broadcloth, although the key is the yarn count (how many pics and ends are in the fabric), which can vary. A highly constructed broadcloth made from high-count single-ply yarn will cost more than a lower-count coarser yarn in the plain oxford weave. Suffice to say, the designer will have an understanding of the textile market and what makes a good fabric.

Today, most dress shirts, regardless of the fabric or weave, are treated with a wrinkle-resistant finish, which varies by product; most tout the fact that the shirts do not have to be ironed after they have been washed and then dried in a dryer. Wrinkle-free finishes and 100 percent cotton fabrics have also taken a large share of the market for casual pants.

Denim is the number one material used to make men's pants. It is made from 100 percent cotton, with the exception of those jeans that find their way to the market with a percent or two of spandex woven into the fabric to offer a little stretch.

For knit shirts, many designers prefer 100 percent cotton knitted in a piqué stitch. Many companies use **blended fabrics** combining two or more yarns made up of different fibers, such as polyester and cotton, to achieve a desired look or texture.

Men's suits, sport jackets, and dress trousers can be made up in various fabrics, with wool being the most used in better-quality apparel. Seasonal fabrics such as linen and cotton can make up beautifully into well-tailored suits.

The importance of fabrics will be discussed further in Chapters 7 to 10, which deal directly with individual product categories.

FUTURE OF TEXTILES IN MENSWEAR

Mr. S. Gray Maycumber has been a textile writer and editor for over 30 years, including 25 years with *DNR*, where he served as managing editor of the textile department, and prior to that as a senior editor and a columnist. *DNR* is considered the bible of the menswear trade. It is released every Monday in a full-color glossy format. (*DNR* is discussed further in Chapter 6.)

Figure 3.12 *Textile expert Gray Maycumber has been writing and editing for trade publications on the subject for over three decades.*

Most recently, Gray has been a contributing editor to *Textile Insight*, which started publication in 2005. *Textile Insight* bills itself as having its eye on the global textile market, reporting news from an American point of view. This magazine is published monthly in full color and is supported by advertisements from textile and fiber companies worldwide.

Gray commented on the future of textiles in menswear, "Designers are always experimenting with new fibers and fabrics, and I see a move back toward polyester in menswear based on the new fabrics that the mills are creating. In addition, blends seem to be back in vogue, as a good blended fabric plays off the best characteristics of each of the fibers in the textile" (S. Gray Maycumber in discussion with the author, October 9, 2006).

Gray sees the continued influence of television and movies in design. The Internet is another form of mass communication to consider. At first, Gray resisted the Internet, but he has come to embrace it, as have many in the industry. Gray sees the Internet as an integral part of conducting business and recognizes its power as an information source. However, given his vast experience in the industry, he still thinks that the power of the written word in the form of daily newspapers will survive, although they may not be as numerous as they are today. He does not see the likes of *Women's Wear Daily* disappearing anytime soon.

ADVANCEMENTS IN THE DEVELOPMENT OF SUSTAINABLE FIBERS

Some of the more contemporary designers, such as Canali and Zegna, are experimenting with sustainable fibers/fabrics. These are being manufactured from natural products that can easily be reproduced; they include materials such as bamboo, seaweed, corn, and soy. As concerns grow about protecting the environment, members of the apparel and textile industries are looking at how they can work to help protect the planet. One way is to use fibers from sources that can be grown with minimal impact on the environment. This group of fibers, as well as conventional fibers such as wool, cotton, silk, and linen, are natural and renewable. Polyester, nylon, and many other manufactured fibers derive from petroleum-based products, which are nonrenewable resources.

According to Gray, "The big catchword at Première Vision [a textile trade show held twice a year in Paris], this past show, was not just sustainable fibers and fabrics, but the talk was centered on any fiber and fabric not made from oil- or coal-based products" (S. Gray Maycumber in discussion with the author, October 9, 2006). The difficulty is educating the end consumer about the value of these products and persuading some of the larger producers to seek new fibers/fabrics for developing new ideas.

There has been a lot of talk in the industry about corn as the next big potential source for textile fibers and fabrics. Gray commented, "Corn has a twofold problem: large amounts of pesticides are used, so how eco-friendly does that make it? Corn is a source of food for humans and animals. It is also used in the production of ethanol, which is currently being touted as an alternative to gasoline, so in all of these instances price becomes an issue" (S. Gray Maycumber in discussion with the author, October 9, 2006).

In general, Gray's feeling is that it is very hard to get consumers excited about the actual performance characteristics of these so-called sustainable fibers. One of the difficulties is related to the additional costs of producing these fibers, which means that garments made from them carry a premium price. As well, with the exception of retailers that are well known for selling apparel produced in environmentally friendly ways, such as Patagonia, it is difficult for retailers to market and sell these products. Take Macy's as an example. It sells many different apparel products under various name brands. If Macy's were to develop a brand of menswear produced from soy, how would the retailer market it to the consumer? What message would the new brand convey about the rest of Macy's apparel offerings? At the same time, there is a lot of buzz in the market about eco-friendly products that will have an effect on the textile industry. It was reported that InVista (formerly DuPont) would like to have at least 25 percent of their fabrics made from sustainable fibers in the near future (Magruder, 2007).

ADVANCEMENTS IN THE DEVELOPMENT OF SYNTHETIC FIBERS

In addition to developments in the area of sustainable fibers, great strides have been made in manufactured fibers. A host of synthetic fibers are being used to create new and interesting fabrics such as the following:

○ Fortrel EcoSpun "is made from 100 percent recycled plastic bottles and has set the standard by which all other environmentally friendly fibers are judged. Bottles collected for recycling are refined and purified, broken down, and processed into spun filament strands. These strands are then knitted or woven into fabrics. This concept was first developed in the United States by Wellmann Inc. This process uses 60 times less plastic, 4 times less carbon dioxide, and 6 times less sulfur against the life span of polyester generated by conventional methods" (Recycled Business Gifts, 2007).

○ Dryline by Milliken "uses a push-pull moisture transport technology to draw perspiration away from the skin to the garment surface, where it evaporates. It is a unique combination of nylon, polyester, and spandex that stays dry and comfortable in all sorts of conditions" (Milliken Apparel Fabrics, 2007).

- Dow XLA is a durable stretch fiber that enhances the way clothes move, look, and feel. "Fabrics enhanced with XLA fiber wrap the body in gentle support with a soft, non-snap stretch that endures multiple washings and dry cleanings while maintaining garment shape" (Dow, 2007).
- Climashield is a lightweight performance insulation that is used in the production of gloves, sleeping bags, outerwear, and hats. The technology is based on a continuous filament technology and provides superior strength, moisture resistance, durability, and thermal properties compared to down or even filament fiber, which is cut into shorter lengths called cut staple (Climashield, 2007).
- Hydroflex by Consoltex is a unique technological development created to offer exceptional protection against the elements. "The Hydroflex coating forces humidity to

Figure 3.13 *Synthetic fibers are being used to create new and innovative fabrics.*

circulate outward thanks to its countless microscopic pores. The result is breathable clothes that protect against wind and rain" (Consoltex INC., 2007).

TECHNOLOGY

A chapter on design would not be complete without a discussion of how technology is changing the way apparel is designed today. When one thinks of designers developing their creations, an image that often comes to mind is someone sketching a garment by hand. Many designers still prefer this method, but recent generations of designers are using new technologies to facilitate the design process. *CAD/CAM,* or *computer-aided design* and *computer-aided manufacturing,* are terms that can be applied to the use of any computer application, both hardware and software, that works to increase the speed, efficiency, and reliability of any processes in the apparel and textile industries. CAD/CAM systems are not new to the industry, but developments in these technologies have exploded in recent years.

Two world-renowned companies that have brought great technological advances to the field of apparel design are Gerber Technology and Lectra. Although these companies compete for the same market in many instances, they each offer the designer something a little different to choose from. Each of these companies also specializes in production and manufacturing solutions that will be discussed in Chapter 4.

Both companies offer three-dimensional technology, which is of special interest to designers.

Figure 3.14 *Computers are an integral part of the fashion design process.*

Using these computer programs, designers can do the following:

- call up a design
- drape a fabric on a virtual model
- rotate that model 360 degrees to see how the garment looks
- change pattern size, colors, and silhouettes, all with the click of a mouse

Three-dimensional technology programs enhance the design process and make it more cost effective to bring new designs to the market.

LECTRA

Lectra is a worldwide organization that develops, produces, and distributes software and hardware for industrial users of textiles, leather, and other soft material. It has more than 17,000 customers. The company was established in France in 1973, and its first big breakthrough came in 1985 when it launched its the first automated fabric-cutting machine. (Gerber had its fabric-cutting machine out in the late 1960s.) Lectra customizes technologies to meet the business needs of specific customers.

Lectra offers PC-based products that designers can use to enhance their work. As retailers and apparel companies increase demands for exclusive print and weave designs, the trend has been to bring the design expertise in-house. Lectra's products allow buyers and manufacturers to make timely decisions on styling, enabling quick turnaround on samples. By supporting these programs, Lectra has positioned itself to assist the industry by improving speed to market and accuracy.

Computer-aided designs and techniques enable realistic simulations of both prints and weaves, and the time saved is considerable. Prior to this technology, weaves were created by first painting the pattern then winding actual yarn onto a card to simulate the weave. The process was similar for a print design: an artist would paint the print, then a printer would be commissioned to produce samples.

Lectra offers the following innovations to the industry:

- **PrimaVision Weave** is a design tool for creating new and innovative textiles using an easy-to-use computer program (see Figure 3.15).

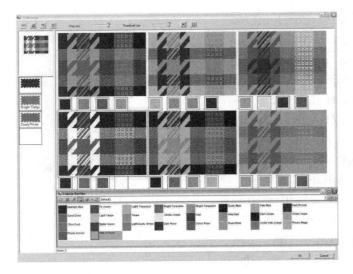

Figure 3.15 With Lectra's PrimaVision Weave program you can create new and interesting weave designs.

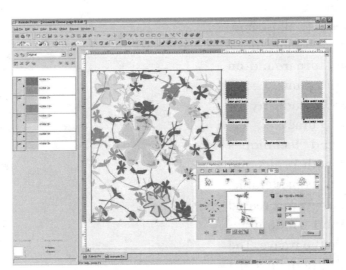

Figure 3.16 Lectra's PrimaVision Print program can increase speed to market by designing new print ideas via the computer.

o **PrimaVision Print** is a comprehensive program used to create print designs on a computer, which cuts down on time and expense (see Figure 3.16).

o **Kaledo Design Management** pulls print and weave designs together to create a successful product lifestyle management (PLM) system. Once the necessary prints

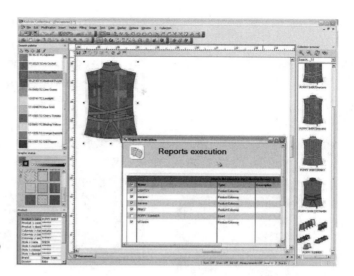

Figure 3.17 *Lectra's Kaledo Design Management system allows the user to transform design into business.*

and weaves have been developed, the Kaledo Style program is used to refine the product line by creating new garments with just a few clicks of the mouse. It is no longer necessary to create large presentation boards to display hand-drawn sketches, fabric swatches, and handwritten notes. Kaledo Style uses high-quality illustrations, allows designers to make quick decisions, and, at the same time, make changes if necessary (see Figure 3.17).

Lectra offers software that can be used in all stages of the design process, from selection of fabrics and prints to final garment designs. All of these programs can be used in concert with each other. Lectra licenses the software, provides training and support for the designers who will be using the software, and follows up to ensure that the products are performing the jobs they were set up to do. Each program requires specific hardware to run, but most upgraded personal computers can support Lectra's software.

Figure 3.18 Gerber Technologies print design program is well suited for any apparel end use.

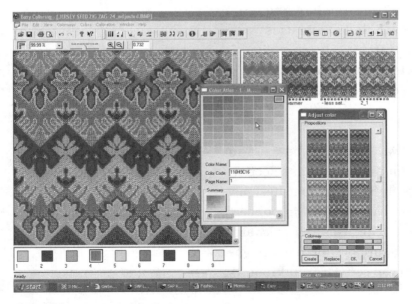

Figure 3.19 Woven designs from the simple to the complex can be created in real time utilizing Gerber's pattern design software.

Gerber Technology was started in the late 1960s by Joseph Gerber, when he invented the S-70 cutter, which automatically cut large amounts of material with a computer-controlled knife. Today, more then 7,000 Gerber cutters are installed in a variety of industries around the world, and Gerber has grown into a $500 million business serving five primary markets: apparel and textile, transportation interiors, industrial fabrics, composites, and furniture.

Compared to Lectra, Gerber Technology is more heavily geared toward the production process and supply chain management, which is the process of planning, implementing, and controlling the operations of the supply chain as efficiently as possible. Supply chain management spans all movement and storage of raw materials, work-in-progress inventory, and finished goods from point of origin to point of consumption. In essence, supply chain management integrates supply and demand management within and across companies. Although Gerber focuses on these aspects of the business, it does incorporate several programs for design, one of which is shown in Figure 3.18.

Gerber's Vision Fashion Studio program places the features of a design studio at the user's fingertips. Using this program, designers can create new styles in a matter of hours rather than days and weeks. Like the products offered by Lectra, Vision Fashion Studio allows the user to custom design textiles, knits, weaves, and prints, and to produce high-quality catalogs and storyboards to communicate information to customers.

THE STONE AGE

Most of you have grown up in a very technologically savvy time. However, when I left JCPenney for my first job in sales, we were not quite into the twenty-first century as far as technology was concerned. This was the early 1980s, the computer age was just starting to have an impact on business, and the Internet was not yet discovered!

The company where I worked had a small office in the Empire State Building on the 32nd floor. We sold and marketed men's knit shirts and sweaters. We were a vertical company, with the knitting, cutting, and sewing produced in our factory in Marion, South Carolina. Long-distance telephone charges were very expensive, so we used a device called a teletype. In order to send information to the factory, we would type the information on what looked like a manual typewriter. It would

(continued)

produce a tape, similar to the kind used to run a player piano. Then this tape was fed into another device hooked into the phone line. It would transmit the information to the mill, and a printed text would appear on the other end. We thought this was high tech! As you can see, we have come a long way in a very short time!

Gerber and Lectra are both leaders in fashion technology. Each company brings a unique perspective to the world of fashion; Lectra focuses more on the design aspect of the business, and Gerber focuses more on the manufacturing sector. There is some crossover as the two companies do compete for similar business with the same customers and end users. Customers' final purchasing decisions are based on price, service, and business needs. The choice of one of these companies over the other can be made only after a thorough investigation of both companies and a decision as to what will most benefit the customer's organization.

CONCLUDING THOUGHTS

The goals of this chapter were to help you learn the following:

o   the steps in the design process
o   how changes in fiber and fabric development affect the textiles designers use to create their lines of apparel
o   how developments in technology affect the design process
o   the potential and business ramifications of entering into licensing agreements

These objectives were met through a series of interviews and discussions about some of the changing and innovative technologies affecting the textile market today. Fibers, yarns, and textiles are the foundation from which all designs originate. By getting a basic understanding of these key elements, you position yourself to better understand how the design process works. Another interesting aspect of the men's fashion business is how and why designers, companies, and retailers enter into licensing agreements. These agreements are extensions of the core businesses and, when handled properly, can be a source of additional profit potential.

In the next chapter, you will look at how menswear is made. Chapter 4 discusses the manufacturing process and reviews sourcing options. The chapter will guide you through the steps used in the industry to make menswear products. It examines how research interacts with design and manufacturing in the industry and what quality control means.

KEY TERMS

blended fabric

designer

inspiration

Kaledo Design Management

licensing

PrimaVision Print

PrimaVision Weave

product developer

DISCUSSION QUESTIONS

1. Use the Internet to research Gerber Technology and Lectra. How are the two companies different? How are they similar? If you were going into production, sales, or marketing in the menswear business, which of these companies would you likely choose to provide the software and hardware you would need to run a successful business? Why?

2. List five menswear designers and describe in your own words who you think their target customers are.

3. This chapter discussed the process of licensing. Describe five menswear designers that have entered into licensing agreements. What products are covered by these agreements?

REFERENCES

Climashield. (2007). Climashield [online]. Available: http://www.clmashield.com [August 14, 2007].

Consoltex Inc. (2007). Consoltex [online]. Available: http://www.consoltex.com [August 14, 2007].

Dow. (2007). Dow [online]. Available: http://www.dow.com [August 14, 2007].

Magruder, Karla. (2007). Today's take on green. *Textile Intelligence,* Vol. 2, No. 6, p. 16.

Milliken Apparel Fabrics. (2007). Milliken Apparel Fabrics [online]. Available: http://www.millikenapparelfabrics.com [August 14, 2007].

Patterson, R. F., and Litt, D. (Eds.). (1993). *New Webster's Expanded Dictionary.* West Boylston, MA: P.S.I. & Associates, Inc.

Recycled Business Gifts. (2007). Fortrel EcoSpun [online]. Available: http://www.recycledbusinessgifts.co.uk/fortrelecospun.htm [August 14, 2007].

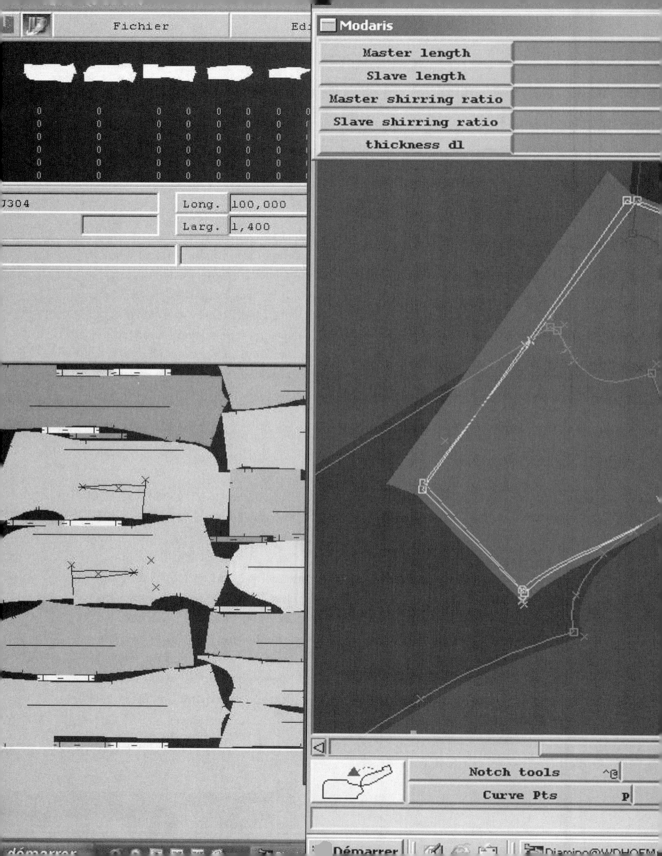

Fichier   Ed:

J304

Long. | 100,000
Larg. | 1,400

Modaris

Master length
Slave length
Master shirring ratio
Slave shirring ratio
thickness dl

Notch tools   ^⊟
Curve Pts   P

démarrer   Démarrer   Diamino@WDHOFM

FOUR

MANUFACTURING

IN THIS CHAPTER, YOU WILL LEARN
THE FOLLOWING:

- o how the manufacturing process operates in the men's apparel industry and various options available when sourcing production
- o how the research process interacts with design and manufacturing
- o the importance of quality control in the overall design and manufacturing process

Have you ever gone shopping and wondered where those clothes actually came from and how they were made? If you are like most consumers, you go to the store, see something you like, try it on, and buy it without giving a second thought to where and how it was made. As students of fashion, it is time to change that thinking. Imagine you are designers with a design and marketing company. How will you get your apparel products made?

PRODUCTION OF GARMENTS FROM DESIGN TO MANUFACTURING

DEVELOPING A THEME

The first step in the process is design. Imagine that the season you are designing for is Spring/Summer 20_ _. You fill in the date. The process never really changes; it is the trends that change. Sometime in the previous January or February, you would have come up with the theme for your **line** or **collection**, which is part of the design process.

A line is defined as "one large group or several small groups of apparel items developed with a theme that links the items together," whereas a collection is "a group of apparel items presented to the buying public, usually by high fashion designers" (Glock & Kunz, 2005, p. 84). The reality is that many designers call their "lines" collections, not because they are being presented to the buying public, but to give the impression that the merchandise has a higher value.

Your line or collection will be based on a theme. For example, you might feature a particular fabric, such as denim, or a particular style, such as nautical attire. The key to developing your theme is to understand the following:

○ the market in which you work
○ the ultimate consumer, otherwise known as your target market

RESEARCHING THE MARKET

After deciding on your theme, you need to shop the market to learn what is new and fresh for the current Spring/Summer season. Generally speaking, you would be shopping the market nine months to one year in advance of the new season. A designer working on fashions for Spring/Summer 2008 would shop during Spring/Summer 2007, when those seasons' fashions are in the retail stores. As an industry person, you are always shopping the market, whether you go to the mall or to your favorite department store. You always have an eye on what is happening and who is doing what, as you never know when that information will come in handy.

While shopping, you should also look in on your competition to find out what new styles they are carrying and their current price points (the selling prices that you would find at retail). The competitors' current price points will help you in planning your own pricing decisions. If your competition is selling jeans at $60, you will use this information to set your own prices. You may want to differentiate yourself and sell at a higher price, or you may want to beat the competition and sell your jeans at a lower price. You do not want to copy the competition, but as a good designer, you always want to know what is going on around you so that you can respond to your customers.

You also need to have a clear understanding of your customer. In Chapter 2, customers were defined based on demographics and psychographics, but to be truly successful, you need to know your **target market**. A target market is "a set of buyers sharing common needs or characteristics that the company decides to serve" (Armstrong & Kotler, 2005, p. 199). In order to get a clear understanding of just who makes up that target market, the designer may need to research or simply use existing information such as sales records. If you undertake a research project, you can do it internally or hire outside consultants. In conducting research, it is critical that you ask the right questions. As you are trying to identify and understand your target market, the demographics of your customers is one important consideration.

Consider the size and scope of today's market. The market is characterized by many shifts in demographics that have an impact on the way business is conducted in the fashion industry. Some of these changes were addressed in Chapter 2, such as the increase in the Hispanic and Asian populations and the potential need to cater to those markets. Another example can be seen in the shift in the population that will occur over the next 20 years in response to increased migration to three states in particular: Florida, California, and Texas. This shift will have a direct effect on outerwear sales as the need for heavy outerwear will diminish with more people moving to warmer climates.

RESEARCHING AND SAMPLING FABRICS

While conducting research at the retail level to see what is out there, you will also be busy with the following:

○ meeting with fabric mills
○ attending fabric trade shows
○ attending fashion forecasting seminars

The trade shows provide excellent opportunities to meet with representatives of fabric mills with which you are currently doing business, as well as representatives of new fabric mills that might carry interesting fabrics that would fit into your upcoming theme. (See Table 4.1 for a listing of fabric shows.)

Première Vision (PV) is a major fabric trade show held twice a year in Paris, bringing together all the top fabric mills from Europe

TABLE 4.1 FABRIC TRADE SHOWS

LIST OF TEXTILE TRADE SHOWS

NAME	LOCATION	MONTH	WEBSITE
Chicago Fabric & Trim Show	Chicago, IL	June/November	www.aibi.com
China Textile Show	New York, NY	June	www.nychinashow.com
Direction Show	New York, NY	June/April/August	www.directionshow.com
European Preview	New York, NY	January/July	www.europeanpreview.com
Expofil	Paris, France	February/September	www.expofil.com
Fabric Fair	Chicago, IL	April	www.mmart.com
MAGIC	Las Vegas, NV	February/August	www.fabricshow.com
Hong Kong Textile Fair	Hong Kong	July	www.hktextilegarmentfair.com
I-Style	New York, NY	January	www.i-textile.com
Ideabiella	Cernobbio, Italy	February/September	www.ideabiella.com
Ideacomo	Cernobbio, Italy	February/October	www.ideacomo.com
Inprints	New York, NY	February/October	www.inprintsny.com
Inatex	Frankfurt, Germany	January	www.inatex.com
Interstoff Asia	Hong Kong	January/October	www.interstoff-asia.com
InterTextile Milan	Milan, Italy	February/September	www.intertexmilan.it
Intertex Textile Shanghai	Shanghai, China	March/October	www.intertextile.com
London Fabric Show	London, England	February	www.londonfabric.com
Material World	New York, NY	September	www.material-world.com
	Miami, FL	April	
Moda Fabric Fair	Milan, Italy	March/September	www.modain.it
Los Angles Textile Show	Los Angles, CA	April/October	www.californiamarketcanter.com
Moda-expo	Moscow, Russia	February/August	www.moda-expo.ru
Munich Fabric Show	Munich, Germany	February/September	www.munichfabricstart.de
Premiere Vision	Paris, France	February/September	www.premierevision.com
Preview	Seoul, South Korea	August	www.previewinseoul.com
Printsource	New York, NY	April/August	www.printsourcenewyork.com
Silk Show	Dallas, TX	June	www.dallasmarketcenter.com
Texworld	Paris, France	February/September	www.texworld.messefrankfurt.com
Tissu-premier	Lille, France	April/September	www.tissu-premier.com
Turkish Fabric Show	New York, NY	September	www.turkishfabric.com

Sample listing of fabric trade shows that are held in any given year.

Please note that where two months are listed the show takes place during each month. As the actual dates/days change from year to year please check the web site for day and exact location.

Source: www.infomat.com, leading Internet information source for the apparel and textile industry.

to show their new fabric collections. Visitors from all over the world attend. While in Europe for the show, visitors have opportunities to observe the trends in Paris and perhaps other European cities, shopping and street watching, and also performing store checks. In the fashion industry, a store check is when you visit shops that you consider trendy or important to your business and window shop for new ideas. Store checks can confirm that you are on the right track or point out that you might have missed an important trend.

Your theme is coming together. You have put your ideas down on paper. You have met with the fabric mills and selected your **swatches.** A swatch is a fabric sample from a mill; generally a swatch is 8 by 10 inches in size and attached to a card that has the following information:

o   the mill's logo
o   fabric description
o   fabric type
o   fabric construction
o   fabric weight
o   fiber content

You will use the information you have gathered to help you decide which mills to work with and which fabrics to sample. Once those decisions have been made, your next step is to write your fabric and sample orders.

Fashion designer Ron Chereskin (see Chapter 3) relies on his licensing partners to make the samples for his line, but he is the one responsible for ordering the sample fabrics. It is not uncommon to have several licensees all creating samples at the same time out of different fabrics representing the different categories. A category of merchandise is best described in terms of the actual product; for instance in menswear, outerwear and tailored clothing are two product categories. Product categories can be defined even more specifically, such as woven versus knit sport shirts. In this industry, there are many companies that specialize in a single product category. You could have a licensing agreement with one company to produce your woven tops, another for bottoms, and yet another for outerwear. The possibilities are limitless and will vary from company to company.

Pause for a moment and review where you are in the process. You have completed the following steps:

o   You created the theme for your line in January/February.
o   In March/April, you did the following:
    o   shopped the market
    o   met with fabric mills and attended fabric shows
    o   selected fabric swatches that would work well with your theme and ordered sample yardage

ENSURING THE FIT OF THE GARMENT

Given the fact that you are working in a design and marketing company, you rely on your manufacturing partners to create the garment samples for you. You are very conscious of the fit of the garment, as this is one of the hallmarks of your line. Thus, you provide all the **spec sheets** along with copies of **make detail sheets,** which include detailed sketches of the garment from several viewpoints. A spec sheet is a list of measurements associated with a garment along with detailed sketches and guidance on how to measure points. These measure points are indicated on the spec sheet and are guides as to where the measurements are to be taken in order to maintain the accuracy and the integrity of the size specifications (see Figure 4.1). A make detail sheet (see Figure 4.2) is a road map of the garment to be made. The make detail sheet gives the factory directions about what will be included in the garment and how it will be sewn.

Some companies still maintain a sample room in their design studios or showrooms. The purpose of a sample room is to make patterns and samples. However, as this can be an expensive proposition, more and more companies are relying on the manufacturer's or contractor's expertise to make the samples. Having a sample room on the premises has traditionally been more popular in the women's wear business than in menswear.

The samples are completed in May/June. The lag in the time from sample fabric order to finished samples can be the result of several factors. The sample fabric you selected may not be available immediately. If the sample fabric has to be made, it can take anywhere from two to four weeks. Perhaps your manufacturing partner is halfway around the world, and it takes time to get everything to where it needs to be.

As the samples come back into the design studio, you take the following steps:

- You review the samples to make sure they adhere to the make detail sheet.
- You measure the samples to check against the spec sheet for accuracy and to make sure they are within **tolerance.** The term *tolerance*

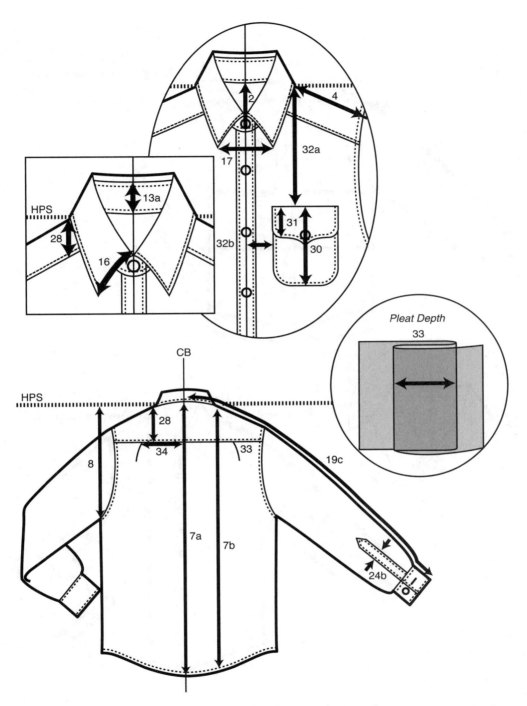

Figure 4.1 *Sample of a specification (spec) sheet that is used to record garment measurements. Each company generates its own version.*

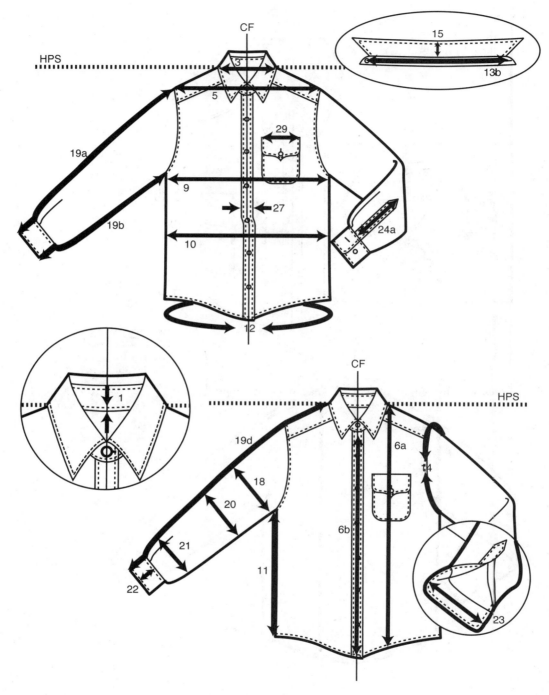

Figure 4.1 *Continued*

2	NECK DROP–FRONT	Measure down from the neckline or collar seam at center back to the neckline or collar seam at center front.
3	NECK – WIDTH	Measure straight across the HPS
4	SHOULDER – LENGTH	Measure along the shoulder seam from the neck seam to the armhole seam.
5	ACROSS SHOULDER total measurement (TM)	Measure from shoulder point (where the shoulder seam meets the armhole seam) to shoulder point front and back.
6	FRONT – LENGTH	There are several methods for measuring front length. Be sure to specify which of the following you used: a. FRONT LENGTH/HPS–Measure from the HPS straight down to the bottom of the garment. b. FRONT LENGTH/CF–Measure down the center front of the garment from the neckline to the bottom.
7	BACK – LENGTH	There are several methods for measuring back length. Be sure to specify which of the following you used: a. BACK LENGTH/CB–With the back of the garment facing you, measure from the center back neckline seam to the bottom of the garment. b. BACK LENGTH/HPS–Measure from the HPS straight down to the bottom of the garment.
8	HPS TO UNDERARM	Measure from the HPS to the bottom of the armhole.
9	ACROSS CHEST (TM)	Measure garment straight across one inch below armhole front and back.
10	ACROSS WAIST (TM)	Measure from side to side at narrowest point front and back. The womenswear waistline can be located by measuring down 17" from the HPS. Drop 18" for men.
11	SIDE–LENGTH	Measure the side seam from the armhole to the bottom of the garment. If the garment has slits, measure to where the slits begin.
12	BOTTOM EDGE OPENING (SWEEP) (TM)	Make sure that any pleats or gathers are fully extended and following the contour of the hem. Then measure bottom edge of the garment.
13	COLLAR BAND	a. HEIGHT–Measure at center back from neckline seam to top edge of collar band. b. LENGTH–Measure along the center of the collar band from center of button to the end of the buttonhole.
14	ARMHOLE CIRCUMFERENCE (TM)	Following the armhole seam contour, measure from the shoulder point to the bottom of the armhole. Multiply this measurement by two for the total circumference.
15	COLLAR WIDTH CENTER BACK	Measure at center back from the collar seam to the edge of the collar.
16	COLLAR WIDTH @ POINT	Measure along the edge of the collar point.
17	COLLAR SPREAD	Measure across between the points of the collar.
18	UPPER SLEEVE WIDTH (TM)	Measure straight across 1" down from the armhole at a right angle to the folded edge of the sleeve.
19	SLEEVE LENGTH	There are several methods for measuring sleeve length. Be sure to specify which of the following you used: a. SLEEVE–LENGTH/OVERARM (FROM SHOULDER SEAMS)–Following the contour of the outside of the sleeve, measure from top of armhole seam at the shoulder to the bottom of the sleeve (including the cuff). b. SLEEVE–LENGTH/UNDERARM–Measure from where the armhole and underarm seam meet to bottom of the sleeve (including the cuff). c. SLEEVE–LENGTH FROM CB–With the back of the garment facing you, follow the contour of the sleeve and measure from the center back of the neckline to the bottom of the sleeve (including the cuff). d. SLEEVE–LENGTH FROM HPS–Following the contour of the sleeve, measure from the HPS to the bottom of the sleeve (including the cuff).
20	ELBOW (TM)	Measure across midpoint of sleeve at a right angle to the folded edge.
21	SLEEVE OPENING (TM)	With the tape measure at a right angle to the center fold of the sleeve, measure straight across the bottom of the sleeve where it attaches to the cuff.
22	CUFF–HEIGHT	Measure straight down from top to bottom of cuff.
24	SLEEVE PLACKET	a. LENGTH–Measure straight down the sleeve placket without including the cuff. b. WIDTH–Measure straight across the sleeve placket.
25	DEPTH OF SLEEVE HEM	Measure straight down to the fold.
26	BINDING–WIDTH/HEM	Measure straight down to the fold.
27	FRONT PLACKET–WIDTH	Measure across the placket.
28	YOKE	Measure down from HPS.
29	POCKET–WIDTH	Measure across the top of the pocket.
30	POCKET–LENGTH	Measure down the center of the pocket. For irregularly shaped pockets, take a second measurement down the side of the pocket.
31	POCKET FLAP	Measure from top to bottom down the center of the flap. For irregularly shaped flaps, take a second measurement down the side of the flap.
32	POCKET PLACEMENT	a. Establish the vertical placement of the pocket by measuring down from the HPS to the top of the pocket. b. Establish horizontal placement of pocket by measuring across from the center front to the side of pocket.
33	PLEATS–DEPTH	Measure the depth of pleats.
34	PLEATS PLACEMENT	Measure the distance of the pleat to the center front/center back.
35	BUTTON PLACEMENT	Measure the distance of the center of the first button to the neckline seam. Measure the distance of the center of the first button to the center of the second button. Typically, buttons are evenly spaced thereafter.

Figure 4.1 *Continued*

Specification and Make Detail Sheet

Style: RZ41986

Fabric: 100% Cotton, Wrinkle Resistant, Relaxed Fit

Description: Khaki Pants

Original Size: 34/30

Specification:

Waist: 33 1/2

Seat: 23 1/2

Knee: 11 1/8

Inseam: 28 1/2

Outseam: 38 5/8

Rise: 10 1/8

Company: Eddie Bauer®	Size Class: Men's Product Type: Khaki Pants
Description	**Measurement**
WAISTBAND:	Width = 1 1/2 inches; Length = 33 1/2 inches
POCKETS:	
Backside traditional besom pocket	Width = 5 7/8 inches; Length = 1/2 inch
Location	2 inches from left and right side seams; 4 inches from the top of the waistband
Depth of pocket (inside of pant)	9 inches from bottom of waistband; 6 1/2 inches from pocket seam; width = 6 7/8 inches
Backside traditional besom pocket button	Width = 5/8 inch; Quantity = 2
Location	1/2 inch from top of traditional besom pocket; 2 3/8 inches from the left side of the pocket; located in both backside pockets
Backside traditional besom pocket	1 inch, Quantity 2
Button hole	
Location	1 inch from top seam; 2 1/2 inches from left side seam of pocket; located on both pockets
SIDE HAND POCKETS:	Length = 6 inches along side crease of pants; Quantity 2
Location	2 3/4 inches from top of waistband
Depth of pocket (inside of pant)	12 1/2 inches from bottom of waistband; width = 6 1/2 inches
FRONT SIDE BELT LOOPS:	Width = 1/2 inch; Length = 2 1/4 inches
Right hand side facing pant, pant loop	3 7/8 inches from button hole flap
Left hand side facing pant, pant loop	6 1/2 inches from inside flap seam
BACKSIDE BELT LOOPS:	Width = 1/2 inch; Length = 2 1/4 inches
Right hand side facing pant, pant loop	1 1/2 inches from right hand seam
Left hand side facing pant, pant loop	1 1/4 inches from left hand seam
Center backside pant loop	8 inches from left hand side seam
HARDWARE:	
YKK metal zipper	Length = 6 5/8 inches
Location	1 3/8 inches from top of waistband; 8 3/4 inches from left side seam
FUNCTIONAL BUTTONS AND BUTTON HOLES:	Buttons = Four Holes; Stitch = Cross stitched; Thread Color = Dyed to match
Inside closing button on top flap	Width = 5/8 inch; 2 3/8 inches from end of flap; 3/4 inch from top of waistband
Corresponding button hole on inside flap	Width =1 inch; 1/2 inch from end of inside flap; 5/8 inch from top of waistband
Closing button on inside flap	Width = 5/8 inch; 2 1/4 inches from end of inside flap; 3/8 inch from top of waistband
Corresponding button hole on outside flap	Width =1 inch; 1/2 inch from end of outside flap; 1/2 inch from top of waistband
LABELS:	
Eddie Bauer logo	Width = 1 3/4 inches; Length = 1/2 inch
Location	On right hand side of back of pant; 1 3/8 inches from right hand side seam; 1 5/8 inches from bottom of waistband
Eddie Bauer logo with Since 1920	Width = 2 1/4 inches; Length = 1 inch
Location	Inside lining of back of pant; 9 1/4 inches inwards from left hand seam; 1/8 inch from top of waistband
Wrinkle Resistant Relaxed Fit label	Width = 2 inches; Length = 5/8 inch
Location	Inside lining of back of pant; 11 5/8 inches from left hand seam; 3/8 inch from top of waistband

Figure 4.2 *Each company creates its own version of a make detail sheet, which conveys all the details necessary to manufacture a garment or accessory.*

refers to the measurements on the spec sheet and is represented by a plus or minus symbol. Apparel sewing is not an exact science, as it is still labor intensive. Thus, a tolerance is created by allowing the garment to be over or under when measured against the spec sheet. For example, on a men's woven sport shirt, the chest measurement on a size medium may be 40 inches with a tolerance of plus or minus 1/2 inch. By creating the tolerance, you allow for the sewer to be over or under and still meet the size specification.

o The last step in this process is to try the garment on a live model or a form to check for proper balance and make any final adjustments.

If you go through all the above steps and determine that several of the samples do not meet your specifications and/or were poorly sewn, you have the following three choices:

o drop the samples from the line
o send the samples back for corrections
o have the samples remade from scratch

What would you do?

TESTING MARKET REACTION

Everything is coming together. You are confident that the line is right and that it is well suited for your target market. The samples look great, they fit well, the theme is cohesive, and it is time to test the waters. One technique is to set up appointments with key customers to get their initial reaction. This can be tricky as you may feel strongly about the line, but your regular buyers might not feel as you do and suggest drastic changes.

If you face a situation with some of your key customers in which they are not in total agreement with your line/theme, you have a decision to make. Do you risk not getting any orders from these important buyers, or do you work together to come to some understanding? If you choose to work together, you might make some token changes that reflect the feelings of the buyers but that will not undermine all the hard work you have put into the line to date. By doing this, you make the buyers partners in the process. Then they have a vested interest in buying the line and helping it to succeed.

SHOWING YOUR LINE AND PLACING PRODUCTION ORDERS

You open up your real selling season in June/July and start calling on your buyers to set up appointments to show the line. At this point, your company will have made one of the following decisions:

o to go ahead and place production orders (this is known in the industry as buying shelf stock)
o to pre-sell the line, collect orders, total them up, and then place production orders

The decision made will vary from company to company. Let us say, for example, that you produce a line of basic T-shirts, which are a commodity item and always in demand. You might go ahead and produce without orders in hand.

You create shelf stock, as your liability is low, and you have a good track record of past sales. On the other hand, if you produce moderate- to better-priced fashion goods, you will most likely collect orders and then manufacture the products. These goods have a much higher risk and a shorter shelf life.

Once you are in the business, you will hear the term **goods** on a regular basis, as in the following examples:

o Where are the goods?
o I need to inspect the goods.
o Are the goods on the water? (Have the goods been put on a ship from overseas?)

Basically, the term *goods* means anything that you can produce and sell. It can be menswear, women's wear, or children's wear. This term gets a lot of use in the fashion industry.

MANUFACTURING AND DELIVERING THE GOODS

Imagine that you have had a successful selling season, and you have collected enough orders to make the production run profitable. Now, the actual manufacturing of the product must take place. Remember that you are a design and marketing company, so you rely on your manufacturing partners for your actual production. As an example, imagine that the key item in your line is a men's woven sport shirt. This is the item you will follow in the production cycle. In general, the principles that apply to the production of a woven shirt will hold true for most menswear items.

What have you accomplished in the process so far? You have designed the shirt, chosen fabrics, sampled the garment, decided to include it in the line, and pre-sold it. Now, it is time to manufacture the shirt and deliver it to the customer. The process started in January, and it is now July/August.

Your customer has set a delivery date. This date can be found on the purchase order, which will indicate when the shirts are needed in the customer's warehouse or store. Most large retailers today will bring the product into their own warehouses for inventory and **quality control (QC)** purposes before distributing to their various retail outlets. This aspect of the business will have an effect on the delivery date required by the buyer, as some warehouses can take up to two weeks or more to process orders through the system and get the merchandise shipped. The retailer also has to allow for transit time to the stores, as well as the time it takes to get the merchandise out on the selling floor.

The delivery date is agreed upon, and the wheels are set in motion. Your manufacturing partner has several options, which would have been taken into account at the beginning of the process, as they have a direct bearing on cost. The options of your manufacturing partner include the following:

- They can **import** the shirts.
- They can produce them domestically.
- They can cut the fabric in the United States, send the cut parts to a country in the Caribbean Basin, Central or South America, or Mexico for sewing, and then bring the completed shirts back to the United States.

As you look at these options in more detail, decide which would be best for your company.

IMPORTING

The manufacturer that you have chosen to work with might own their own production facilities here in the United States or they could produce products in a factory they own in another part of the world. A third option would be to contract with a third-party manufacturer to produce the woven shirts. Then the fabric and **findings** (trim items such as buttons and zippers) are arranged, and the manufacturer proceeds to produce the shirts according to your specifications. Then, the finished product is shipped to the United States. Remember, a large majority of the factories only cut and sew the garments, so the fabric has to come from someplace else. The fabric mills that supply the **piece goods**, which is another name for fabrics, could be located in a different country.

If the manufacturer you chose is using a third party, or a **contractor**, to make the shirts, you could arrange to purchase a finished product. This means that the third party will be responsible for the following:

o   providing all the fabric (which would be sourced from a fabric mill) and trims (findings)
o   producing the shirts
o   shipping the finished garments

The term *contractor* generally refers to a company or factory that provides sewing and other specialty services. In today's industry, the term is applied to any company or factory that provides production of apparel. Another option is to buy the fabric and trims and ship them to the factory. Then the factory is responsible only for cutting the fabric and making the garments.

In the author's opinion, the best option is to buy the **full package**, as it puts the responsibility on the factory to make sure everything runs smoothly. When you buy a full package, you issue a contract or purchase order for a specific number of garments. For this example, imagine the order is for 2,000 woven sport shirts. The factory will be responsible for providing everything to complete the sport shirts, including cartons, hangers, and anything else required to complete a full package.

If you choose to buy the fabric and trims yourself, the factory will be providing **CMT**, which stands for "cut, make, trim." In this case, you provide the factory with all the materials to make the shirt—not only the fabric and trims, but also the necessary patterns and markers.

- **Patterns** are diagrams of the pieces of the garment. These include all the parts of a shirt, such as fronts, backs, yokes, sleeves, pockets, collars, cuffs, plackets, and so on.
- A **marker** is a diagram or arrangement of the pattern pieces as they will be placed on the fabric before it is cut. Picture a jigsaw puzzle; all the pattern pieces are arranged in the most efficient manner so that the pieces fit together in the best way possible. You can never get them to fit exactly as you must leave room to cut the fabric. The task is to arrange the pattern pieces so you waste as little fabric as possible in between them. Today, markers

are often generated by computer, and have a high degree of efficiency, thereby minimizing any waste of fabric. As anyone in the fashion industry knows, fabric is money.

When the factory provides CMT, it does the following:

- cuts the fabric
- sews the pieces together
- trims the garments by applying buttons, labels, and tags
- presses the garments
- places the garments in polybags
- prepares the garments for shipping

How do you pay the factory for the production of the shirts? If you own the overseas factory, you will most likely use an internal accounting mechanism. If you are importing a full package, you will most likely use a financial instrument called a **letter of credit (L/C)**. The letter of credit can be a complicated financial document that is executed between your bank and a bank nominated by the factory with which you are doing business. The exact terms and conditions vary by transaction. For your purposes, you need to know that once you or your company opens the L/C, the dollar amount of the transaction is frozen in your account. In this case, the amount of money frozen in your account will be the amount of the purchase order that you have agreed on with the factory, and that amount will be held until such time as the L/C is negotiated.

The L/C is usually negotiated at the time of shipment, as long as all the conditions set forth

In my 28 years in the industry I have done my fair share of traveling, and on some days, I have asked myself "why am I doing it?" Long plane flights, eating unfamiliar foods, and traveling to countries that lack drinkable water are just a few of the challenges.

On one trip in particular, I found myself acting as co-pilot—with zero piloting experience! My company had just started producing men's shirts in the Dominican Republic for Eddie Bauer, and the buyers wanted to visit the factories to make sure that they met with Eddie Bauer's **code of conduct** and quality requirements. The code of conduct is a document that almost all companies require suppliers and contractors to sign before doing business. The code is the company policy that defines the firm's expectations for policies and behavior (of employees and contractors/factories) concerning

(continued)

in the agreement have been satisfactorily met. The main considerations are whether the shipment is on time, and whether it has been approved from a quality control standpoint. Quality control includes "the efforts applied to assure that the end product/services meet the intended requirements and achieve the customers' expectations" (Glock & Kunz, 2005, p. 641). The most likely scenario is to have a representative from your company and/or a third-party inspection service audit the shipment prior to release. Companies will require a signed certificate of inspection approving the shipment to accompany the necessary documents to release the L/C.

Once the L/C has been paid to the factory, it is very difficult, if not impossible, to get your money back, should you encounter problems with the shipment once it arrives in your warehouse. Thus, you need to take as many precautions as possible. Goods have been shipped and L/Cs paid where quality issues were overlooked or missed at the factory level. One recourse is to negotiate a lower cost on your next order, provided you want to keep doing business with that factory.

Importing is a way of life in the apparel industry, especially in the menswear business. With importing, travel usually is a part of the job. This can be a good thing or a bad thing. Traveling as part of the job is good in the sense that you do get to visit some great places. You can also find yourself in some unusual situations.

DOMESTIC PRODUCTION

Fewer companies today than in the past have the luxury of **domestic production**, or being able to produce apparel in the United States. The latest figures cited were 30 percent of the country's total apparel consumption, which means that $28 billion worth of apparel, is still produced here in the United States. The main reason for the decline in domestic production is the high cost of labor in the United States, and to a lesser degree, the cost of materials. Just as in the case of importing, a company could own a factory in the United States or it could choose to contract the job of manufacturing the product to a third party.

If your company owns a factory in the United States, you will pay for the goods in the same way as in the example of the company-owned factory overseas. If you contract with a third-party manufacturer, you will arrange your terms of payment, which can be a domestic letter of credit, cash terms, or net terms, which refers to a condition of sale when a cash discount is neither offered nor permitted. If you purchase something on net 30 terms, your payment is required within 30 days.

Advantages to manufacturing in the United States include the following:

o You have greater control over the production process. Producing in the United States means you are no more than several hours away from any city at any given time. If you have a production problem, you can travel to the production facility within a relatively short time versus sitting on a plane for 14 hours if you are producing in the Far East.

o Reduced transit time can be a critical factor in getting your product to the retailers. If you

---

human rights issues. More recently, these codes have been expanded to include environmental issues.

I was the salesperson responsible for the account, so it was my responsibility to travel with the buyers. As a vice president for the company, I was also responsible for my company's decision to work in these particular factories. The buyers arranged to stay in one of the resort areas on the island. Since it was a resort, we decided to fly down on Saturday, play golf on Sunday, and visit the factories on Monday.

Monday arrived, and we met to visit the factories, which were on the other side of the island. I had arranged for a car to pick us up, but when I inquired to the concierge, he refused to allow us to travel that way. He explained that if we traveled the route that we had planned, the car would be stopped in the mountains by banditos and we would be robbed.

(continued)

A wave of panic swept over me. I was on the island with one of my biggest customers, not looking very smart for failing to anticipate this situation. The concierge told me not to worry; we could hire a plane and fly to the other side of the island. I told the folks from Eddie Bauer that we had to fly, but it would have to be Tuesday as I needed to check with my boss first. The arrangements were made for Tuesday. I alerted my contacts in the factory of the situation, and we were set.

Tuesday arrived. We went to the airport, which was a grass strip in the back of the resort. The pilot approached the four of us and asked who made the arrangements, so I advised him that I had. He promptly said, "Señor, today you are the co-pilot." The color drained from my face and the faces of my traveling companions. The pilot told me to climb in the front seat but not to touch anything!

(continued)

have the garments produced in the Far East, it will take at least four to five weeks to receive your merchandise once it is shipped, whereas if they are produced in the United States, you can always use Guaranteed Overnight Delivery (GOD) or one of the other freight expediters, such as UPS or FedEx if you are in a real hurry.

Of course, it will generally be more expensive to have the goods made here in the United States.

807 PRODUCTION

The other option is to use a system called Item 807. That is the original designation given to this program by the U.S. government; today it is formally known as 9802.00.80. The concept of **807 production** was first established to keep more apparel and textile businesses here in the United States and, perhaps, help stem the tide of imports. In order to take advantage of this program you are required to do the following:

○   buy and cut your fabric in the United States
○   purchase your trims in the United States
○   send the entire package, including sewing thread, to a country specified to participate in the program

Originally, under the 807 designation, countries located in the Caribbean Basin and Mexico were allowed to participate in the program. With the change in designation to 9802.00.80, countries in sub-Saharan Africa were also covered by the program.

Once the fabric pieces, trim, and thread arrive in the country of choice, the workers sew the garments. They also prepare the finished garments for the retail stores by pressing and pinning them and putting them into polybags.

Your company will pay **duty** only on the value added, which is the cost of the labor used to sew and finish the garments in this case. *Duty* is another word for tariff; the term *duty* is more commonly used in the industry. In effect, it is a tax, or fee, levied by the government on imports. The cost of the duty is passed on to the customer; a markup is applied to the cost by the seller, and the retailers who purchase the products also apply their own markup. What starts out as a $2 duty can become $4 by the time it reaches the retail level. Duties are not limited to 807 production; they apply to all products that are imported into the United States, which will be discussed later in this chapter.

COMBINATION PRODUCTION

When deciding where to get your goods made, your choices include the following:

o   direct import
o   domestic production
o   807 production
o   a combination of direct import, domestic production, and 807 production

How would a combination work? Imagine you have just received an order for 100,000 woven sport shirts. The buyer needs his initial delivery in the stores in three months, and the balance of the goods can flow over the next six months.

If fabric is available in the domestic market, you can arrange to have the first portion of the production for the buyer's initial delivery

As it turned out, the flight was uneventful and the scenery was gorgeous. The trip over the island took less than 20 minutes, and we were met by my contact from the factory in an old Toyota Land Cruiser. This Toyota had an extra accessory that I had not seen on any vehicles in the United States. It was a double-barreled shotgun bolted to the dash. The part about the banditos must have been true.

The return flight was also uneventful. We returned to the resort, and the buyers at Eddie Bauer placed a big order so, all in all, the trip was a success.

made in the United States, or 807 production, with the balance of the shirts being imported. This way, you can take the order and cost average the difference between the import and the domestic/807 production. Keep in mind that this method has to be monitored very carefully, so that the product that is made domestically and/or under the 807 program matches the imported product. Through careful quality control, you can eliminate the risk of mixing the stock.

Avoiding such a mix of stock is important. If you receive a mixed lot, it will be very obvious at the retail level and it can have negative effects on sales. A mixed lot can be made up of the same garment with the same base fabric, but due to the variations in dying and other finishing techniques, the fabrics might not be matched in terms of colors and/or shades. Have you ever encountered a rack of shirts or other garments that were selling for the same price and made of the same fabric but looked quite different? Most likely, these were the result of a mixed lot.

NEW TECHNOLOGIES

The process outlined on the preceding pages is by no means the definitive way of doing business; in fact, every company has its own way of designing, marketing, and producing goods. In the menswear trade, there are many variations among companies; some consist of two or three people while others employ thousands of people and produce diverse products that are sold all over the world.

For large manufacturers that can afford the latest technology, companies such as Lectra and Gerber Technology have created a host of products to make the manufacturing process flow more smoothly. This section identifies several solutions that are used in the industry today. There are other software and hardware companies providing technical systems for the apparel and textile industry, but Lectra and Gerber Technology are two of the best in the business.

LECTRA

Lectra supports Gallery Web, which manages collections from start to finish. Figures 4.3 to 4.5 are examples of products that Lectra offers to help its customers compete in the global market.

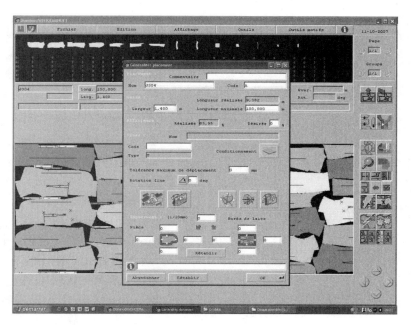

Figure 4.3 Visual display of Lectra Diamino program.

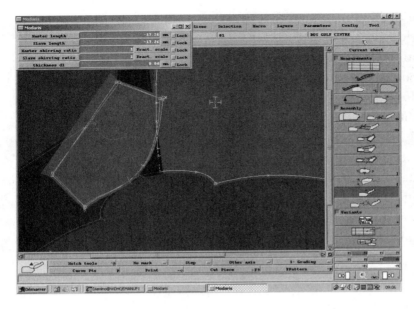

Figure 4.4 Modaris is part of Lectra's CAD program.

GERBER TECHNOLOGY

Gerber Technology's tag line is "Expect more," and they deliver on that promise in the products that they offer to the industry. Figures 4.6 to 4.8 are examples of many of the products that Gerber offers to the industry.

POLITICAL AND GLOBAL INFLUENCES

It is a fact of life that if you are involved in the apparel/textile industry, you will be involved in an import situation. For that matter, as a consumer, you already are. Just look at the men's clothing and accessories that you or a family member own. I challenge you to find five items with country-of-origin labels stating "Made in the U.S.A." Why is that? As mentioned earlier in the chapter, it comes down to economics. As a designer, you have to ask, "Where can I get my

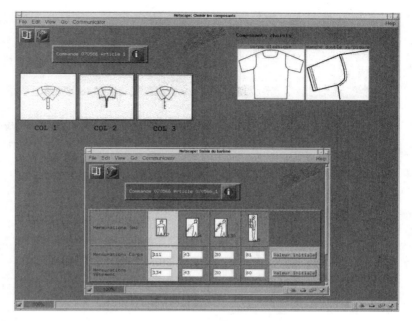

Figure 4.5 FitNet, Lectra
Technology.

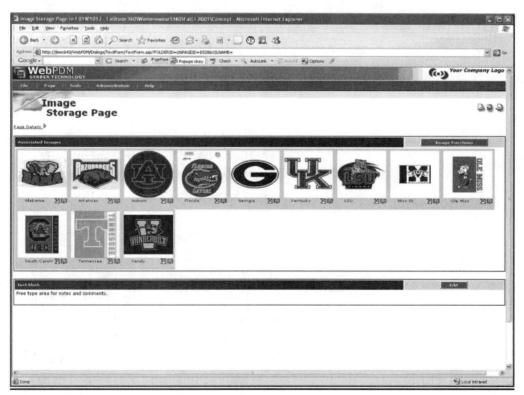

Figure 4.6 Gerber Web PDM image.

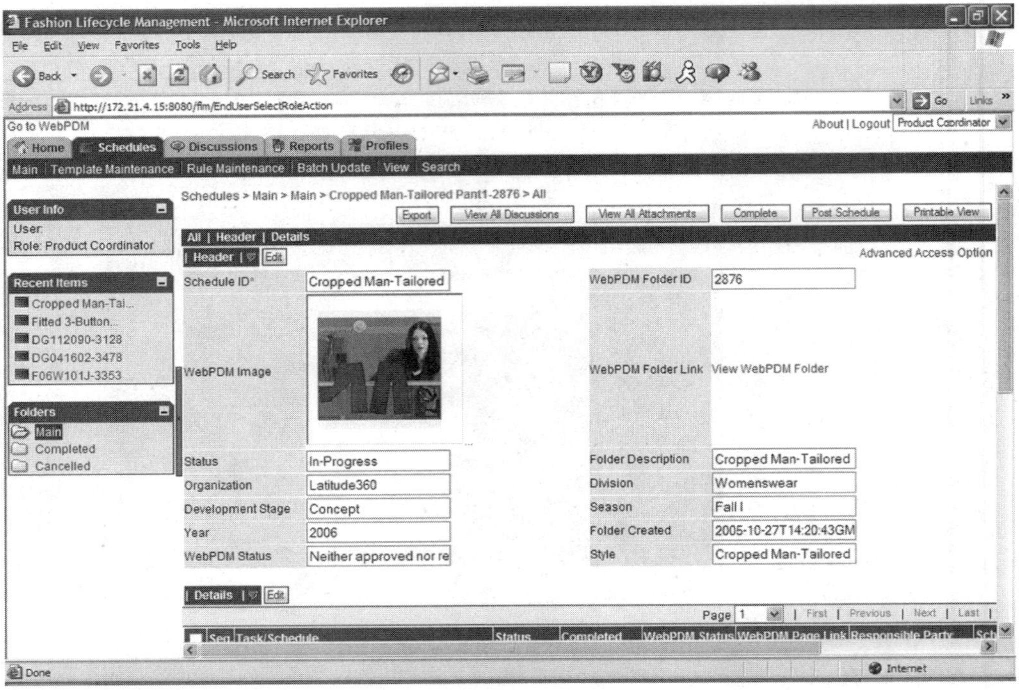

Figure 4.7 *Image storage page from Gerber program.*

goods produced that will allow me to meet my profit goals and deliver a quality product to the retailer that will, in turn, meet their target market?" The most likely answer is to import. Conversely, as a multinational business, you might also be in the position to export your product to another country.

CHOOSING A TRADING COUNTRY

From which country should you import? You always have to keep your target customer in focus. If you are Wal-Mart, will you choose to import ties from Italy? If you are Neiman Marcus, would you import ties from Vietnam? There are no easy answers to these questions. Ties made in Italy

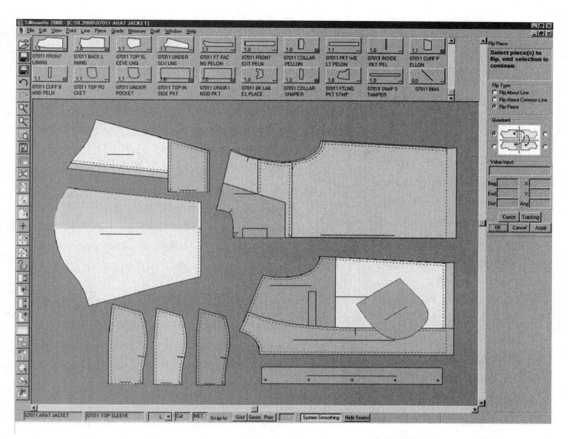

Figure 4.8 Preparing pattern pieces for marker making using Gerber technology.

normally imply expensive goods and will probably not fit with Wal-Mart's target market. Vietnam implies inexpensive production where the workers are not yet highly skilled, and so it would not be the best fit for Neiman Marcus. Each manufacturer and retailer must use the resources at its disposal to seek the country that best fits its needs.

What should you consider when choosing a country from which to import? Criteria could include the following:

o   Stability of the government: Have there been any recent political upheavals that would cause concern about traveling there?

o Ease of travel to the country of choice: Sometimes it comes down to direct flights versus connecting flights. Another consideration is whether the factories are accessible by car once you arrive in the country (see side bar "On a Wing and a Prayer").

o Availability and willingness of the labor force: Not all labor forces are willing. Our industry is labor intensive, and not all populations want to take on manual labor.

o Availability of technology: Laundry facilities might be an important factor to consider, for example. Some dyeing and finishing techniques require very technical equipment that may not be available in all countries being considered.

o Employee safety issues: Do the facilities have proper fire exits? Is there proper ventilation for the workers?

o Technical expertise: If a machine breaks down, is there a person on site that can make the necessary repairs?

o Code of conduct, human rights, and environmental issues: Today more than ever, dealing with human rights and environmental issues is critical for success. Would you produce in a sweatshop atmosphere or in ways that are highly damaging to the local environment?

o Production capacity: Can the factory produce garments in the amounts you require and at the time needed?

- Language/cultural issues: Working in foreign countries can be difficult when there are language and cultural differences.
- Availability of materials: Are the necessary fabrics and trims readily available, or do they have to be sent in from another country?
- Transportation issues: Some factories are in remote areas, and goods have to be transported to the seaport by truck before they can be loaded onto ships. This is not always as easy as one might think. In addition, container ships can be backed up in ports at any given time, especially during a busy shipping season.
- Weather-related issues: Monsoons can affect shipping production. In some countries, the trucks transporting goods are not covered, and shipments can get wet.

These are just some of the criteria to think about when choosing your trading partner/country.

GLOBAL ECONOMIC ISSUES

In addition, there are other issues to consider regarding the global economy. In 1995, the **World Trade Organization (WTO)** was created out of the General Agreement on Tariffs and Trade (GATT). The World Trade Organization, which is headquartered in Geneva, Switzerland, is the global international organization dealing with the rules of trade between nations. At its heart are the WTO agreements, negotiated and signed by the bulk of the world's trading nations and ratified by their governments. The goal is to help producers of goods and services, exporters, and importers conduct their business.

DOING THE LAUNDRY

I know it may sound obvious, but you do need to investigate all aspects of your production before placing your orders. On one occasion, I had placed an order for rugby shirts that were to be garment-washed with a factory in the Dominican Republic. The factory staff assured me that everything was okay with the job, and, as I had used this factory before for other products, I was not unduly worried. When it was time for a factory visit, I entered the factory grounds to see all of the beautiful rugby shirts that Eddie Bauer had ordered hanging on clothes lines. The workers at the factory were able to wash the garments, but they lacked the necessary equipment to machine-dry them! Suffice to say, you need to ask all the right questions before placing your business with a factory in another country.

For the apparel/textile industry, the most significant action came by way of the **Uruguay Rounds** of GATT that reduced and eventually eliminated **quotas** on apparel and textile products. A quota was a limit set by a government on the amount of a particular product that could be imported into that country. All quotas were abolished as of January 1, 2005.

GATT was created by the Bretton Woods meeting held in Bretton Woods, New Hampshire, in 1944. The purpose of this meeting was to set out the plan for recovery after World War II by encouraging the reduction in tariffs and other international trade barriers, or quotas. It took from 1944 until 2005, but the quotas are gone and tariffs have been reduced somewhat. However, tariffs are still a major source of revenue for many governments. Remember that a tariff, also known as duty, is a tax that is imposed on any product being imported into a country.

As a result of the elimination of quotas, the United States has witnessed a tremendous surge of imports, particularly apparel and textiles from China. This surge caused concern on the part of the apparel and textile industry in the United States. Within the body of the agreement to eliminate quotas, there is a mechanism that allows for **safeguards** to be put into place to stem such a surge. Congress petitioned the president to impose safeguards as a way to slow down the increase in several categories of merchandise that had the potential to disrupt the business of domestic producers. The safeguards were, in effect, a form of quota.

The product categories that were affected by this measure were textiles made from certain synthetic filament fabrics, brassieres, and other body-supporting garments. Other categories are also under consideration for safeguards, including the following:

o   cotton and man-made fiber sweaters
o   cotton and man-made fiber dressing gowns and robes
o   men's and boys' wool trousers
o   knit fabric

It remains to be seen if these newly established safeguards will have any long-lasting benefits to the industry.

IMPORTING INTO THE UNITED STATES

In order to properly assess tariffs, the U.S. government has created the **Harmonized Tariff Schedule of the United States (HTSUS)**. This publication is thousands of pages in length and classifies every conceivable product that one would want to import into the United States (see Figure 4.9).

The page from the HTSUS in Figure 4.9 deals with the importation of woven shirts. Earlier in the chapter, a woven sport shirt was selected as the example to be followed through the production process. In this case the shirts are 100 percent cotton. You designed the 100 percent cotton woven shirt. You went through the entire sample process, from fabric to findings, and you selected where you wanted to make the shirts (domestic, 807, import). You had ample lead time, so you chose to import from China.

The shirts are now complete, and the workers at the factory in China want to be paid. Before you

CHAPTER 62

ARTICLES OF APPAREL AND CLOTHING ACCESSORIES, NOT KNITTED OR CROCHETED 1/

Notes

1. This chapter applies only to made up articles of any textile fabric other than wadding, excluding knitted or crocheted articles (other than those of heading 6212).

2. This chapter does not cover:

    (a) Worn clothing or other worn articles of heading 6309;

    (b) Orthopedic appliances, surgical belts, trusses or the like (heading 9021).

3. For the purposes of headings 6203 and 6204:

    (a) The term "suit" means a set of garments composed of two or three pieces made up, in respect of their outer surface, in identical fabric and comprising:

    -    one suit coat or jacket the outer shell of which, exclusive of sleeves, consists of four or more panels, designed to cover the upper part of the body, possibly with a tailored waistcoat in addition whose front is made from the same fabric as the outer surface of the other components of the set and whose back is made from the same fabric as the lining of the suit coat or jacket; and

    -    one garment designed to cover the lower part of the body and consisting of trousers, breeches or shorts (other than swimwear), a skirt or a divided skirt, having neither braces nor bibs.

    All of the components of a "suit" must be of the same fabric construction, color and composition; they must also be of the same style and of corresponding or compatible size. However, these components may have piping (a strip of fabric sewn into the seam) in a different fabric.

    If several separate components to cover the lower part of the body area presented together (for example, two pairs of trousers or trousers and shorts, or a skirt or divided skirt and trousers), the constituent lower part shall be one pair of trousers or, in the case of women's or girls' suits, the skirt or divided skirt, the other garments being considered separately.

    The term "suit" includes the following sets of garments whether or not they fulfill all the above conditions:

    -    morning dress, comprising a plain jacket (cutaway) with rounded tails hanging well down at the back and striped trousers;

    -    evening dress (tailcoat), generally made of black fabric, the jacket of which is relatively short at the front, does not close and has narrow skirts cut in at the hips and hanging down behind;

    -    dinner jacket suits, in which the jacket is similar in style to an ordinary jacket (though perhaps revealing more of the shirt front), but has shiny silk or imitation silk lapels.

    (b) The term "ensemble" means a set of garments (other than suits and articles of heading 6207 or 6208) composed of several pieces made up in identical fabric, put up for retail sale, and comprising:

    -    one garment designed to cover the upper part of the body, with the exception of waistcoats which may also form a second upper garment, and

    -    one or two different garments, designed to cover the lower part of the body and consisting of trousers, bib and brace overalls, breeches, shorts (other than swimwear), a skirt or a divided skirt.

    All of the components of an ensemble must be of the same fabric construction, style, color and composition; they also must be of corresponding or compatible size. The term "ensemble" does not apply to track suits or ski-suits of heading 6211.

1/ See Section XI, Statistical Note 5.

Figure 4.9 *Page from the Harmonized Tariff Schedule of the United States. This is just one of thousands of pages illustrating the information provided by the U.S. government regarding tariffs.*

send payment, you must have someone inspect the shirts to make sure they meet with all of your specifications, from garment quality to packing materials. You elect to use your own quality control person, who happens to be in the region. Your other choice in this case would be to hire an outside firm to carry out the final inspection, which would result in an additional cost.

The certificate is signed, and the manufacturer draws down the L/C at the same time as the goods are shipped. Since they were bought on a **Freight on Board (FOB)** basis, you own the goods the minute they ship. Therefore, you are responsible for any insurance, freight, duty, clearing costs, brokers fees, and any additional costs that might arise. Other ways to set up the purchase include the following:

o **Net Terms:** You negotiate the purchase, take possession of the goods, and agree to pay at some specified time in the future. The payment due date can be net 30, 45, or 60 days from receipt of the goods. This works well for a domestic purchase, and even an 807 purchase, but with an import on net terms, the manufacturer is required to pay for the duty, transportation, brokers fees, and other miscellaneous costs associated with the shipment.

o **Landed Duty Paid (LDP):** You take possession of the merchandise once it has arrived and cleared customs. Here, the cost of the merchandise as indicated by the dollar amount on your invoice will be higher than the FOB, as the duty and transportation charges are paid by the exporter. As in the case of the FOB purchase, your invoice will not reflect any freight charges or duty costs as these cost factors are your responsibility. Although the government sets the duty rate, you have control over the method and carrier used to transport your freight.

o **Cost, Insurance, Freight (CIF):** In this instance, you are paying for the cost of the goods, any insurance you might have on the shipment, and the freight. You are also responsible for the duty once the goods arrive.

There is no easy answer as to which method you should use to purchase the goods, as each has advantages and disadvantages. Most companies use the FOB method, which gives them control over variables such as freight charges and clearing costs—although not duties, which are set by the government and paid at the same rate by everyone.

ADDING IT ALL UP

In this chapter's hypothetical situation, you are importing woven shirts from China that you designed. Total **costs** will be as follows:

o The first cost is what you pay the manufacturer for the full package. This cost is $10.00 per shirt on an FOB basis. As a full package, this cost includes the fabric, trims, packaging, and finishing.

o Freight to the United States by ship will cost about $0.20 per shirt.

o In the HTSUS, the duty, or tariff rate, on the woven shirts falls under category 340 at the rate of 19.7 percent. On your $10.00 shirt, that duty comes to $1.97 per shirt.

o Brokers fee is $0.10 per shirt.

- Miscellaneous charges include items such as drayage, which takes into consideration the cost of moving the freight out of the port once offloaded from the ship and the eventual transporting of the merchandise to your warehouse. This charge is $0.15 per shirt.

Add the costs up, and you get a cost of $12.42 per shirt.

You need to make a profit on these shirts, so you add your profit margin of 40 percent, or $4.98, so now each shirt costs at $17.40. The $4.98 is your gross profit. Based on the history of the company, by selling the shirt at $17.40, you will wind up with a net profit of 5 percent or $0.87 per shirt. Remember that your original purchase was for 100,000 shirts so the net profit on this one order would be $87,000.00.

There is one last number to consider. You sell that $17.40 shirt to a department store that marks it up 63 percent. The retail price becomes $47.00. A garment whose first cost was $10.00 is now sold to the consumer for $47.00!

CONCLUDING THOUGHTS

In this chapter, you looked at the manufacturing process in the menswear industry. The goals of this chapter were to help you learn the following:

- how the manufacturing process operates in the men's apparel industry and various options available when sourcing production
- how the research process interacts with design and manufacturing
- the importance of quality control in the overall design and manufacturing process

The author used research and his understanding of the menswear business to achieve these objectives. Personal anecdotes set in sidebars were included to highlight interesting details about conducting business in the menswear industry. In addition, current technologies were discussed, including key programs from both Gerber Technology and Lectra. Financial instruments were introduced, and a costing exercise was undertaken to illustrate how a garment that is imported into the United States is brought to market.

In Chapter 5, the topic of retailing will be introduced. The chapter will look at the origins and history of retail in the United States, from the early settlers to modern times. The various segments that make up retail business will be discussed, as well as some of the key players. As with the design and manufacturing aspects of the menswear business, retail has also been influenced by new technologies; Chapter 5 will consider some ways in which technology has affected retail trade.

KEY TERMS

807 production
CMT
code of conduct
collection
contractor
cost
Cost, Insurance, Freight (CIF)
domestic production
duty
findings
Freight on Board (FOB)
full package
goods
Harmonized Tariff Schedule of the United States (HTSUS)
import
Landed Duty Paid (LDP)

letter of credit (L/C)
line
make detail sheet
marker
Net Terms
pattern
piece goods
quality control (QC)
quota
safeguard
spec sheet
swatch
target market
tolerance
Uruguay Rounds
World Trade Organization (WTO)

CLASS EXERCISES

1. You are looking for a new source of supply for your menswear company. Choose an article of menswear that you want to source. Using the examples of a spec sheet and a make detail sheet in Figures 4.1 and 4.2, create your own spec sheet and make detail sheet for this product. The manufacturers you work with will use these documents to calculate the cost and create a sample of the product you wish to develop. Remember to include every detail, or you will have to answer many questions later, which will delay the process. Note

that creating a spec sheet and a make detail sheet is not an exact science, and the terminology you use may be different from that used by your classmates. The main purpose of this exercise is to get you thinking about all the details that go into creating a garment and to practice verbalizing these details so that you will become more familiar with the process.

2. Look up a current menswear designer.
   a) Describe their target market.
   b) Report on the current state of the designer's business.

3. Look up a menswear manufacturer.
   a) Who are their customers?
   b) What level (low end, middle, high end) of menswear do they sell?
   c) What are their key products?
   d) Do they have any licensing agreements? If so, who are the partners?

4. Case Study: Mr. Michael O'Shea is the president and founder of XYZ Menswear. XYZ has been manufacturing, marketing, and selling men's sportswear for over 30 years. The products have always been produced domestically. XYZ owns two factories in the southern part of the United States. The company employs over 500 people in its two factories. Many of the employees have been with the company from the start. In fact, in each of the factories, there are three generations working on the same sewing line, grandmother, mother, and daughter!

   The company has lost market share and money for the last five years. Prior to that, it had seen double-digit increases for many years. However, in 2001, its fortunes started to turn. The company continues to receive compliments on its styles, fabrics, and designs, but it is no longer cost-competitive. In addition, several key salespeople have recently left because they could no longer satisfy their customers' needs.

   a) What can Mr. O'Shea do to try to save the business?
   b) Identify steps Mr. O'Shea should have taken as soon as the company started to lose money.
   c) What is the future for companies like XYZ?

REFERENCES

Armstrong, G., and Kotler, P. (2005). *Marketing: An Introduction*. Upper Saddle River, NJ: Prentice Hall.

Glock, R., and Kunz, G. (2005). *Apparel Manufacturing Sewn Products Analysis*. Upper Saddle River, NJ: Prentice Hall.

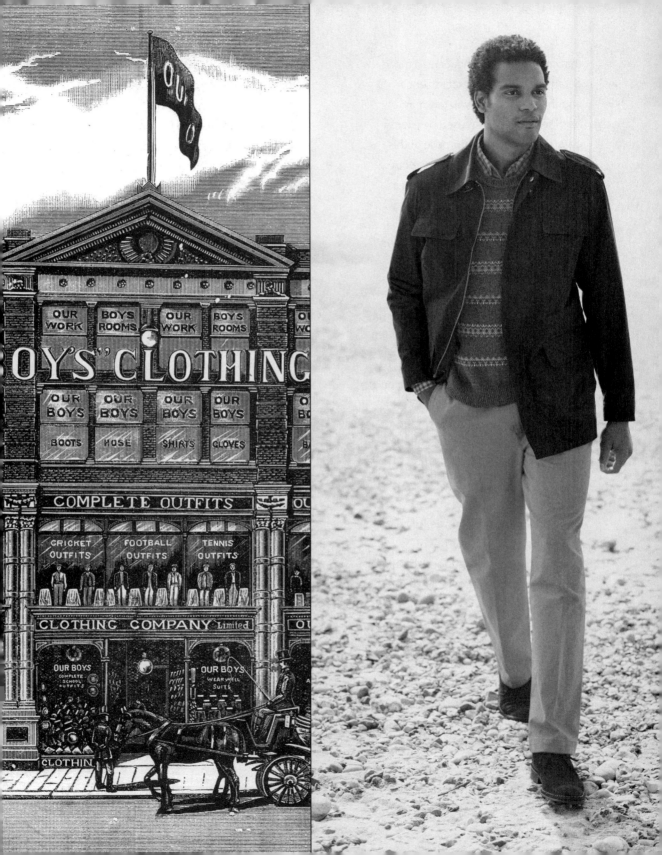

FIVE

RETAILING

- o the origins of the retail industry and the segments that make up today's menswear retail landscape
- o information related to the buying function and how it differs among retail operations
- o how technology has changed the way retailers conduct their business

Where do you shop for menswear? Have you ever given any thought to the origins of the retail trade? Can you describe the various retail institutions that exist today? What are the functions of buyers? How has technology changed how buyers perform their jobs? These and other questions will be answered in this chapter.

What is a retailer? A **retailer** is defined as "a business that sells products and services to consumers for their personal or family use"; **retailing** is "a set of business activities that adds value to the products and services sold to consumers for their personal or family use" (Weitz, 2004, p. 719). Each of these definitions focuses on the consumer. The key difference arises on the retailing side as "a set of business activities" created to add value to the shopping experience. As a consumer, you have most likely experienced the various levels of what retailers call "activities," and these activities have affected your own shopping experiences, perhaps in both positive and negative ways. Activities such as return policies, availability of alterations, hours of operation, sales practices, and home delivery can have a major impact on how you view your shopping experience.

In this chapter, you will look at the different retail segments. Then, as a consumer and a student of fashion, you can determine which retail segment lives up to the true definition of retailing.

THE ORIGINS OF RETAILING

The roots of retailing go back thousands of years. However, as this country is not that old, we will not go back quite that far, as we explore the question of how retailing took root in the United States.

With immigration to the United States in the 1700s, people needed to purchase food, clothing, and other supplies. Most families were largely self-sufficient; they grew their own crops, spun yarn for fabric, and made their own clothes. However, not everyone had the ability or the resources to meet all their own needs; that is where peddlers and trading posts came into play.

PEDDLERS AND TRADING POSTS

Peddlers carried their wares in wagons and traveled from homestead to homestead offering for sale the items that they had with them and taking orders for future delivery. In fact, the expression "drumming up business" originated with the peddler. As the peddler approached a homestead, he would bang on a wash basin to make the sound of a drum. This approach had two purposes: it alerted the occupants of the

Figure 5.1 In rural America, itinerant peddlers were the retailers of their day.

homestead that the peddler was arriving, and it protected the peddler from being shot at. Remember that this was back in the day when people lived far apart from each other and had to be wary of strangers approaching. Today, retailers and salespeople often remark that they need to go out and drum up some business. The difference is that today the saying is used more in the sense of using marketing and sales techniques to attract business.

With the movement of people throughout the newly established colonies, the need for a more formal method of buying was established in the form of trading posts. These trading posts were set up in more populated areas. Some folks had to travel for hours by horse and buggy in order to reach the trading posts to buy the necessary staples. When new clothes were needed, there were no racks of ready-made items to choose from. At that time, every item of menswear had to be hand made, as modern manufacturing techniques were still years away.

READY-MADE CLOTHING

"The term *clothier* was originally used to describe a finisher of wool cloth. But by 1790, it had come to mean a dealer in ready-made clothing" (Boswell, 1993, p. 40). In the next phase, menswear progressed from hand-tailored, individually fit garments to clothing made by tailors and offered for sale as manufactured garments. These garments were still hand sewn against a set of measurements, although they were not made for anyone in particular. They were the precursor to modern ready-to-wear.

"The gradual change in name designation as retail selling practices evolved could be exemplified by following the career of one Adam Chirnside of New York City. In 1790, the New York City directory listed Adam Chirnside, located at 5 Old Slip, merely as a retailer. During the years of 1791–94, he was listed as a tailor and shopkeeper, and in 1795, he was listed as a dealer in ready-made clothes. The successive changes in listings were indicative of the growing importance of ready-made clothing and the need to be known as a seller of such clothes. The term *clothing store* spread to Boston where it made its first appearance in public notices in 1813 under the name of Thomas Whitmarsh" (Cobrin, 1970, p. 42). Although Thomas Whitmarsh was the first to advertise as a clothing store, it was not the first retailer to appear on the scene. Credit for the first retailer would have to go to the general store.

Figure 5.2 *Early retailer located in downtown setting.*

These retail operations were set up in strategic geographic locations to cater to a growing population in the United States.

MAIL-ORDER CLOTHING

In 1872, Aaron Montgomery Ward established the first mail-order catalog. It offered 163 items for sale and delivered them via the postal service. Montgomery Ward later established itself as a major retailer in the United States with many stores and a strong catalog presence lasting until 2001, when it was forced to close due

Figure 5.3 *Montgomery Ward produced the first mail-order catalog in 1872.*

to a downturn in sales and antiquated catalog facilities. The only presence Ward's has today is as an online retailer offering select catalogs. It is now based in Cedar Rapids, Iowa. Unfortunately, it offers little to no apparel.

Sears Roebuck went into the catalog business in 1896 and continues as a major retailer to this day. However, like Montgomery Ward, Sears Roebuck has a significantly reduced presence in the mail-order business today. The poor state of the plant and equipment at Sears' distribution centers contributed to the decline of the company's mail-order business; these facilities were almost 100 years old and had not been updated with modern systems over the years. Also, a growing number of companies were getting into the specialty mail-order business. These companies offered new and interesting products, as well as some of the traditional products offered by Sears; they also offered better customer service and sometimes better pricing.

The advent of the Industrial Revolution and the ability to produce apparel in large quantities resulted in more retail establishments. Several inventions helped to foster this growth, including the following:

o   1791—Samuel Slater opened the first spinning mill in the United States.
o   1794—Eli Whitney patented the cotton gin.
o   1813—Francis Cabot perfected the power loom to weave fabric.
o   1845—Elias Howe invented the sewing machine.

From the 1700s until the mid-1800s, population increases created a need for mass-produced apparel, and technological improvements made such mass production possible. Particular groups of men, including sailors, slaves, and miners, had a need for cheap ready-made clothes, and the expanding middle class wanted good-quality clothing at reasonable prices.

With the establishment of mass-produced apparel, a distribution system was needed; the retail sector as we know it today was born. In 1818, Brooks Brothers first opened its doors, and 10 other major department stores followed its example through the mid-1880s:

o   1826—Lord & Taylor
o   1842—Gimbels

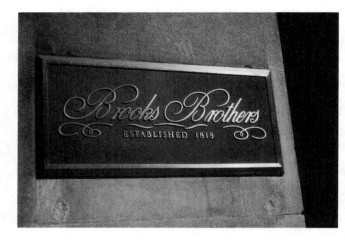

Figure 5.4 Brooks Brothers was the first of many major department stores selling menswear.

- 1849—Famous Barr
- 1851—Jordan Marsh
- 1852—Marshall Field's
- 1854—Carson Pirie Scott & Co
- 1857—Macy's
- 1862—Stewart's
- 1867—Rich's
- 1869—John Wanamaker and Co

All of these major department stores, with the exception of Macy's and Lord & Taylor, have disappeared from the retail landscape. The physical stores themselves have not gone by the wayside, but the names have changed. Federated Department Stores, now officially called Macy's, bought the majority of the stores on the list and now controls the largest market share in the department store category. The department store remains a destination for shoppers looking for the latest trends in fashion, just as it was when these stores first appeared on the scene.

The United States Census Bureau separates the menswear industry into five categories as follows:

o   clothing: suits, sport coats, topcoats, overcoats, dress slacks
o   furnishings: shirts, ties, underwear, socks, pajamas
o   heavy outerwear: windbreakers, snowsuits, ski jackets, heavy sportswear
o   work clothes: uniforms, overalls, work shirts
o   other: hats and miscellaneous

Although the government breaks the industry down into the above categories, for our purposes and those of the retail industry, this chapter will concentrate on three categories: clothing, sportswear, and furnishings.

CLOTHING

To the average consumer, *clothing* usually means any type of garment that can be worn. "In the strictest sense of the word, however, this is not true in menswear. Everyone might wear apparel, but only men wear clothing" (Boswell, 1993, p. 41). Therefore, the term **clothing** usually means mid- to higher-quality tailored garments, such as suits, sport coats, dress slacks, and tailored outerwear. These garments carry a higher price tag and are more likely to be subjected to the process of tailoring or some degree of alteration so they will better fit the customer. The topic of clothing and the individual articles of apparel that make up the clothing industry will be covered in more depth in Chapters 7 through 10.

What do you think of when you hear the term sportswear? Nike? adidas? Reebok? If you do, you are half correct. From an industry perspective, sportswear is broken down into subcategories, including the following:

o activewear, which includes the following:
  o spectator sportswear, which covers a wide range of garments that consumers may buy to affiliate themselves with a sports team or school; most of these products are sold under licensing agreements (see Chapter 3) and are, for the most part, not used in any actual sports activity
  o participatory sportswear, a subcategory of activewear, which is actually worn while participating in a sport or exercising
o casual wear, including casual pants, shorts, knit and woven tops, and sweaters; these types of garments, once considered for weekend and leisure wear, have become a mainstay in most men's everyday wardrobes, especially with the casualization of the workplace in America

Casual wear and activewear, including spectator sportswear and participatory sportswear, have become extremely large businesses and will be reviewed in more depth in Chapter 10.

Furnishings make up the final category. This category is the most comparable to the women's wear market. Items that are housed in the furnishings area include the following:

o dress shirts and ties
o pocket squares and handkerchiefs
o belts and suspenders
o socks and underwear
o pajamas and robes
o jewelry
o umbrellas
o scarves, hats, and gloves
o other items that do not reside in any other department

Furnishings have taken on a much more meaningful place in the industry over the past several decades. This is evident when you visit a local department store and look at the amount of floor space dedicated to the furnishings department.

Dress shirts, which are sold by neck size and sleeve length, are the only type of shirts that you will find in the furnishings department. Sport shirts, knit and woven shirts in sizes ranging from S to XXL, are sold in the sportswear section.

The furnishings area has increased in popularity as more designers and retailers continue to emphasize the importance of accessories in dressing. The choices have increased tenfold. It is easier and more cost effective to go out and buy a new tie, dress shirt, pocket square, or piece of jewelry to complement a suit that you already own than to go out and buy an entire new outfit. As men continue to increase their fashion awareness and venture more fully into the furnishings area, this department will become more important. We will revisit this topic and explore it in more depth in Chapter 8.

Just as the industry identifies three main categories of menswear, there are different categories of retailers that sell menswear products.

DEPARTMENT STORES

The United States Census Bureau (Stone & Samples, 1985) defines a **department store** as one that employs 25 or more people and sells general merchandise in the following categories:

○ furniture, home furnishings, appliances, radios, and television sets
○ general lines of apparel and accessories for the family
○ household linens and dry goods

The fashion industry takes a somewhat different view. "Department stores are large retailers that divide their functions and their merchandise into sections, or departments. Department stores have a fashion orientation, follow a full markup policy, and operate in stores large enough to be shopping center anchors" (Burns & Bryant, 2002, p. 457). Given this definition, can you name several department stores? Certainly, the number-one player in the field today is Macy's, a division of Federated Department Stores. Others that fall into the industry definition include the following:

○ Dillard's
○ Nordstrom
○ Belk Stores

Figure 5.5 *Many department stores, such as Macy's, serve as shopping center anchors.*

- o Saks Fifth Avenue
- o Neiman Marcus (which was once classified as a specialty store)

There are also other stores that would be considered regional department stores, but like many department stores throughout the country, they have been bought by Federated and have been changed over to Macy's. Two examples are Burdines in Florida and Marshall Fields in Chicago.

Although the department store has been criticized in the past for being boring, confusing, and old-fashioned, its image has been revitalized in recent years as more emphasis has been placed on fashion that is appropriate for the stores' target markets. There has also been a strong push for more private labels (labels that can be purchased exclusively in one store and are owned by that store).

For example, Macy's has built successful private-label programs to support four lifestyles, which it has identified as key components in its merchandising strategy. The lifestyles are as follows:

○ The Traditional customer takes a conservative approach to life. He cherishes tradition and distrusts change.
○ The Neo-Traditional customer has traditional values and mainstream taste, but he is open to change. Convenience and comfort are critical due to his busy lifestyle.
○ The Contemporary customer is an independent thinker who looks for functional design and whose career is a high priority.
○ The Fashion customer thrives on change and is constantly looking for the next fashion statement. This customer will settle for design over quality and will have moved on to the next fashion long before his purchases wear out.

Lifestyle segmentation is the organizing principle behind Macy's private-brand strategy and individual brand development. In menswear, the key labels include the following:

o	Alfani	Neo-Traditional
o	American Rag	Fashion
o	Club Room	Traditional
o	Exceed	Neo-Traditional
o	INC	Contemporary
o	John Ashford	Traditional
o	Material London	Neo-Traditional
o	Tassa Elba	Traditional

Each label can be purchased only at Macy's and represents a specific brand lifestyle of their customers.

In addition, department stores have placed a renewed emphasis on customer service as a way to increase and maintain their customer base. Of the retailing activities mentioned at the beginning of the chapter, those related to customer service are the ones that stand out. Important questions to be answered in terms of customer service include the following:

o When you shop, is there adequate sales staff on the selling floor?
o Does the salesperson take good care of you?
o Was your shopping experience pleasant?
o Will you return to this retailer?

If staff members who deal with customers perform their jobs properly, then the answer to these questions will be yes. If not, they can count on not having you back in their store. Even a discount store like Wal-Mart has greeters at the entrance to welcome you to the store and help

Figure 5.6 Specialty stores such as Gap limit their merchandise to a single category or a single brand.

direct you. However, after that, you are strictly on your own.

The government definition states that a **specialty store** carries a limited line of merchandise, or may specialize in selling one or very few types of merchandise (Boswell, 1993). The industry takes a similar view. As the name implies, to be considered a specialty store, the store must do one of the following:

○ specialize in a single category of merchandise or a few closely related categories targeted to a well-defined market
○ carry the merchandise of one manufacturer or brand

Specialty stores have a limited selection of a merchandise category, but they carry full size and color assortments. Generally, one or possibly two **price zones** will be found in specialty stores. A price zone is a retail strategy of pricing merchandise to fall between two set prices. For instance, you could price all your merchandise between $80 and $100, and this would establish your price zone. Within the zone, you could have multiple prices for your products, but none would be lower than $80 nor higher than $100. Some stores specialize in higher-end designer looks; these stores are often called boutiques. Given our definition, specialty stores include the following:

- GAP
- Banana Republic
- Hollister
- Abercrombie & Fitch
- Eddie Bauer

Brooks Brothers was founded in 1818 as the first ready-to-wear fashion emporium in America. Known for its high-quality merchandise, personal service, and exceptional value, Brooks Brothers continues to be a major force in the menswear market to this day. Based on its superior reputation, quality, and service, the prices it commands are a bit higher than the average consumer will usually spend. Over the years, Brooks Brothers has boasted among its clientele Abraham Lincoln, Ulysses S. Grant, Theodore Roosevelt, Herbert Hoover, Franklin D. Roosevelt, John F. Kennedy, Richard Nixon, and Bill Clinton. In 2006, Brooks Brothers introduced a line of suits dedicated to John F. Kennedy, and the line will carry his name. Brooks Brothers has a very long history; some of the more recent events that have shaped the retailer include the following:

o   Marks & Spencer of England acquired the chain in 1988.
o   In 2001, Retail Brand Alliance, headed by Claudio Del Vecchio, purchased Brooks Brothers from Marks & Spencer and continues to run the business today.
o   Also in 2001, Brooks Brothers was the first retailer to introduce body-scanning technology that allows customers to customize their suits, sport coats, trousers, and dress shirts. The result was great-fitting custom-made clothing, precisely tailored to fit the body's unique contours and specific proportions.
o   In 2006, Brooks Brothers continued to uphold its fine tradition and commitment to quality and extraordinary customer relationships.

Family Britches is a local specialty store with locations in Chappaqua, New York, and New Canaan, Connecticut. Family Britches has been in business for a little over 36 years and has fine-tuned their retail assortment to fit the target market in each area. The fine-tuning that has occurred over the years is the result of careful selection of the merchandise that they carry in their stores. In order to make the best merchandise selections, Family Britches does the following:

o   carefully listens to customers' wants and needs
o   responds to customers' suggestions about what merchandise to carry

Figure 5.7 Family Britches is a small, two-store retailer that is customer-focused.

The two towns where the stores are located have similar demographic makeups, and the stores cater to the affluent male consumer. As a small retailer, Family Britches can be much more customer-focused than a large chain. Some of the salespeople are actually the owners; if a client makes a suggestion about a brand or designer, these salespeople have the power to make the decision to stock the store with that brand or designer. Of course, there has to be a consensus that the products they are investing in will sell to more than one customer. Additional research is generally conducted with other customers, or a small amount of the product may be brought in on trial.

Family Britches publishes an entertaining, educational magazine that doubles as a direct mail piece and their main form of advertising, with over 92 pages of editorial content and brand advertising.

Barry Mischkin and Rick Buggee, two of the three partners of Family Britches (the third is

Mark Gust), attribute their success to having the right product at the right price when the customer needs it. The store carries brands from Zegna, Corneliani, Polo, Hickey Freeman, Paul & Shark, David Chu, Gimo's, Ballin, Robert Talbott, Zanella, Bills Khakis, Vineyard, St John, Scott Barber, Hiltl, and Canali, to name a few. These brands are geared toward an income demographic that usually fits into the top 10 percent of the nation. Barry and Rick know who their customers are and what their customers want from them. Family Britches caters to the customer in the following ways:

- It is built around lifestyle brands.
- It is easy to shop there.
- It is staffed with professionals.
- If they don't have it and you want it, they will get it for you (Barry Mischkin and Rick Buggee, Partners, Family Britches, in discussion with the author, December 5, 2006).

CHAIN STORES

Chain stores are a group of retailers that are centrally owned and controlled by a central office, and that handle similar merchandise. It is a commonly held belief that, in order to be considered a chain store, the chain must have 11 or more stores. Given this definition, most specialty stores and department stores, as well many discount and off-price stores, would be considered chain stores. However, from a sales and marketing standpoint, especially in menswear, the industry has traditionally considered three major

Figure 5.8 Two of the leading retail chains are **(a)** Sears and **(b)** JCPenney.

retailers when discussing the "chains." They are as follows:

- JCPenney
- Montgomery Ward
- Sears

If you were working in the menswear industry, and you were assigned the job of selling to the chains, these would be your accounts. Montgomery Ward is no longer in business as a retail store, which leaves Sears and JCPenney as the true chains, as far as the industry is concerned.

The following characteristics are typical of chain store organization:

o centralized buying (Sears buys in Chicago; JCPenney buys in Plano, Texas)
o no single flagship store
o centralized distribution
o typically standardized store decor and layout

Private-label merchandise plays an important part of the merchandise mix in these retailers. Name-brand designers have always been reluctant to sell to this tier of the market for fear of diluting or even losing their department store placement. JCPenney features private labels such as the following:

o Worthington
o Arizona
o Stafford

Along with its private labels, Sears has also purchased Lands' End and installed shops within its stores to market the Lands' End brand.

DISCOUNT RETAILERS

Discount retailers sell brand-name merchandise at less than traditional retail prices. Retailers such as Wal-Mart, Kmart, Target, and Kohl's buy large quantities of merchandise at discounted prices and generally work on lower margins than other retailers, passing on the savings to consumers. Discount retailers are not typically known for their menswear. The discounters are more likely to stock staples such as underwear, hosiery, and flannel shirts in the winter and knit shirts in the spring/summer for men. The exception to this rule has been Target and Kohl's, which have earned the nickname "upscale discounters," or, in Kohl's case, "the neighborhood department store." These two store groups carry some better brands of menswear and have become a shopping destination for the value-oriented consumer. These stores are categorized as self-service with strong emphasis on promotional pricing practices.

FACTORY OUTLET STORES

Factory outlet stores are used by manufacturers to sell the following:

o   their own seconds
o   their irregulars (damaged merchandise)
o   their overruns (merchandise produced in excess of their orders)
o   their customer cancellations (orders canceled by other retailers)

Once primarily located close to the actual factory where the item was being produced, factory outlets can now be found all over the country. They can be found near major highways, tourist resorts, and many places in between, although they are generally located several miles away from any major full-price mall. With the advent of such large-scale operations, it has become common practice to manufacture product specifically to sell in the outlets, as there are not enough seconds, irregulars, and overruns to sustain an ongoing retail venture the size of the factory outlets.

OFF-PRICE RETAILERS

Off-price retailers also buy irregulars, overruns, and seconds, but they buy these products from other manufacturers and even retailers. This group of stores specializes in offering national brands, designer labels, or promotional goods for sale at discount prices. Companies that operate in this manner include the following:

o Burlington Coat Factory
o Marshalls
o T.J. Maxx
o A.J. Wright
o Ross Stores
o Syms

Given the extreme competition for goods in the market, these retailers have also resorted to making products under specific labels to sell in their stores. A buyer will go into the market and work with manufacturers, who might have made an opportunistic buy on fabric, to create a garment for one of these retailers to sell in their stores. When buyers who work for these retailers go into the market, they generally have the ability to write an order on the spot. The theory is that if they do not take advantage of a good deal when they see it, the next off-price buyer to come through the door most likely will. The opportunity to buy the goods will be lost for the buyer that hesitated.

This buying practice can often lead to inconsistent merchandise assortments and products that change on a regular basis. From the consumer's standpoint, this means frequent trips to these retailers to constantly check to see what new arrivals have been put out on the selling floor. Private-label merchandise is not a big part of the merchandise mix with these stores. However, Burlington Coat Factory, which was owned by the Milstein family and was recently purchased by another party, has started to add private labels to the merchandise mix.

OTHER RETAIL TRADING AREAS

There are other types of retail establishments and/or retail trading areas that can be considered, such as the following:

o   kiosks
o   flea markets
o   yard sales
o   consignment shops
o   thrift shops

Vending machines have even been used to sell men's dress shirts, socks, and T-shirts! For the most part, these other types of retail establishments constitute a very small part of the industry. However, they are places where men's apparel can be purchased, and they should be taken into consideration, as they provide opportunities in the marketplace for buying and selling.

THE NOW INFAMOUS QUILTED FLANNEL

As you know, I started my career with JCPenney as a Catalog Inventory Control Specialist (CICS)—sounds like a powerful position! One of the CICSs' responsibilities was to track sales and report to the buyers when we thought we needed to buy more products. We used early computer-modeling technology back then based on a percent-done method, which looked at the length of the catalog and computed what percent of the catalog was completed against the number of sales captured. Basically, each product in the catalog was assigned a rate of sales, which was typically based on a historical comparison. However, the quilted-flannel shirt was a new item and we did not have any history. Thus, we winged it.

As I recall, we used a woven-plaid sport shirt that was sold in a previous catalog as the basis to determine the number of shirts to buy for

(continued)

the new item in the upcoming catalog. Boy, were we wrong! Our estimates were way too low! In the first week, we blew through 50 percent of the season's estimate, and we had what we called a "runner." As a CICS, it was my responsibility to work with the buyer to capture as many sales as possible. As it turned out, we got lucky. The domestic shirt industry was not doing well, and there was plenty of production available.

We put two additional suppliers on the project, and in the end we wound up selling 83,000 shirts. Our initial estimate had been 12,000 shirts. At the same time, we captured 93 percent of the sales, which represented over $1million in sales generated for just that one page in the entire catalog. I am proud to say that this earned our department the designation of having a $1-million page, which was a big deal back then. This success garnered all of us a nice bonus, as well as a really swell plaque.

Nonstore retailers include any retailers that distribute products to consumers by means other than traditional brick-and-mortar retail stores. For menswear, the three most important and growing nonstore retailers include the following:

o   television
o   the Internet
o   mail-order catalogs

The growth in these areas can be attributed to the following factors:

o   increased demand by consumers for convenience, product quality, and overall selection
o   an extremely fragmented market
o   the continued shift in demographics, such as the increasing number of women in the workforce, single-parent households, time pressures, and increasing family incomes
o   the availability of credit extended by credit card companies
o   increased speed of delivery through parcel package services as well as the U.S. postal system
o   technological advances in encryption and security procedures, which make more consumers feel comfortable using the Internet to make purchases

MAIL-ORDER/CATALOG RETAILERS

Mail-order/catalog retailers "sell to the consumer through catalogs , brochures, or advertisements, and deliver merchandise by mail or other carrier. Apparel is one of the top-selling items bought through catalogs with nearly one in five Americans buying apparel through catalogs" (Burns & Bryant, 2002, p. 466). Mail-order catalogs now offer the consumer the convenience of ordering in the following ways:

- by mail
- by telephone through the use of toll-free numbers
- by fax
- over the Internet

Examples of mail-order retailers for the menswear market include J Crew, Lands' End, and Eddie Bauer.

TELEVISION RETAILERS

Television retailers do not play a big part in the menswear business and are more geared toward women's wear, accessories, and hard goods. The three main channels of distribution include the following:

- QVC (Quality. Value. Convenience.)
- HSN (Home Shopping Network)
- Shop at Home

Although some menswear products do pop up on these channels, it is not a regular means of selling menswear. These venues enable consumers to purchase right from the comfort of their homes. Technology has advanced to the point of allowing consumers to use their remote controls to place an order; they no longer even have to phone the order in to the retailer.

MOM'S ADDICTION

Home Shopping Network, better known as HSN, burst onto TV screens back in 1982 as the Home Shopping Club. My mom loved HSN. Living in the original Leisure Village in Lakewood, New Jersey, she had never learned to drive. The UPS driver quickly became her best friend!

Mom would turn on the TV and watch HSN for several hours at a time. She would invariably order something, as they had great bargains back in those early days. Everything she bought could be spread out over five or six easy payments of just $19.95 plus shipping and handling. Each Christmas, my brothers and sisters and I (there are six of us in all) knew where our presents were coming from and, regardless of what they were, we loved them all!

(continued)

On a serious note, home shopping via the TV can become an addiction, one that can have serious financial repercussions. Thankfully, my older sister intervened and cut up Mom's credit cards before it was too late. It really didn't matter by then, as they were maxed out anyway!

Back when Mom was buying up a storm, she had to dial her phone to place her order. Now all you have to do to click your remote control without ever taking your eyes off the TV, and then wait for the UPS truck to arrive!

Internet/e-commerce is the selling of goods over the Internet. Since the mid-1990s, the use of the Internet to market and sell products, including menswear, has grown consistently and continues to grow. In 2006, Americans spent over $100 billion shopping on the Internet. Industry experts suggest that this will increase to $225 billion by 2011. Many traditional brick-and-mortar retailers have added Web sites to their merchandising mix. Stores involved in Internet selling include the following:

o   JCPenney
o   Macy's
o   Sears
o   GAP
o   Wal-Mart
o   Target

Many retailers use the Internet as an extension of their regular retail operations. Some retailers report up to 10 percent of sales now coming from the Internet.

In addition, many manufacturers, designers, and brands have developed extensive Web sites. Some allow consumers to purchase products, while others continue to use the Internet for informational purposes. For example, Nike allows consumers to go online and purchase a pair of customized athletic shoes directly from its Web site. It appears easier to buy menswear online than women's wear, given the more consistent size specifications in menswear versus women's wear. As many women can attest, one retailer's size 8 could be another retailer's size 6, 10, or even 12. With men's size specifications, the chances are greater that garments sized as small, medium, large, or extra-large will be consistent from one retailer to another. Thus, men can be more confident that items they buy online will fit.

Continuing advances in technology, coupled with the younger generations' familiarity with technology, makes the potential of Internet-based sales virtually unstoppable. Will the Internet make traditional retailers obsolete? No, but Internet-based sales will become more important to many retailers, and the Internet will need to become part of retailers' overall marketing strategy. The Internet will challenge some of the weaker retailers and, perhaps, force further consolidation in the retail community.

BUYING PRACTICES OF THE RETAILER

The buying practices of retailers vary and are determined by several factors, the most important being size and type. The size of the retail operation helps determine how much merchandise a retailer can carry. The type of retail operation helps shape the buying methods.

MATRIX BUYING

Matrix buying is a term you will hear in large department store operations. For the most part, matrix buying is determined by committee within the retail organization, and it is a

Figure 5.9 *Matrix buying is determined by committee within the retail organization. Pictured here are a diverse group of buyers reviewing merchandise on open see day.*

coveted determination for suppliers to achieve. Each store determines what factors will qualify a supplier to be included in their buying matrix. One consideration is the brand name or designer label.

By way of example, imagine you are just starting your business, you sign a major licensing agreement with a national brand, and the department store carries that brand. This arrangement will most likely get you onto the matrix as this is a product/label that the department store already carries. On the other hand, if you open a new business and do not have any star power or do not represent a national brand, it will be difficult for you to break into the department store trade and to get on the matrix. Not all suppliers achieve the status of "being on the matrix."

Once approved, the advantages to suppliers can be substantial. Approval will guarantee distribution of the supplier's product to all the stores within the buying matrix, as most department stores operate on a centralized buying system. This set-up can also prove very frustrating for suppliers who are not on the matrix, as many buyers will not even grant suppliers an appointment to show their lines of apparel unless they appear on the matrix list.

BUYING FOR SMALL SPECIALTY STORES

As a retail buyer, you may find yourself buying for a small specialty store, or boutique, with one or maybe two stores. In this scenario, you are very limited as to how much you can buy and from what suppliers. In most of these situations, you are buying from designers or top brands that cater to small-size retailers. Consider how the scope of the buying decision varies from the boutique to a discount retailer like Wal-Mart. The boutique may buy 12 pieces of a style, while the buyer for a company like Wal-Mart might have an opening buy for 600,000 units! The general principle is the same, however; it involves getting the right merchandise for the target customer at the right time. It is just the scale that changes.

BUYING AND PRIVATE-LABEL PROGRAMS

Another change that has had a drastic effect on the retail buyer's function is the advent of large private-label programs. In the past, retailers would rely on the various manufacturers/ wholesalers they did business with to produce private-label programs for them. Now, it is the retailer who has built large infrastructures to

Figure 5.10 *Today, retailers deal directly with manufacturers of their private-label programs.*

deal directly with the factories to produce their own private-label programs. This practice cuts out the middle man, and retailers enjoy more control and profit with their private labels. In effect, the buyer works in conjunction with the product development department to do the following:

o provide input into what styles are appropriate for the selling season
o instruct the product developers on decisions such as size assortment and color selection

o   decide how much to buy and for what delivery, with input from the planning analyst

Technology has changed the way the buyer operates. It is not uncommon for retailers to record selling volumes in the billion-dollar range, and this money has to be budgeted down to the buyer level. Computer modeling using historical references makes it easier to create a top-down budget, which starts with a dollar figure and is subsequently divided amongst all the departments within the organization. The goal of top-down budgeting is to have all of the selling departments record enough sales to achieve the budgeted amount. Without this technology, the job of the planning analysts would be impossible.

Many retailers have added positions titled **planning analyst** to their organizations. The responsibilities of the planning analyst include the following:

o   telling the buyers how much money they can spend in any given time frame
o   telling the buyers how much merchandise to order and when to deliver the goods

In instances where an individual buyer has large buying power and is responsible for hundreds of millions of dollars, planning analysts can make the difference between profit and loss. Each planning analyst can control several buyers and untold millions of dollars.

Retailers in the off-price category buy in a different manner. Their main focus is finding opportunistic buys in the market on a regular basis. These buyers are literally out calling on manufacturers every day, as there is fierce competition among buyers to get the best deals at the most advantageous time. As mentioned earlier, the buyer for the off-price retailer can make the buy right on the spot, usually writing up an order at that time. This differs from buying for other types of retailers, who might take samples from the suppliers and go through an extensive line review before committing to purchasing any products.

One off-price retailer, Burlington Coat Factory, had a unique way of ensuring that they saw any and all suppliers. They held what they called an "open see day." That meant that if suppliers had products to sell, they went

Figure 5.11 Burlington Coat Factory is a leading off-price retailer.

to Burlington Coat Factory's offices on 38th Street in Manhattan with samples during the prescribed time (for menswear, it used to be Wednesday from 9:00–11:00 a.m.). The suppliers were guaranteed an audience with the buyer. Of course, that did not mean that the buyer would buy what suppliers had, but at least they were able to see someone.

WHO HAS THE POWER?

The retailers are in the driver's seat when it comes to offering products for sale to the consumer. The key issues always come back to knowing their target market and having the right product at the right price and in the right place at the right time. As the retail landscape continues to evolve with consolidations and mergers, the level of service that is demanded by the retailers continues to increase. The bottom line is that if suppliers want to sell to any or all of the retailers in their trading area, then they must abide by the retailers' rules. For every company that wants to sell, or is selling, in retail today, there is always someone waiting to take their place. The burden is not so much on the retailers as it is on the suppliers to get it right.

THE ROLE OF TECHNOLOGY IN RETAILING

Technology will play an ever-increasing role in the way retailers operate. Technology-based acronyms form a veritable alphabet soup: RFID, EDI, QR, SKU, UPC, and so on. What do they all mean? How do retailers use these systems and benefit from the technologies these acronyms

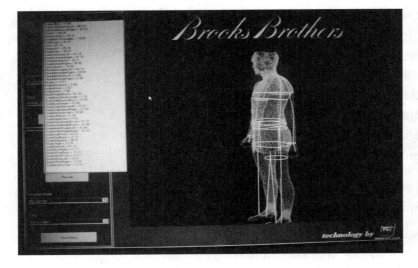

Figure 5.12 Technology is playing an increasingly important role in menswear retailing. For example, Brooks Brothers has introduced body-scanning technology to create a perfect fit for its clients.

stand for? As practitioners in the apparel industry, you will hear about one key issue: speed to market. This concept involves having the product on the shelves when the consumer wants to buy it. Several practices have helped put this issue into focus, with **Quick Response (QR)** at the forefront.

QUICK RESPONSE

Quick Response is a process created by U.S. manufacturers that allows retailers to replenish stock at virtually the same rate at which consumers are purchasing it. The use of technology and systems such as **Electronic Data Interchange (EDI)** makes QR possible. Although you may not have realized it, you have seen this system at work. You go to your favorite retailer and select an item to purchase. You take it to the cash register, where the cashier scans the bar-coded ticket to read the **Universal Product Code (UPC)**, which determines the **Stock-Keeping**

Unit (SKU) level. The scanned information is then transmitted to a computer. Depending on the model stock module in the system, a purchase order may be created, which is then electronically transmitted to the manufacturer or retail warehouse for immediate shipment.

The system is programmed to keep accurate stock information. The buyer or planning analyst sets a default in the system to tell the computer that, when the stock on the floor reaches a certain level, it is time for the system to create a new order to replenish the depleted stock. This system greatly reduces the need for human interaction. In the past, individuals would track stock and determine when to place new orders. Each order would have been handwritten and faxed or mailed to the vendor for shipment. This process was not only time-consuming, but it had a stronger potential for errors.

RADIO FREQUENCY IDENTIFICATION (RFID)

Once the product is shipped, the RFID system comes into play. This is a relatively new system, and it is not heavily used in the apparel market. However, once the problems are ironed out and companies see the profit potential, more and more companies will start to use this technology. **RFID, or radio frequency identification,** uses tiny microchips implanted in the actual product or packing materials to track the exact location of individual garments or the entire shipment. These chips contain no batteries; they respond by transmitting a unique identification code that is powered by the initial radio signal transmitted to the chip. RFID technology

Figure 5.13 *Microchips implanted in the product or the packing material allow continuous tracking of an apparel shipment.*

is so advanced that the chips are actually half the size of a grain of sand!

RFID tags are a useful development and a compelling technology. By using these microchips, retailers are able to reduce inventories and also reduce theft, which is estimated to cost the industry $50 billion per year. Even a 10 percent or $5 billion reduction in theft through the use of the microchips can have a major impact on retailers. One retailer that has embraced this new technology is Wal-Mart. Although they are starting off slowly, the potential savings for a mega-retailer such as Wal-Mart is staggering.

As with many new technologies, some controversy does surround the use of RFID. The key issue is privacy, specifically when the RFID microchip remains active after the consumer leaves the store. Will people have the capability to read the chips from any distance and thereby be able to track customers? With this technology, the potential for abuse does exist.

In an article titled "RFID Tags: Big Brother in Small Packages," journalist Declan McCullagh

(2003) presented the following four simple guidelines for retailers:

- ○ Consumers should be notified when RFID tags are present in what they are buying. A notice on a checkout receipt would work.
- ○ RFID tags should be disabled by default at the checkout counter.
- ○ RFID tags should be placed on the product's packaging instead of the product when possible.
- ○ RFID tags should be readily visible and easily removable.

CONCLUDING THOUGHTS

The goals of this chapter were to help you learn the following:

- ○ the origins of the retail industry and the segments that make up today's menswear retail landscape
- ○ information related to the buying function and how it differs among retail operations
- ○ how technology has changed the way retailers conduct their business

The chapter began by establishing a historical perspective on the retail trade, tracing the origins from the early settlers to modern-day retail. This chapter also presented information on the buying function. You learned how buyers carry out their jobs and how the buying position differs from one retailer to the next. Through interviews and research, you developed an informed view of what it means to work in the retail trade. You also took a peek at how technology has altered the retail landscape with new innovations that, at times, have created controversy.

In Chapter 6, you will learn how the media affects the menswear industry. The media plays an increasingly important role in getting the message out to the consumer. You will look at the various types of media used today, as well as the differences between the practices of advertising versus public relations. You will examine how marketing to the menswear customer fits into the overall media plans established by designers, manufacturers, and retailers.

CHAPTER EXERCISES

1. Choose a retailer to research from any level of distribution discussed in the chapter. Who is their target customer? What is their marketing strategy, including advertising? Name three other retailers that would be considered competition for your selection. Present your findings to your class.

2. Use the Internet to research ways that e-tailers are trying to reach consumers. What marketing strategies are they using?

3. Visit a retailer, introduce yourself to the store manager, and interview the manager to determine the retailer's target customer. What are some of the shopping habits of the customer? What are some of the visual merchandising techniques that the retailer uses to attract customers?

4. In this chapter, you have examined the different retail segments. Review the definition of retailing at the beginning of the chapter. Which retail segment lives up to the true definition of retailing?

5. RFID is a relatively new technology— one that can potentially be abused. From an ethical standpoint, how could this technology be abused? Could retailers and/or governments use RFID to track purchases you make? Some pet owners are already using these devices to keep track of their pets, so what is next? Can you foresee a world in which RFID chips are implanted in humans? Research the issues surrounding RFID technology further and debate the pros and cons of its use.

REFERENCES

Boswell, Suzanne. (1993). *Menswear: Suiting the Customer*. Englewood Cliffs, NJ: Regents/Prentice Hall.

Burns, L.D., and Bryant, N.O. (2002). *The Business of Fashion: Designing, Manufacturing, and Marketing* (2nd ed.). New York: Fairchild Publications, Inc.

Cobrin, Harry A. (1970). *The Men's Clothing Industry: Colonial through Modern Times*. New York: Fairchild Publications, Inc.

McCullagh, Declan. (2003). Perspective: RFID tags: Big brother in small packages [online]. Available: http://news.cnet.com/2010-1069-980325.html [December 12, 2006].

Stone, E., and Samples, J. (1985). *Fashion Merchandising: An Introduction* (4th ed.). New York: McGraw Hill.

Weitz, Levy. (2004). *Retailing Management* (5th ed.). New York: McGraw Hill.

NS | FASHION | GEAR | FEATURES | FORUMS | VIDEO | DET

scribe | features | fashion | politics | women | style guy | blog

GQ

OK SHARP // LIVE SMART
nday, October 15, 2007

BSCRIBE TO GQ
UBSCRIBE NOW
VE A GIFT
ENEW

YLE

GQ 100:
The Best Stores in
America

Suit Your Shape: Watch the
Video
GQ Rules: Building Your
Perfect Business Wardrobe
GQ Endorses
How to Buy a Watch
The 10 Best Suits Under $500
25 Style Secrets
The Style Guy: 500 of Your
Most Pressing Sartorial
Questions, Answered
How to Buy a Suit: Watch the
Video
The Style Guy Online: Weekly
Dispatches from Glenn O'Brien
The Sartorialist
The 10 Commandments of
Style
The Perfect Shirt-and-Tie
Wardrobe
How to Buy a Topcoat

ITICS

The Best of Our
Inside-the-Beltway
Coverage

MEN OF GQ

(WOME
WATCH
SEXY C
CRAWL
VIDEO

And see
of the ico
supermoe

(GALLE
THE CO
PORTF

From JFK
Alba, see
cover in
history…

(FOOD
THE SE
TEMPL
THE FO
WORLD

Alan Ric

E GENTLEMAN

nd to be noticed," says artist Richard Merkin,
y Dintenfass Gallery on West 57th Street and
ere, he wears a black bowler from Lock & Co.,

SIX

MENSWEAR AND THE MEDIA

- the different forms of media used in the marketing of menswear
- the difference between public relations and advertising and their impact on the industry
- how to use media effectively to market and sell menswear products

If you were to develop a new line of menswear today, what form(s) of media would you use to market and advertise your line? The answer to that question depends partly on the type of line you want to market (e.g., clothing, sportswear, or athletic wear) and more importantly, who your target customer is. What would be the most effective way to communicate your message to your target market? Before trying to answer that question, you need to look at the various types of media that could be used to accomplish your goals.

FORMS OF MEDIA

There are many different forms of media, including the following:

- **print media,** which includes consumer publications, trade publications,

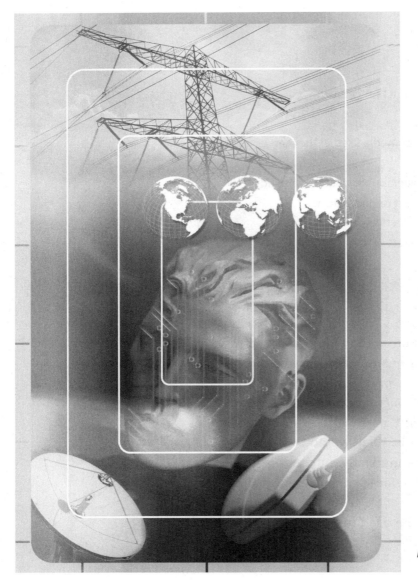

Figure 6.1 Menswear is marketed through a wide variety of media.

daily newspapers, direct mail, and catalogs

- **broadcast media,** which includes radio, television, video, billboards, the Internet, and other types of electronic media, such as cell phones

In addition, there are industry productions, such as trade shows and fashion shows that can be considered forms of media. These aspects will be covered in Chapter 12, when the supporting cast to the menswear trade is discussed.

The various media opportunities can have a strong impact on the promotion of fashion today. Think for a moment about the last time you looked in a magazine, turned on the TV, or surfed the Web. What did you see? No doubt you saw some form of advertising. Can you remember what the content was? Maybe you can, and maybe you cannot. However, if you saw an outfit that you liked, you would remember the outfit. This would get you thinking about how great you would look in the outfit if you bought it. That is the power of the media: to communicate a message to the consumer. That message can be informational in nature, or it can send a signal for action—in this case, the action of making a purchase.

PUBLIC RELATIONS AND ADVERTISING

Not all that you see in the media is considered advertising; some of what you see is **public relations**, or **PR**, as it is called in the trade. What is the difference between PR and **advertising**? "Public relations is the process of building good relations with the company's various publics by obtaining favorable publicity, building up a good corporate image, and handling or heading off unfavorable rumors, stories, and events" (Armstrong & Kotler, 2007, p. g6). "Advertising is defined as any paid form of non-personal presentation and promotion of ideas, goods, or services by an

Figure 6.2 Edward L. Bernays is considered to be the father of modern public relations.

identified sponsor" (Amstrong & Kotler, 2007, p. g1). What lies at the core of these definitions is really free versus paid forms of marketing.

The publicity generated by PR does not cost your company money out-of-pocket, although the PR department that puts out the stories about your company has a cost associated with it. Imagine a full-page story in a major newspaper or consumer magazine that discusses your company or a fashion trend that benefits your company. If you had to buy that same space, it might cost a considerable amount of money, but since it is PR, there is no out-of-pocket expense involved.

PRINT MEDIA

Several different types of print media are important to the industry. Each has its own specific purpose, but the ultimate goal is to communicate fashion news. Types of print media include the following:

o   consumer publications
o   trade publications

- daily newspapers
- catalogs
- direct mail

CONSUMER PUBLICATIONS

As the name suggests, the consumer is the primary target market for consumer publications. The publications that fall into this category focus on educating the consumer about the latest fashions and important trends. In addition, they offer general information on sports, travel, transportation, technology, sex, investments, world news, and politics. Some of the more popular consumer publications are noted in Table 6.1.

Each of these magazines targets a specific audience, although there is overlap among the readers. *GQ* caters to the fashion-conscious reader, and the content of the magazine is dominated by the men's fashion industry. *Esquire*, on the other hand, carries articles that are of an editorial nature, and they generally focus on non-fashion topics. *Esquire* does cover fashion-related topics from time to time, and the magazine is supported by advertisers from the men's fashion industry.

Recently, *Esquire* introduced a new publication titled the *Big Black Book, The Style Manual for Successful Men*. *Esquire* has lent its name to various other publications in the past, and this publication was viewed as an excellent opportunity to extend *Esquire*'s brand presence. Fashion writer David Lipke (2006a, October 2) interviewed publisher Kevin O'Malley, who stated, "This is a brand extension for us, a hybrid between a coffee table–style book and a magazine;

Figure 6.3 Consumer magazines such as GQ focus on educating the consumer about the latest fashions and trends.

it is very visually driven, it has no back ads and it's meant to be kept as a source book" (p. 12). Aimed squarely at the high-income man, the publication offers advice on timeless luxury, from five-figure watches to six-figure sports cars, as well as more practical advice like how to polish your own shoes. *Esquire* has promised advertisers that it will sell at least 100,000 copies at $9.95, and they hope with its success they will be in a position to publish the *Big*

Black Book twice a year starting in 2008 (Lipke, 2006a, October 2, p. 12).

In addition to *Esquire* and *GQ,* several other men's consumer publications have made it to the newsstands in recent years. Many of these are listed in Table 6.1. All of these magazines are geared toward the male consumer, and each tries to target a specific market. However, as mentioned previously, there is some overlap between several of the magazines. For example, both *Cargo* and *Stuff* target the male who is interested in sex, sports, jokes, gear, and fashion.

Regardless of the differences among the various publications, they all share a common purpose: to attract a male audience and, with the help of the advertisers who support these publications, to try to get them to buy the products that are advertised and otherwise featured in the magazine. In addition to advertising, the editorial content of magazines can also express favorable or unfavorable opinions about certain products and therefore can have an effect on the purchase of the products.

TRADE PUBLICATIONS

"Trade publications are those which address business issues important to the fashion and garment industries, including manufacturers, retailers, designers, suppliers and so on" (Boswell, 1993, p. 10). Only a handful of trade publications have survived over the years. The most important trade publication in the men's fashion industry is the *Daily News Record* or *DNR.*

Fairchild Publications publishes *DNR* and distributes it on Mondays each week in the form of a glossy newspaper, somewhat like

TABLE 6.1 CONSUMER MAGAZINES

GQ, or *Gentleman's Quarterly,* was launched in 1957. *GQ* is a monthly men's magazine focusing on fashion, style, and culture for men. Articles cover topics including food, movies, fitness, sex, music, travel, sports, technology, and books. The magazine has a monthly circulation of just under 800,000 and targets the upscale, sophisticated male.

FHM (For Him Magazine) first appeared on the newsstands as *For Him* in the United Kingdom in 1985. Later, its title was changed to *FHM.* It is currently published monthly in 28 different editions around the world; each edition accounts for a different language. Circulation is stated at 700,000 per month. *FHM* targets the young, trendy male through topics such as sports, movies, music, gadgets, gossip, men's fashions, the "bar scene," and extensive discussions on sex. *FHM* discontinued its print edition in the United States in March 2007 in favor of an all-digital format.

Esquire was founded in 1933. It began as a racy publication for men and has since transformed itself into a more refined publication with an emphasis on men's fashions, and the inclusion of contributions by famous authors. Circulation is pegged at around 2 million, and the magazine targets a similar demographic as *GQ.*

Stuff is a men's magazine featuring interviews, pictorials, and other articles of interest to its target market of 18- to 30-year-old males. *Stuff* uses product reviews for computers, video games, sports cars, and cell phones as a focus to attract readers. Like *FHM, Stuff* ceased its print version in October 2007 in favor of an online version.

Details is an American monthly men's magazine that was started in the 1980s and has a circulation of approximately 500,000. It is primarily devoted to men's fashion and lifestyles. The target is males in their 20s and 30s who are looking for an irreverent fashion magazine and who aspire to be affluent.

Cargo was founded in March 2004 and was created for the fashionable and trendy segments of the male demographic. Metrosexualism was a hot commodity, and *Cargo* boasted a paid circulation of 373,727 for a six-month period that ended on December 31, 2004. Unfortunately, the trend did not survive, and the publisher, Conde Nast, decided to shut down the publication in April 2006. This title is included to show the fickle nature of consumer magazines.

King is a monthly men's magazine geared toward African-American and urban male audiences. It features articles on hip-hop and rhythm and blues, as well as sports and fashion articles.

Maxim is an international men's magazine based in the United Kingdom with a reported circulation of 2.5 million readers. Aside from female pictorials, none featuring nude photographs, the magazine features short articles on subjects such as sports, movies, television, video games, fashion, cars, and alcohol—subjects that are considered to be of interest to an audience primarily made up of males between the ages of 21 and 45.

Men's Vogue is a fashion magazine based on the success of women's *Vogue.* It has a readership of 300,000 per month and is a relative newcomer to the scene; its first issue is dated September 6, 2005.

an oversized magazine. When the author first started in the industry, *DNR* was published five days a week in a newspaper format. Then it went to three times a week, and it finally settled into publication once a week in its current glossy format. Its counterpart in the women's wear business, *Women's Wear Daily,* is still published five days a week, since the women's wear business is larger than the

Figure 6.4 *DNR is the most important trade publication in the menswear industry. It has been covering the menswear industry for quite some time.*
DNR Then

BRIONI: EBIT Jumps 157% in First Public Earnings Release

DNR

DEFINING MEN'S FASHION $10 WWW.DNRNEWS.COM   MONDAY, JULY 23, 2007

Be Cool
New Shades, Techno Fabrics and
Five Other Trends for Spring '08—
See DNR TREND REPORT, Page 33

BARTLETT TO OPEN STORE; HAGGAR DEAL ON HOLD
BY JEAN SCHEIDNES

NEW YORK—John Bartlett is downshifting. The designer, once famous for having sent naked men down the runways, has canceled plans for a spring runway show, and the better collection he was planning with Haggar Clothing Co. has been halted.

There will be a spring John Bartlett collection, including all the requisite licensed product, but it will consist of just 20 looks.

Amid these changes, Bartlett is forging ahead with his first store, in the West Village. The designer has mellowed considerably

See BARTLETT, page 9

RAF SIMONS

Behind the
Scenes at
Garys
64

Top 10
Accessory
Categories
97

Figure 6.4 *Continued*
DNR Now

menswear business, and more industry news is generated by women's fashions. The menswear industry is much smaller in scope with fewer designers and name brands accounting for a larger share of the market.

Like any magazine, *DNR* sells advertising space. However, it differs from consumer publications in that the advertisers are targeting concerns that relate specifically to their own industry. *DNR* boasts a readership of 15,310, which comprises manufacturers, retailers, designers, and product developers. Its readers include the following:

○ company presidents and vice presidents
○ company owners

- general and divisional merchandise managers
- store managers
- buyers
- advertising display managers
- sales and marketing managers
- manufacturing and production managers
- purchasing managers
- other titled and non-titled personnel (Fairchild Fashion Group, 2006)

The numbers themselves may not seem impressive, but keep in mind that this is a small industry, and this publication reaches all the key decision makers.

MR (Menswear Retailing) Magazine is another publication that merits mention. "Retailers and menswear professionals turn to *MR Magazine* for accurate information, insightful analysis, bold ideas and real-world fashion, as well as humor, 'Schmoozing' and a look at the people who drive the men's business" (MRketplace.com, 2006). *MR* is published monthly and reaches a demographic similar to that of *DNR*. It boasts a subscriber list of over 18,000. *MR* considers itself the industry's most trusted source for information about everything from jeans to sportswear to suits and furnishings.

As *MR* and *DNR* are produced by different companies, it would appear that they are in direct competition, not so much for readership, but for advertisers. However, many of the key companies advertise in both publications in an effort to cover the market and to ensure that their message is properly conveyed to their target market.

Daily newspapers are not known primarily for their fashion coverage, particularly menswear. However, these publications are still important to the consumer. Daily newspapers can be found in every major city and many small cities throughout the country, with their primary focus being local news. Many of these newspapers address the topic of fashion in their lifestyle or human interest sections. The size of the paper will determine whether it has a fashion editor on staff or whether it uses the various wire services to pick up news items the editors think will interest their readers. Most fashion coverage focuses on women's wear, as it is the larger aspect of the fashion business and is considered more interesting. Menswear garners mention only when it is deemed important enough to displace women's wear.

In addition to fashion-related items, daily newspapers carry information on major manufacturers and retailers in the business section, particularly if there is local interest centered on plant or store closings or the announcement of a new company or retailer moving into the neighborhood. The business section also carries news related to the stock performance of various companies in the apparel trade. This section also highlights issues such as the U.S. trade deficit from time to time, as the trade deficit has been greatly affected by the global nature of our industry.

CATALOGS

Catalogs serve two main purposes: selling products and educating consumers.

Over the last several years, there has been a proliferation of mail-order houses whose sole purpose seems to be to mail out as many catalogs as possible. Every day, people open their mailboxes to find several catalogs offering all sorts of merchandise.

Several very reputable companies offer quality men's apparel through the mail, including the following:

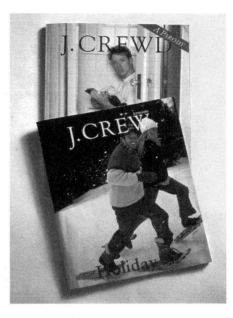

Figure 6.5 *Quality menswear can be ordered from mail-order catalog companies.*

o   Lands' End
o   J. Crew
o   Eddie Bauer
o   JCPenney
o   Bachrachs

In many instances, catalog companies also provide trend information in a subtle way. By showing the feature items on the pages, the catalog companies are telling consumers what products are in fashion for that season. Some also offer editorial comments. For example, Lands' End usually features an item prominently in each issue of their catalog. This company has been known to go to great lengths to explain where the product comes from, why it is an important product, what the fiber content is and why that is important, and most of all, why the consumer should buy it. The idea behind this marketing technique is to give consumers a sense of ownership about the product and give them more of a reason to buy.

Catalogs today allow customers to submit their orders in the following ways:

o   by mail
o   by telephone using a toll-free number
o   by ordering online at the catalog company's Web site

The mail-order business continues to grow in spite of the growth of online sales and the added cost of shipping and handling. Prestigious companies such as Neiman Marcus mail out a much-anticipated catalog every year at Christmastime. This catalog has items for sale ranging from the most outrageous to the simplest. One Christmas, the catalog offered customers a private island, and another time, his and hers matching helicopters were for sale!

DIRECT MAIL

Direct mail is a form of media because, like the catalog, it can be used as a selling tool as well as a way to communicate information to consumers. This form of communication is not widely used in the menswear industry, because it is more effective for selling individual items such as hard goods or perfumes.

BROADCAST MEDIA

Today more than ever before, broadcast media has become a major force in helping to shape consumers' opinions of fashion. The key elements that make up the broadcast media segment include the following:

- television
- video
- billboards
- radio
- the Internet

TV is by far the strongest element in the group. Prior to the 1950s, radio and print media were significant sources of information about

Figure 6.6 *Movies and their stars have often had an enormous impact on fashion and style.*

new fashions. Movies also had an impact. Due to the long lead times required to produce a feature-length movie, the fashions in them were slightly dated once they reached the public. However, every once in a while, something magical occurs in film that has an impact on the fashion industry. (See Table 6.2.) Journalist Vicki Vasilopoulos (2006) reported on this phenomenon: "Over the course of cinematic history, it has happened a handful of times. A few films are so stylish, so richly evocative of an era or time, that there can be no mistaking what happened. Style played a leading role" (p. 43).

TABLE 6.2 IMPORTANT FILM FASHIONS OF THE TWENTIETH CENTURY

American Gigolo (1980)	Richard Gere glided across the screen in an unconstructed tan Armani jacket and steel-gray silk shirt in this time capsule of men's high style circa 1980. *American Gigolo* launched Giorgio Armani into wider public consciousness (he was featured on the cover of *Time* magazine two years later). This movie essentially put Armani on the map, and jump-started his love affair with Hollywood stars.
The Thomas Crown Affair (1968)	No list of great fashion films would be complete without this Steve McQueen effort. McQueen played a Boston Brahmin with a butler and a life of moneyed leisure. The elegant businessman wore tubular three-piece suits with side vents and slim trousers. He also favored tortoise-rimmed blue aviator sunglasses and a pocket watch on a chain. Following the release of the movie, designers around the world picked up on these details and incorporated many aspects into their own collections.
Goldfinger (1964)	This was arguably the definitive James Bond film. Sean Connery, as 007, was the personification of suave in the third film of the Bond series. The tough and sexy ladies' man looked impeccable on every occasion without trying too hard. From a style vantage point, the quintessential Bond scene was when he stripped off his wetsuit to reveal a white dinner jacket with a red carnation. You could not help but smile. It is notable that every bit of his tailored wardrobe in this 1964 film could be worn today. His office attire, a slim navy suit with a white French-cuff shirt and skinny tie, looks like it stepped off the runway today. A country look that Bond wore while driving his Aston Martin in Switzerland is exceedingly contemporary: a tweed tan jacket with angled flap pockets that was paired with a knit tie and slash-pocket trousers.
A Hard Day's Night (1964)	This film was about 36 hours in the life of the Beatles, and it included seven sublime songs that the Fab Four had just recorded. *A Hard Day's Night* may have been the first mockumentary ever made, as it poked fun at the band's influence. On the fashion front, the film cemented the influence of Carnaby Street, Swinging London, and mop-top hair. The new direction came from British tailor Dougie Millings, who created about 500 outfits for the Beatles, including their signature round-neck jackets with braided edges. The film featured those short four-button jackets with pegged trousers and skinny ties, as well as distinctive gray sharkskin stage jackets with inset black velvet collars and vertical pleats and panels in the back. Millings himself appeared in one scene. Believe it or not, the suits are still being reproduced by a company in Maryland.
Saturday Night Fever (1977)	As John Travolta strutted down the street to the tune of the Bee Gees' "Stayin' Alive" in the opening credits, the camera tilted up from his red shoes to reveal his bell-bottoms, short black leather jacket, tight red open-collar shirt, and gold medallion necklace. Right away, that Brooklyn beefcake Tony Manero telegraphed that we were in for some seriously stylish male swagger. Not since Gene Kelly graced the screen had an actor practiced dancing as such a virtuoso macho exercise, albeit in tight pink polyester bell-bottoms and a printed polyester shirt. Who can forget that three-piece white suit, which created a menswear trend that lasted past the disco era?

(continued)

TABLE 6.2 (CONTINUED)

Chariots of Fire (1981)	*Chariots of Fire* won four Oscars in 1982, including Best Picture and Best Costume Design for Milena Canonero. This story of two track athletes running for Great Britain in the 1924 Olympics was one of those rare cinematic achievements: visual poetry from start to finish. The clothing and costumes were so stunning that you could literally watch the movie with the sound turned off and still enjoy it. At Cambridge, we saw tweed suits paired with double-breasted vests, rich belted raglan-sleeve overcoats, bi-swing back jackets, knickers, cable-stitched pullovers, and regatta looks such as a braid-edged blazer worn with an intarsia vest and bow tie. As if that weren't enough, there was a boatload of scarves wrapped around necks and artfully flung over men's shoulders; hats of every kind, from fedoras to newsboy caps; plus-fours worn with argyle socks; and spectator shoes galore.
Wall Street (1987)	Michael Douglas, in his Oscar-winning turn as Gordon Gekko, a piranha of the financial world, inspired much admiration from style mavens. This Mephistophelean character required aggressive power clothes for his rarefied and cutthroat world of insider deal making. Alan Flusser, who helped design Douglas's wardrobe, put him in sharply tailored custom-made double-breasted suits, silk foulard ties, a gold tie pin, and striped suspenders. Slicked-back hair and a cigar finished off the 1980s power look for the alpha male.
The Thin Man (1934)	William Powell and Myrna Loy played amateur sleuths Nick and Nora Charles with great aplomb in this classic comedy. This glamorous, urbane pair engaged in some of the wittiest badinage ever to hit the silver screen. The body-skimming pinstriped peak-lapel suits, dressing gowns, and luxurious topcoats of this 1934 film were just the icing on the cake for what was essentially an excuse to look at swells drinking, smoking, and having a ball. (*Swells* is a 1930s slang term for hip people with money.)
The Wild One (1953)	Riding around with the Black Rebels Motorcycle Club, Marlon Brando made an indelible image as a tough, laconic nonconformist who was hugely appealing to young people of the generation. Believe it or not, this film was banned in Britain until 1986. However, Brando's style and attitude in that role have become enshrined in men's fashion. The leather motorcycle jacket, denim jeans, and ringer T-shirt are now a standard uniform of both real rebellion (the rock band, the Ramones) and the faux variety seen on suburban streets.
Top Hat (1935)	With Ginger Rogers at his side, Fred Astaire summed up the film when he sang, "I'm stepping out, my dear, to breathe an atmosphere that simply reeks with class." Did it ever! Watching *Top Hat* is like eating a rich dessert. It is a frothy confection, but it is one of the most sublime musicals in movie history, with songs by the inimitable Irving Berlin. Astaire can be seen in his signature looks for day and evening: a double-breasted tux with a white boutonniere; and his soft-shoulder tweed two-button sport coat tapered in the waist, worn with relaxed gray flannel trousers, and finished off with a striped tie, a fedora, and suede oxfords.

(continued)

TABLE 6.2 (CONTINUED)

The Sting (1973)	This picture about con men in Depression-era Chicago continued the long Hollywood tradition of stylish gangsters. It earned seven Academy Awards, including Best Picture and Best Costume Design for Edith Head. She was the most honored costume designer in Academy Award history. The clothes were an integral part of the plot and helped maintain the "front" by which Redford and Newman scored their intricately plotted sting. Every man who was part of this operation had to look the part in order to be convincing. Hence, it is one of the most gorgeous films for menswear, a tailored clothing tutorial of the 1930s, a high point of men's style. The most stunning outfit may be seen on the character of Kid Twist, who wore a navy shadow-stripe peak-lapel suit with a pearl-gray double-breasted vest edged in white, a luxurious cream-colored overcoat, and gray gloves that matched his gray homburg. Of course, Redford and Newman conducted the big sting while wearing elegant tuxes.
The Great Gatsby (1974)	Theoni Aldredge won an Oscar for Best Costume Design, but this film was a critical and commercial dud, an empty vessel compared to the other 1920s period film, *Chariots of Fire*. The ladies' clothing was absolutely gorgeous, but, except for Robert Redford's wardrobe (which Aldredge commissioned from Ralph Lauren), the men's costumes looked oddly contemporary. Writer Tom Wolfe, a natty dresser in his own right, supposedly dismissed *The Great Gatsby* as "Fitzgerald as interpreted by the Garment District." The story goes that there was some bad blood between Aldredge and Lauren; she did not thank him when she accepted her award because Lauren was allegedly taking credit for the costume design in the press. Redford's clothing was undeniably beautiful and evocative of the Roaring Twenties. His pink three-piece summer suit with a French blue tie was a stunner. The obligatory fashion scene came when Redford as Jay Gatsby, attired in a three-piece white suit, told his love interest, Daisy Buchanan, "I've got a man in London who buys all my clothes." Then, in a gauche new-money display, he proceeded to throw his multi-hued shirts around the room like so many scoops of sorbet.

Source: Adapted from Vasilopoulos, V. (2006). Lights, camera, fashion. *Family Britches Magazine*, 43–48.

Aside from the movies described in Table 6.2, it was left to daily newspapers and magazines to promote the fashions of the day. Radio did play a small part, but of course it is hard to get a visual from a radio announcer.

TELEVISION

Today, the overwhelming majority of households in the United States have more than one television. In many instances, households have three or more TV sets. With the advent of cable and satellite television systems, making hundreds of channels available, programmers can now target specific markets with individual topics. Prior to cable and satellite television, mainstream programming was carried on only five channels, and marketing was extremely expensive.

In addition to watching the many award shows on which celebrities can be seen in various modes of dress, consumers tune in to regularly programmed shows that feature cast members in outfits that were picked specifically for their characters. Many of these outfits are also credited at the end of the programs, giving recognition to designers, brands, and retailers. Much time and energy goes into creating an image for each character. In turn, this encourages consumers to dress like the characters they admire and, consequently, to go out and buy the fashions.

Aside from regular television shows, the following cable shows have sparked popular interest in fashion:

- *Project Runway*
- *America's Next Top Model*
- *Fashion House*
- *Queer Eye*

As with much of the media, television tends to focus on the women's wear industry, although menswear has started to make inroads into programming. Shows like *Queer Eye* have developed a strong following. *Fashion TV*, also a popular program, started in France in 1997. This program brings the viewer instant access to over 300 catwalk shows per

Figure 6.7 *There are several television shows, such as* Queer Eye, *that report on men's fashion.*

year. M2BTV, which has over 40 channels of on-demand programming, features many topics. Titles include the following:

- *SNAG*
- *For Men & Their Interests*
- *Men's Fashion Programming*

In addition to the television programs themselves, the big money is in the advertisements that are shown during programs. When cable first burst onto the scene, it was billed as commercial-free television—but that didn't last. In 2007, a 30-second commercial spot during the Super Bowl cost $2.6 million! Television is a big business, and, for the most part, only the big brands and retailers can afford to include television advertising in their overall marketing strategy. However, one option for smaller businesses is advertising on local television and community cable stations.

Who pays for all that advertising? The simple answer is you do, provided you are buying the products that are advertised. Every time an

Figure 6.8 In 2007, a 30-second commercial during the Super Bowl cost $2.6 million.

advertised product is purchased, part of the money spent on that item goes into the retailer's marketing budget. If the advertised product is sold by the retailer, that money is built in to the cost of the goods. This is a very simplified version of what happens. Therefore, it is usually a better value to buy the private-label product than the advertised name brand, provided you can live without the name brand.

Two other areas of television broadcasting have had an impact on the consumer: television shopping and infomercials. Two channels dominate the home-shopping area: QVC and Home Shopping Network. Once again, these channels are not really known for carrying menswear; the products they feature tend to consist overwhelmingly of women's apparel and accessories, and beauty aids. However, from time to time, they do feature a group of menswear products from a designer.

Infomercials rarely feature menswear; they more often focus on home appliances and exercise equipment.

As a medium for broadcast, video has been waning over the last several years. Once thought to be a good method to deliver a concerted message to the public, it has lost favor because of the fast-paced world in which we live. Retailers used videos (first tapes, and later DVDs) and **video catalogs** as a means to deliver a consistent message to the consumer. In most instances, the videos were set up in a store department to demonstrate a particular product or, in the case of fashion, to illustrate how the consumer would look if the outfits were purchased. One of the negative aspects was that these videos usually ran for several minutes (up to 10 minutes or more), and the average consumer would lose interest before making the purchase decision. The retailers also had to deal with machines breaking down and tapes/DVDs being mishandled.

Figure 6.9 Menswear retailers use video to demonstrate various aspects of fashion.

Some companies would provide a video to be viewed in the consumer's home to help encourage the purchase or to give information on various features. This method was not considered very effective for encouraging sales of men's apparel.

Esquire revisited the idea of using visual media to deliver a message to consumers through the use of newer technology. The magazine included a DVD featuring five designers that sold products in Macy's. Each designer gave tips on how to dress using their styles. The DVD was a group effort to promote the magazine, the retailer (Macy's), and the designers, and it was inserted into copies of the magazine. The effort was paid for by Macy's, *Esquire,* and the manufacturers who made the apparel for the designers. The DVD ran for approximately 30 minutes and proved effective as a communication tool, provided the consumer was interested in the five designers that were featured on it.

BILLBOARDS

Billboards include outdoor signage that displays a wide variety of messages to the viewing public. In recent years, the use of billboards has increased as part of the overall marketing strategy of several apparel companies, including menswear companies. The following companies have used billboards as a vehicle to advertise:

o   Polo Ralph Lauren
o   Calvin Klein
o   Weather Proof Garment Company

Figure 6.10 *Billboards are an effective way to communicate fashion to the male consumer.*

This method of advertising has the following drawbacks:

○ The message remains constant for the life of the advertisement.
○ The advertisement is subject to the elements of weather, which can cause damage if it is not properly maintained.
○ Billboards are generally changed on a monthly basis and can become dated if left up too long.

However, billboards do appear to be an important aspect of media broadcasting. Because of the number of potential exposures that they can provide, billboards will continue to have an impact on the consumer.

RADIO

Radio must be considered in any discussion of broadcast media as this form of broadcasting provides a solid base of consumer advertising. Most notably, you can tune in to your favorite radio station and listen to the broadcast for its main content and, at the same time, hear advertisements for a wide variety of products. Many retailers and some name-brand manufacturers and designers of apparel use radio to spread the word about their products. Radio allows the advertiser to target specific markets based on the listening audience and broadcasting range of the station. As mentioned earlier, radio is not a main advertising medium because of its limited ability to create a "picture" in the consumer's mind. Therefore, radio is used mainly as a vehicle for advertising.

THE INTERNET

Ask anyone today to identify the fastest broadcast media and the answer will be the **Internet.** The computer has changed the way the world does business by offering virtually immediate access to vast amounts of information, and by ensuring access to timely, up-to-date information.

Anyone with a computer can be online instantly and have access to millions of pages of information. Think of a company that you want to research, plug that name into your favorite search engine, and you will have more information at your fingertips than you know what to do with. Not only is the Internet an excellent vehicle for research, but it can also be used to buy and sell products through various portals such as eBay.

If you are in the fashion business and cannot travel to all the shows that are staged worldwide, you can view many of them online. Several are even offered in real time. Most trade publications mentioned in this chapter also have Web sites that you can visit, and, in many instances, you can obtain an online subscription for a fee. Web sites that focus on men's fashion news include the following:

- AskMen.com
- Shark.com
- SharpMan.com
- King-Mag.com

Even the popular site MySpace.com has morphed into a form of broadcasting as it starts

Figure 6.11 *Menswear and men's fashion are covered in several Web sites.*

to incorporate advertising into its media content. According to DNR writer Amy Wicks (2006), "MySpace isn't just for teenagers; its largest audience is adults over 35 years old, and 80 percent of the world's top 100 brands are already delivering their messages via the social networking Web site" (p. 23). Later in her article, Wicks interviewed Ross Levinshon, president of Fox Interactive Media, a division of News Corp., which purchased MySpace in 2006. During that interview, he stated: "Since News Corp purchased the site last year for approximately $600 million, it has grown from 17 million unique users to 80 million. Some 230,000 new people join MySpace every day, equivalent to the population of Buffalo, NY. The average user looks at 650 pages per month and there were 35 billion page views last month, a number second only to Yahoo" (p. 23).

MySpace is experiencing extraordinary growth. Levinshon concluded the interview by saying that he is "not entirely sure what the future holds for MySpace, but online businesses will continue to flourish for years to come; creative people and risk-takers are going to win" (Wicks, 2006, p. 23).

The Internet is also a source of advertising opportunities for designers, brands, and retailers with streaming videos, pop-ups, and banners all announcing products that are intended for consumption. Many sites are supported by advertising, with the content being secondary. Recall the discussion in Chapter 5 of the importance of e-tailing or e-commerce as means of conducting business. In 2006, the estimated volume from Internet sales was pegged at $26.5 billion, with a continuing growth trend in 2007 and beyond.

Figure 6.12 *Online shopping for menswear from the comfort of your home or office.*

With the increasing popularity of the Internet, the following questions must be raised:

- Will the Internet make brick-and-mortar retail establishments obsolete?
- Will the Internet make the printed page obsolete?

Clearly, the Internet will not make brick-and-mortar retail establishments obsolete. People like to shop; they like to try things on, feel them, and test them out. In many instances, the Internet is used as a source of information or a supplement to the retail store as we know it today. Some retail organizations may suffer, and perhaps even close, due to increased competition from the Internet. However, if they are that susceptible to competition, they probably do not have a chance for long-term success anyway.

The question about the effect of the Internet on the printed page is more difficult to answer. Perhaps the full extent of the technology will not be known for years to come. In an article titled "Whither magazines?" David Lipke (2006b, October) wrote, "Magazines, as we know them are dying. That's the rather portentous first sentence in a book to be published this winter, titled *The Last Magazine*, which predicts the inevitable decline of printed periodicals, as magazine distribution moves onto new digital platforms. The materials that have defined magazines for over 250 years are dissolving gradually into digital bits and bytes. This evolution will have profound implications for how publications are conceived, sold, and consumed" (p. 14).

Lipke also writes that the author of *The Last Magazine,* David Renard (a former Gartner Group analyst who now owns MU INC./Netcirculation) and others predict that the number of periodicals will decrease by 15 percent through 2016, and within 25 years, only 10 percent of the paper-based magazine industry will remain, sustained by collectors and aging consumers (Lipke, 2006b, October). As technology moves forward, new means of creating e-papers are being developed with the goal of making the publications easier to read and more consumer-friendly. Who knows?

Sometime in the not-so-distant future, you may be reading this very textbook via an e-reader.

Other new and developing technologies are emerging that will constitute broadcast media. The following technological devices are all capable of carrying some form of broadcast advertising to the consumer:

o cell phones
o MP3 players and iPods
o Palm Pilots
o GPS systems
o BlackBerries
o other handheld devices

As technology continues to develop, there will be new avenues for communicating directly with consumers. The savvy marketing companies will find ways to tap in to new technologies to target specific markets down to the individual level. As younger generations become more comfortable with these devices, it will be easier for companies to reach out and touch each and every one of them.

CONCLUDING THOUGHTS

The goals of this chapter were to help you learn the following:

o the different forms of media used in the marketing of menswear
o the difference between public relations and advertising and their impact on the industry
o how to use media effectively to market and sell menswear products

This chapter identified two main types of media: print and broadcast. Components of the print category were discussed, including consumer versus trade publications, catalogs as a vehicle to communicate with consumers, and the use of direct mail. Broadcast media, particularly television, radio, video, the Internet, and billboards, were presented as primary means of communicating fashion news to individual consumers. Working definitions were developed for *public relations* and *advertising*, and examples of each were reviewed.

In the next chapter, you will focus on developing an understanding of the men's tailored clothing industry. The chapter will be product specific, and it will provide you with a framework to understand key aspects of the various apparel segments that comprise the tailored clothing market. You will also look at specific design features that are unique to this part of the industry.

KEY TERMS

advertising
billboard
broadcast media
catalog
daily newspaper

direct mail
Internet
print media
public relations (PR)
video catalog

DISCUSSION QUESTIONS

1. Choose a form of media that was discussed in the chapter and discuss current trends in marketing as they pertain to that specific form.

2. Choose a menswear consumer publication. Bring a copy to class and discuss the editorial and advertising content. Who is the target market? What brands are represented in the publication?

REFERENCES

Armstrong, G., and Kotler, P. (2007). *Marketing: An Introduction*. Upper Saddle River, NJ: Pearson Prentice Hall.

Boswell, S. (1993). *Menswear: Suiting the Customer*. Englewood Cliffs, NJ: Regents/Prentice Hall.

Elliot, Stewart. (2007). "30 seconds of fame at Super Bowl XLI will cost $2.6 million." *New York Times*. [online]. Available: http://www.nytimes.com/2007/01/05/business/media/05adco.html. [November 7, 2007].

Fairchild Fashion Group. (2006). Circulation/ Demographics. [online]. Available: http://www.fairchildmediakit.com/dnr/circulation.cfm [November 1, 2006].

Lipke, David. (2006a, October 2). Inside *Esquire's Big Black Book*. *DNR*, p. 12.

Lipke, David. (2006b, October 2). Whither magazines? E-paper may imperil the printed page. *DNR*, pp. 14–15.

MRketplace.com (2006). About MR. [online]. Available: http://www.mrketplace.com/content/About-MR.36.0.html [January 2, 2007].

Vasilopoulos, V. (2006). Lights, camera, fashion. *Family Britches Magazine*, pp. 43–48.

Wicks, A. (2006). MySpace. *DNR*, p. 23.

SEVEN

TAILORED CLOTHING

- the various classifications that make up the tailored clothing industry
- the products that make up the tailored outerwear business
- design and make features of the products in the tailored clothing and tailored outerwear business

Chapters 1 to 6 examined several different aspects of menswear: history, demographics, design, manufacturing, retail, and the media. In this chapter, the focus will shift to more product-specific elements of the menswear market. Tailored clothing will be discussed, as well as tailored outerwear. The following categories make up the **tailored clothing** industry:

- suits
- sport coats
- vests
- pants
- tailored outerwear

Each of these categories has specific characteristics that are unique and vary from designer to designer. Designers try to create looks and styles directed toward their intended target customers.

As discussed in Chapter 5, men's tailored clothing is housed in a separate area, away from sportswear, usually adjacent to furnishings (discussed in Chapter 8). Tailored outerwear hangs in a separate department and is distinguished from other outerwear products.

SUITS AND SPORT COATS

Noted author Mark Twain once said that "clothes make the man." Truer words have never been spoken, especially when it comes to a man's suit. Historically, the suit comprised three pieces: jacket, pant, and vest. This is termed a **nested suit**. All the pieces match and are sold on the same hanger. In today's society, the vest has been reduced in importance and is subject to the whims of designers, who try to resurrect it as a fashion statement from time to time. Currently, vests are found more in the casual arena, as an accessory coupled with casual slacks and a sport shirt.

THE MAKE OF A SUIT

What makes one suit stand out from the next? The first thing to look at is the **make** or **grade** of a suit. These terms are interchangeable; the term *make* will be used in this chapter. The make of a suit refers to the number of hand-sewing operations involved in its construction. A lower number indicates fewer hand-sewing operations and, conversely, a higher number indicates more hand-sewing operations. The term *hand sewing* refers to sewing operations that do not use any machines at all; think of a tailor stitching an entire suit by hand.

Figure 7.1 *This nontraditional three-piece suit includes a matching jacket and pants paired with a solid vest.*

The make has a direct bearing on the cost of the suit. This chapter refers to a numbering system to distinguish the make of a suit; there is also an X-make.

○ **X-make:** This suit is made predominantly by machine with no hand-sewing operations. The X-make is produced by individuals sitting at sewing machines joining seams together by pushing fabric through the machines. This is the least costly method of producing a suit.

- Make #1: This make uses few, if any, hand-sewing operations and is the next lowest in terms of quality and cost of producing a suit.
- Makes #2, 4, 4+, and 6: These numbers indicate varying grades of make with each one accounting for more hand-sewing operations than the previous one.
- Make # 6+: This would be considered the top of the line, or highest quality, in terms of make and grade of a suit. These garments will require anywhere from 120 to 150 separate hand-sewing operations. The cost of these suits is commensurate with the number of hand-sewing operations, and a good 6+ can range from $1,500 to $15,000. Check out Kiton suits online and see the prices for yourself. For a more modest hand-tailored suit, you can visit Hickey Freeman or Oxxford Clothes. These sites allow you to build your own suit and price it accordingly.

THE DROP OF A SUIT

Another important characteristic of the nested suit is the **drop**. The drop is the difference in inches between the chest measurement of the suit jacket and the waist of the pants that accompany the jacket on the hanger. The most common drop for a men's suit is a 6-inch drop. For example, if you were to buy a suit that was marked as a 40 regular, the pants would have a 34-inch waist. Of course, few men have the exact physique to be able to buy a suit and walk out of the store without any alterations. In fact,

Figure 7.2 *A tailor takes measurements in preparation for alterations.*

all nested suits will require at least one alteration. The pants are sold with an open bottom, meaning there is no hem or cuff. Thus, even if the jacket and the waist of the pants fit perfectly, the pants will still need to be hemmed or cuffed.

As for other alterations, it is not uncommon to have one or more of the following done:

o   take in or let out the pants
o   adjust the sleeves
o   take in or let out the waist of the jacket

In addition to the 6-inch drop, other styles of suits carry different drops. A 7-inch drop can be considered a younger man's style, although with more men becoming health conscious, this is becoming a more popular model and more readily available in better stores. Another style is the 8-inch drop, which is not all that usual. In the industry, this style, with its broad shoulders and narrow waist, is often referred to as an athletic cut.

Customers often wonder what size suit to buy. You purchase a suit in the same size as your actual chest measurement. If your chest measures 40 inches, you should purchase a suit in size 40.

Many manufacturers and retailers are getting around the challenges of fitting different body builds by selling and marketing **suited separates**. This could be called mix-and-match, where the customer can select a suit jacket from one rack in one size and pair it up with matching pants in a different size from another rack.

This concept is not new; JCPenney, for example, has been in the suited separates business for over 30 years. In recent years, many other retailers have picked up on this trend in an effort to capture younger customers and put them into a suit at a relatively inexpensive price point. Today, you can buy suited separates at the following retailers:

- o Target
- o Kohl's
- o Zara
- o H&M
- o Express

Consumers need to be careful when selecting suited separates. Some companies that try to market suited separates do not do a very good job of matching the jackets and pants. In order to offer the consumer a quality suited-separates package, manufacturers must have very high quality standards for both fabric and dyeing techniques. In menswear, this is a critical factor. Jackets that were made in one country and pants that were made in another country and were supposed to be the same color, matching each other to mimic a nested suit, can at times be very inconsistent, with different dye lots not matching at all. Companies like JCPenny do this right, by cutting the jackets and pants in the same country and the same factory out of the same dye lot, guaranteeing an ideal match every time.

SUIT JACKETS AND SPORT COATS

There is one main difference between the suit jacket (or suit coat, as some call it) and the sport coat. The suit jacket is bought with a matching pair of pants, and the sport coat is sold separately. Both articles of clothing will be housed in the same department within the store, with the sport coat generally offering more variety in patterns, colors, and fabrics. Unique to the sport coat are some styling features, which may include the following:

- patch pockets, with or without flaps
- elbow patches
- a belted back

One other term that is associated with the sport coat is the **blazer**. The traditional blazer has the following characteristics:

- navy in color
- patch pockets

Figure 7.3 A casual sport jacket.

- o brass buttons
- o made in wool or a wool-blend fabric
- o fully lined

The style can be either single breasted or double breasted. Today, the term *blazer* is used to refer to any solid-color sport coat, and it can have different styles and colors of buttons.

Have you ever wondered when to button the buttons on a sport jacket and how many buttons to button? The style advisor at Menstyle.com offers the following advice:

> I usually button the buttons when I put on the jacket and unbutton them when I take it off. (lol) As a high-roll, three-button wearer, I fasten the top and middle buttons, leaving the bottom one open. When I sit down at the dinner table, I often unbutton the middle button, because the jacket hangs better. Wearers of low-roll, preppy-style, three-button jackets usually fasten only the middle button. Two-button wearers usually close only the top button. Buttoning all of one's buttons looks a little too buttoned-up, giving one a sort of Pee Wee Herman or Nutty Professor feeling. Think of the bottom one as the panic button and never button it. (menstyle.com, December, 2002)

DESIGN FEATURES

In this part of the chapter, you will look more closely at key designs and features that help define the styles and give the garments their unique looks.

THE CUT OF THE GARMENT

The first area to look at is the **cut** of the garment. The cut relates to the proportion and silhouette of the garment. There are five cuts that designers choose from when interpreting which cut is best for their customers. Remember that the key to success is to always understand who your target customer is and to design styles that will work for that customer.

DRAPE

"The **drape** is the full, easy cut initially associated with clothing of the 1930s, popularized by the Duke of Windsor. It had additional ease, or fullness, in the chest and shoulder blade area in the back. There was a softness to the coat with a slightly extended shoulder and less padding overall" (Boswell, 1993, p. 63). Today, this styling is often referred to as the slouch suit and is copied by many of the top design houses. This style affords the wearer a more comfortable look and feel to the suit coat while making a statement of confidence.

TRIM EUROPEAN CUT

The **trim European cut** was first made popular in the 1970s and 1980s and can still be found today. This cut emphasized the slimmer European body type and carried a 7-inch drop. The suit sold particularly well to those customers who considered themselves health conscious and, at the same time, fashionable. This cut was made over a slimmer size specification than traditional suits and was generally more padded in the shoulders.

AMERICAN CUT

The consumer concerned about comfort will like the **American cut.** This consumer is

Figure 7.4 *The drape style suit was popular in the 1930s.*

generally of average build and height and can fit into a suit that offers a 6-inch drop. To help create the comfort feature, the suit coat is cut with a lower-than-normal armhole to allow for ease of movement. The shoulders are not as built up as the European cut and have a soft to medium padding. Therefore, this cut is often called the soft or natural-shoulder model.

MODIFIED AMERICAN CUT

The **modified American cut,** "sometimes referred to as the modified European cut, falls in between American and traditional European in styling and silhouette" (Boswell, 1993, p. 64). The look became popular in the 1970s when American men wanted to dress like the Europeans, but with that extra room for comfort. The drop came in either a 6- or 7-inch

(a)

Figure 7.5 (a) *A traditional American-cut suit.* **(b)** *A European-cut suit in a double-breasted model.*

(b)

model, depending on what the designers determined was right for their customers.

The cut that is considered the most traditional of all, with its straight lines, no shape, and minimal shoulder padding, is the **British cut.** Based on the style and look of this cut, it has earned the nickname the "sack coat." In the 1980s, there was a resurgence in this cut, and its influences can still be seen today. The minimalist styling also created an offshoot in the

Figure 7.6 This British-cut suit has minimal construction.

industry: the unconstructed jacket. (Think of the jackets worn on *Miami Vice*.) This jacket was basically sewn together like a woven shirt with no linings, padding, or interfacings to give it any shape whatsoever.

STYLING FEATURES

These features do not affect the fit of the garment but offer the wearer the unique styling that has been designed into the garment.

COAT FRONTS

The choice here is simple: **single breasted** or **double breasted**. The majority of the suits and sport coats sold today are single breasted. The double-breasted models do project a particular image and are not for everyone. In order to pull off the double-breasted look, you need a certain body type: average to tall in height and average to slim through the chest. The single-breasted front can be adapted for almost all body types and comes in an array of button models. One button is considered fashion-forward, with more of a young or European look, while the two-button model is the most common. There are also three- and four-button models, which come and go, based on trends in the market.

The double-breasted jacket, like the single-breasted jacket, comes in a variety of button models as well, each with one or two functioning buttonholes. The two-button front will have one functioning buttonhole, providing a lower stance on the front of the jacket. The four-button and six-button models provide for a more

(a)   **(b)**

Figure 7.7 *The jacket in **(a)** is single breasted; **(b)** shows a double-breasted model.*

fitted garment with higher button stances, and, therefore, the closures are placed higher on the jackets.

LAPEL STYLES

The lapel is a focal point of the jacket and can affect the overall look of the jacket depending on the style and model one chooses. Three key lapel styles are in the market today. These styles are as follows:

○ **Notched:** The notched lapel is the most popular style and can be varied by differing the degree of the angle of the notch.

- **Peak:** The peak lapel is a bit more stylish and can be found on double-breasted models as well as formal wear.
- **Shawl collar:** This style is called a collar instead of a lapel because of the rounded effect it presents to the wearer. This style is seldom seen, except on formal wear or a casual smoking jacket.

The lapels/collars can be further enhanced by applying one of the following types of stitching to the garment:

- **Topstitching** is most common and is usually about 1/4 inch from the edge of the lapel.
- A **bluff stitch** is a very clean edge where no stitching can be seen. Creating the bluff stitch requires a skilled tailor, and this type of stitch is often associated with more expensive suits.
- The **pick stitch** is used only on the finest hand-tailored garments. Some new machinery today can reproduce the look of the pick stitch, but it still remains the mark of a truly expensive hand-crafted suit.

POCKET STYLES

"There are two basic pocket styles in tailored clothing: **besom** and **patch**. But both styles have many variations. When the garment is purchased, often the pockets are basted (sewn) closed. This is for the manufacturer to press the garment more easily and to avoid having the consumer stretch the fabric in try-ons and after purchase" (Boswell, 1993, p. 70). The besom pocket looks like a very long buttonhole. It is also referred to as a **slash, inset,** or **double-welt pocket.** The patch pocket can be considered more informal and comes in many variations. The flap pocket is an informal design; whether or not it is used depends on what the designer is trying to convey in his or her jackets.

A variety of stitches can be used to attach the pockets. The stitch detail can be used as a design feature, just as flaps can.

SHOULDER TREATMENTS

The four basic shoulder treatments that are used when constructing suit jackets and sport coats are as follows:

- **Rope shoulder:** The rope shoulder treatment appears on highly stylized jackets and gives the appearance of an actual raised rope running across the top of the shoulder. It is not a popular style, and is considered very fashion-forward.
- **Square shoulder:** The square shoulder treatment gives the illusion of height by the building up of the padded shoulder; it can be found in jackets sold in the European market.
- **Padded shoulder:** The padded shoulder treatment can be found in the modified American and European cuts with a modicum of padding to accentuate the shoulder area.
- **Natural** or **soft shoulder:** The natural or soft-shoulder treatment is the most common and can be found in the British and American cuts. This is a more conservative styling and works well with most body types.

Vents can be used on the sleeve and the back of the jacket. Most sleeve vents are purely decorative. They can have any number of buttons, with three being the most common. In some instances, the sleeve vent may be functional with buttons and buttonholes to open and close the vents. This is a nice feature, but it is rather impractical, as there is no value in having a sleeve vent that opens and closes.

The rumor is that sleeve vents, and particularly vents with buttons, were invented by Napoleon during a cold winter campaign. He became disgusted with his soldiers for constantly wiping their noses on their sleeves so he had the army tailors add buttons to prevent this nasty practice from continuing.

Back vents come in one of the following options:

o   center back single vent
o   side vents, one on each side

The purpose of back vents is to create ease of movement, although many designers have opted for the ventless back look as a style feature.

Other features that can be incorporated into suit jackets and sport coats are inside pockets, colorful linings, pen slots on the inside of the jackets, locker loops, and pocket flaps on the inside pockets as well. Most well-made suits will also offer the customer an extra button or two sewn into the inside lining or placed in one of the pockets.

(b)

(a)

Figure 7.8 *A suit jacket can have **(a)** one center vent or **(b)** two side vents.*

VESTS

The **vest** is a close-fitting garment with no sleeves to allow for freedom of movement. Historically, the vest was worn to keep the wearer warm. The vest was *de rigueur,* or worn according to fashion convention, up until World War II. During the war, there was a piece goods shortage, so the vest lost its popularity and never fully recovered. Vests have been relegated to the whims of designers, who see fit to try and revive them from time to time. When a vest is purchased as part of a suit, the ensemble is called a three-piece suit (jacket, vest, pants). The styling

Figure 7.9 *Making a fashion statement with a vest.*

of the vest varies by number of buttons, darts, and types and number of pockets. Six-button vests with four besom pockets (two up, two down) and five-button models with two patch pockets are seen from time to time. The back of the vest can also sport a belt that is adjustable to snug the garment closer to the body for additional warmth. As with the jacket, it is a fashion *faux pas* to button the bottom button on any vest, regardless of the number of buttons.

PANTS

Pants, slacks, trousers—what you call them probably depends on your age and viewpoint of the industry. *Trousers* is the traditional term, and it dates back many years. *Slacks* is a relatively new term, which was derived from the term "**slack time**," which originated after World War II. *Pants* is also a term associated with the past and is a derivative of the word *pantaloons*. Like many terms in the English language, it was shortened to fit our vocabulary. When referring to a suit, the term pant is most often used, but any of the other terms are quite acceptable.

Although there are many different kinds of pants in the market today, this chapter addresses dress pants. The dress pant has unique features that set it apart from a casual pant, which will be discussed in Chapter 10. The dress pant will accompany a suit or can be worn with a sport jacket. If you have chosen a nice pair of dress pants to go along with a sport jacket, most likely they will be a solid color. However, there are no hard and fast rules when it comes to fashion.

Figure 7.10 *Nicely creased and cuffed dress pants.*

WAISTBANDS

The exposed portion of the waistband (what you see on the outside of the wearer's pant) can come in the following styles:

○   a pant with belt loops
○   a pant with no belt loops
○   a pant with expandable tabs on the sides that allow the wearer to adjust the pant when necessary

The number of belt loops and the actual placement of the loops, as well as the width and height of the belt loops, can vary depending on the look the designer was trying to achieve. Most dress pants remain relatively conservative. If the pant does not have belt loops, there might be an extended tab closure with a button or two to keep the pants closed.

The inside of the waistband (what you cannot see) is where there is a distinct difference between a dress pant and a casual pant. The dress pant will have a split waistband, which allows a tailor to take the pant in or let it out while performing alterations. In addition, there will be extra fabric in the seat of the pant, called the outlet, which also allows for proper alterations. A casual pant will have a continuous waistband with no split. Therefore, it cannot be altered. To see this difference, look at a pair of denim jeans or khaki pants and then look at a pair of dress pants.

The inside waistband may also have a curtain, and that is the sign of a well-tailored pant. The curtain will be an additional piece of fabric that runs around the inside of the waistband of the pant and extends below the existing waistband approximately 1/4 to 1/2 inch to give the pant a finished look.

In addition, the inside waistband may have buttons attached, four in the front with two on each side and two in the center rear of the waistband to accommodate the use of suspenders. If you choose a suit that does not come with this feature, and you enjoy wearing suspenders, then it is an easy modification the tailor can complete during the alteration process.

PANT FRONTS

Basically, there are two choices: **pleats** or no pleats. Within these choices, there are variations from which you can choose. If you choose a pant with no pleats, it is said to have a plain front. If you choose pleats, the pant can have one, two, or even three of them. If you choose one pleat, the proper term is *single pleated*, two is *double pleated*, and three is *triple pleated*. The single and double pleats are most common; the triple-pleated front would be considered very fashion-forward. Unfortunately, when buying a suit that you like, you are restricted to the style that is on the hanger. If you are buying a pair of dress pants to coordinate with your sport jacket, you can choose the style of pant front that you want.

PANT HEM FINISHES

The pants that you buy as part of a nested suit will need to be altered; at the very least, the length will be adjusted as these pants generally come with an unfinished bottom. When you purchase suited separates, however, the pants will come with a finished bottom. When purchasing a pant with an unfinished bottom, the consumer has to decide whether to have the bottom hemmed or cuffed. This choice is subjective and will depend on the following:

o   the wearer
o   the style of the suit
o   the current fashion

When purchasing a suit, it is important that you wear the proper shoes in order to ensure that the pants are altered to the correct length.

POCKET STYLES

As with pleats, the designer dictates which style pockets are on the pants in nested

Figure 7.11 *The quarter top pocket is one of the most popular pocket styles.*

suits. Front pockets can either be **on seam, quarter-top, half-top,** or **western style.**

Back pockets can be besom on both sides or just the wearer's right. Some dress pants will have one pocket on the wearer's right, which will be a besom with a button-through flap. Once again, the number of back pockets and the styles are determined by the design of the pant. One other type of pocket that can be found on some dress pants is the watch pocket, which will be on the front of the pant under the waistband; it can be a version of the besom with or without a button-through flap.

For pants that are part of a nested suit, the waist size is determined by the drop of the suit. Thus, the waist size is predetermined, while the length is altered to fit the individual customer. If you are purchasing a suited separates pant, you will have the choice of waist and inseam. For example, the size could read waist 32, inseam 30; this would be expressed on the waistband ticket as 32X30, with the waist size always coming first. The rise of the pant can also vary depending on the styling and the design. It can be expressed as a regular, long, and short rise. The rise is the distance from the waist to the crotch and should be in proportion to the build of the wearer.

THINGS TO CONSIDER FOR YOUR FIRST INTERVIEW SUIT

An online article from *Style* magazine presented tips on buying an "interview suit." According to Norman Fryman, former CEO of The Grief Companies, makers of fine tailored clothing, "The suit is the vehicle by which you create a first impression ... [A] suit's silhouette, drape, and color provoke a conscious thought in the mind of the recruiter of what you are all about" (MBAStyle.com, 1996). Fryman and members of *Style* staff developed the following checklist for choosing your interview suit:

1. Decide on the type of job for which you are interviewing. What is the industry? Advertising allows greater flair; banking is more conservative.

2. Allocate a full day for shopping and be sure to wear proper shoes, trousers, and dress shirt. If you try on a suit in a tee shirt and high tops, the tailor will not be able to properly fit you.

3. Go to a store. This sounds simple, but in reality, you need to find a store that will fit your personality and, of course, your wallet. Try on a really expensive suit to get the feel of it and then find one you can afford that feels and looks close to the expensive one you tried.

4. Choose natural fibers, preferably wool or a wool-blend one that has a high wool content. You cannot go wrong with a nice worsted wool.

5. Have a price range in mind, but try on suits in a variety of prices.

6. *If the suit does not fit, do not buy it, even if it is on sale*. Never sacrifice fit for color, fabric, or price.

7. You can change a suit's fit, but not its design. This means that you can alter the sleeves and hems, but shoulders and lapels should not be changed.

8. Look in a three-way mirror, no matter how painful it might be to see yourself in your full glory. This is the only way you will be able to see yourself as others see you. (MBAStyle.com, 1996)

TAILORED OUTERWEAR

When the consumer hears the term *outerwear*, the immediate response is to think of cold weather and what the industry considers casual outerwear: pea coats, down jackets, hooded parkas, fleece-based jackets, and stadium coats. This is where the difference arises. The term *tailored outerwear* refers to overcoats, topcoats, and rainwear (or trench coats, as most call them in the menswear industry). As far as retailers are concerned, this category of merchandise is housed in a separate area away from, but sometimes adjacent to, casual outerwear. Tailored

Figure 7.12 *Tailored outerwear makes a fashion statement on the runway.*

outerwear is most often merchandised within the tailored clothing department.

Most tailored outerwear sold in the United States today is manufactured overseas due to the high cost of labor in producing these garments domestically. The same applies to suits, sport coats, and dress pants. One company that can still boast that they manufacture in the United States is designer Joseph Abboud, who makes suits under his own label in Bedford, Massachusetts. Although there is a lot of talk about overseas manufacturing in this book, there are still companies that do produce in the United States. There are various reasons, such as Quick Response and serving a niche market that can afford to pay the higher price.

OVERCOAT

The overcoat is the heaviest of the tailored outerwear, and is available in single-breasted and double-breasted models. This coat has lost favor due to the expense of its construction and the cost of the fabric. In addition, many consumers have opted for the "all-weather" coat as a replacement for the overcoat.

TOPCOAT

In the industry, the topcoat is considered a lighter version of the overcoat. It has similar styling to the overcoat. In fact, most retailers, designers, and manufacturers rarely distinguish between the two designations and produce what would be considered a dress coat to be worn with a suit, or with a sport coat and dress pants. Regardless of what the industry calls these coats, consumers know what will work for them and what will not.

No well-respected member of the menswear industry would ever be caught asking a retailer where their rainwear section is. It must be called by the name that the industry, as well as the consumer, knows it best: the **trench coat**. This article of clothing gets its name and its roots from a very practical application. The original design was created by Burberry for the troops during World War I. It was so named due to the fact that the soldiers wore these rather large cumbersome coats in the trenches in which they were fighting. They had the following features, which can still be seen on today's version of this popular coat:

o   gun patches on the shoulders
o   epaulets on the shoulders
o   metal rings on the belt, from which to hang hand grenades
o   the wide belt to keep the coat closed during cold times

This coat survived several wars and, during World War I, the trench coat earned the nickname of "spy coat."

The trench coat, like the topcoat and suit, has undergone many transformations based on style and design of pockets, flaps, patches, and the like. However, one thing that has remained constant is the coat's availability in both single- and double-breasted models. The double-breasted trench coat is more popular today, although single-breasted models are seen on the racks. These vary in style as well. A single-breasted trench coat might have a fly front, where the buttons are hidden under a flap of material. However, the single-breasted models are much more austere than the double-breasted models in terms of design elements.

Regardless of the coat-front styling, in order to be considered a trench coat, it must be three-quarter length. Depending on your size, you can usually buy the trench coat in regular, long, or short lengths. These differences are not great and will affect the sleeve and coat length only, not the dimensions of the chest. Like the suit and top coat, you buy this garment in the exact size of your chest measurement. Many people are under the impression that you need to go one size up from your chest measurement. However, the industry has already compensated for the fact that you will be wearing something under the coat, such as a suit, sport coat, or sweater, and it has adjusted the sizing accordingly.

The following additional features can be incorporated into single- or double-breasted trench coats:

o   the type of sleeve treatment: set-in, raglan, or split raglan

o   the sleeves: cuffed or belted sleeves; either style can be functional or ornamental, with the number of buttons on the sleeve left to the designer

o   the back of the coat: belt, side vents, or single vent in the center back

o   pockets: besom, angled besom, or flap pockets

Given the nature of the overcoat, topcoat, and trench coat, most designers opt for a more conservative look. Of the three forms of tailored outerwear, the trench coat is where you will find the most variation.

Designers can also do different things with the insides of these coats. An overcoat and topcoat will most definitely be fully lined with some sort of pocketing on the inside. The trench coat can be fully lined with a removable lining attached with zippers or buttons. This lining can be full or three-quarter length.

ADDITIONAL TAILORED OUTERWEAR STYLES

Several other tailored outerwear styles have endured over the years and have earned their own names. They are as follows:

o The **British warmer** is a double-breasted style with set-in sleeve.

o The **reefer** is a single-breasted version of the British warmer; this style fits closer to the body and has a slimmer silhouette.

o The **polo coat,** a six-butt on, double-breasted model similar to the British warmer, is traditionally made of camel hair in a tan color with a belted back and patch pockets.

o The chesterfield coat is single breasted and generally solid grey with a black velvet collar. It can be in topcoat or overcoat weight and is considered the dressiest of the topcoats or overcoats.

o The **Balmacaan** is a heavy overcoat with rounded collar and raglan sleeves and is fuller in the body. The Balmacaan name is derived from an estate in Scotland and is nicknamed the "bal."

WHEN IT RAINS IT POURS

A good friend of mine, whom I have known from the industry for over 30 years, liked to dress well and buy the latest fashions. I will never forget how proud he was of a new trench coat that he purchased from Macy's. The brand name was Drizzle, and I admit it was a nice looking coat. My friend paid a lot of money for it.

Shortly after making the purchase he had occasion to try it out. He got caught in a typical New York City downpour and proceeded to get soaked to the skin in his new trench coat. He called me up to tell me about his experience and how unhappy (my word not his) he was with the product. He said that he had called the regional sales manager in New York to complain. He told me the fellow's name and remarked that he was getting angrier by the day as this guy was not returning his calls.

The next day, I phoned my friend and disguised my voice, *(continued)* impersonating the regional sales manager for Drizzle. I listened patiently as my friend recounted his experience. After he went on for awhile, I interrupted him and I called him an idiot. Well, he almost came through the phone! I asked, "What is our brand?" He replied, "Drizzle." That's when I said, "So what did you expect? Our coats are only good in a drizzle, and you wore it during a downpour!"

He started to yell, and that's when I lost it and he finally realized what was going on. We both had a good laugh, although I don't think he ever really forgave me for pulling the proverbial wool over his eyes!

Many of the changes in the tailored clothing industry are a direct result of changes in society at large. Historically, men in the United States wore suits during work and leisure time alike. After the 1950s, society became much more relaxed, and men became more casual in their dress. It was no longer necessary for men to wear suits wherever they went. Even in the workplace, where suits had been the uniform of the day, change was in the air. The 1970s, 1980s, and 1990s saw more and more companies abandoning formal dress codes in favor of casual clothing, and this trend continues today.

The trend toward more casual dressing has changed the face of the tailored clothing industry forever. With fewer men wearing suits, the need for tailored clothing designers, factories, and retailers has decreased significantly. Those that have survived are challenged regularly to stay in business. It is not all gloom and doom; those that are still in business are there because they have figured out the right product and deliver it at the right time for the right price. Additionally, these tailored clothing companies are continuously looking for ways to attract new customers through innovative product developments. A few of those companies are highlighted below.

LANIER: LEADING THE WAY

Lanier Clothes is one of the leading manufacturers in the tailored clothing industry. Lanier is a division of Oxford Industries, one of the largest apparel manufacturers in the world. Lanier produces more than 2 million pairs of pants and over 2.5 million coats annually, many of which are marketed and sold as nested suits. State-of-the-art technology and innovative Quick Response systems are used to deliver a consistent and quality product. Lanier's customers include all levels of the retail trade, from discounters to high-end specialty stores. Lanier has many licensing agreements with top designers,

Figure 7.13 Sport coats worn in a casual style.

such as Oscar de la Renta, and it produces many private-label programs as well.

Dana Verrill is the Branded Division President with Lanier. Mr. Verrill has been with Lanier for most of his career and has seen the industry go through many changes, from the leisure suit to today's designer brands.

> There are several key issues that are driving the tailored clothing business today: designer brands, the casualization of America, and lifestyle branding. Just look at what Macy's has done; they have segmented their business into key lifestyle brands to better serve the consumer [see Chapter 5]. As for the casualization issue, it has taken a major toll on our industry, putting several top labels out of business. Luckily, we were strong enough and smart enough to react to this shift, and we now see a trend toward dressing up. That is welcome news for the tailored clothing business. (Dana Verrill, Branded Division President, Lanier, in discussion with the author, November 19, 2006)

In the fall of 2007, Lanier added a new licensing agreement to produce and distribute tailored clothing under Kenneth Cole's New York, Reaction, and Unlisted labels. The collection included suits, suited separates, sport coats, trousers, and rainwear. The items in the collection were distributed in tailored clothing departments at major department stores and select specialty stores. "Kenneth is a unique and talented designer that the American consumer truly respects," said Dana Verrill in a press release. "This deal presents a tremendous opportunity to build a substantial tailored clothing business around the Kenneth Cole label. We have coveted the Kenneth Cole brand for some time and believe they are an excellent fit with our branded business strategy" (IntegratIR, 2007).

THE YOUNGER CUSTOMER

Often when we think of suits we tend to picture a businessman going to the office, or someone attending a formal affair. Today's designers and manufacturers are aiming their sights at a younger market. Even though casualization is entrenched in the young contemporary male customer, scores of younger customers are becoming attracted to tailored clothing as a way to express themselves and set themselves apart from their peers. NPD Group's latest tailored clothing survey confirms the dramatic changes in the clothing market at retail. *DNR* writer Stan Gellers noted, "A younger customer is buying this category, with year-over-year unit sales of men's tailored clothing up 25.5 percent for the 18- to 24-year-old group for the 12 months ending October 2006" (Gellers, 2006, p. 21). In the same article, Gellers interviewed Marshal Cohen, NPD chief industry analyst, who stated, "Young guys have discovered suits as a tool to enhance their image and separate themselves from the pack. Now the younger generation has gone back in time with dressing up, because dressing up with suits is cool again" (Gellers, 2006).

Figure 7.14 *Young men create their own sense of style with the suited look.*

Along the same lines, Elizabeth Lazarowitz (2004) wrote a piece in *USA Today* titled "More Men Suit Up as Jackets, Ties Make Comeback." Lazarowitz talked about designers, such as Prada and Dolce & Gabbana, doing "really serious suits." In the same article, Lazarowitz interviewed Jim More, creative director at *GQ*, who stated, "Not too long ago, everyone was saying, 'The suit is dead. The tie is dead,' and they came back with a vengeance." Marshall Cohen of the NPD group lent his voice to this conversation and stated, "It's not good enough to try to show you could make a million dollars in your pajamas like during the dot-com era. Now it's about showing people that you rise above the rest, and dress is one of the important parts of the equation" (Lazarowitz, 2004).

PUTTING A NEW TWIST ON AN OLD STYLE

Several companies are looking to put a new twist on a very old style: washable and waterproof suits. This is not a new phenomenon.

Figure 7.15 *Joseph Haspel shows off his washable suit.*

During the 1950s, a clothier from New Orleans was successful in developing a blended polyester and cotton seersucker fabric that retained its shape after many machine washings. Joseph Haspel was the clothier, and he fashioned the fabric into a men's suit. To demonstrate his point, while at a convention in Florida, he donned the suit and walked into the ocean. Later that night, he wore the same suit, proving beyond a shadow of a doubt that his suit would stand up to his claim of being washable. To this day, Joseph Haspel is known as the father of the washable seersucker suit.

The new twist to the story is that companies are now doing what Haspel did with a blend of polyester and cotton with wool. JCPenney has a washable wool suit with their Stafford Brand, as well as the Italian brand, Isaia, with a big difference in the price tag. JCPenney's Stafford brand retails for under $300, while the Italian suit, which has been named the Aquaspider Suit, retails for $2,495. The Aquaspider is 100 percent merino wool with a fine coating of Teflon, which results in a suit that looks great and will also keep the wearer dry during the occasional rain shower. How is that for marrying new technology with the classic menswear category of suits!

THE GREEN MOVEMENT COMES TO TAILORED CLOTHING

Bagir Ltd., a tailored clothing manufacturer based in Israel, has developed a new collection called EcoGir. This new collection not only uses organic cotton in the manufacture of its suits; it has stepped up the green movement by weaving

Figure 7.16 *Bagir Ltd. goes green, using post-consumer waste to create a great-looking suit.*

fabric out of post-consumer waste (PCW). The PCW used in this product comes from recycled plastic bottles. The discarded plastic bottles are washed, melted, and converted into a yarn. The yarn is blended with natural fibers to create a unique fabric that will reduce the environmental footprint of Bagir. How's that for innovation!

CONCLUDING THOUGHTS

Chapter 7 investigated styles, design features, and companies that are important to the tailored clothing market. The goals of this chapter were to help you learn the following:

o   the various classifications that make up the tailored clothing industry
o   the products that make up the tailored outerwear business
o   design and make features of the products in the tailored clothing and tailored outerwear business

Classifications were established, and distinctions were made between the suit jacket in a nested suit and a sport coat. Suited separates were also explained. You learned the difference between general outerwear and tailored outerwear, and you delved more fully into specific product features such as pocketing, sleeves, hems, and cuffs. The differences between the casual pant, the dress casual pant, and suit pant were examined. The chapter also included an interview with a leading manufacturer of tailored clothing and helped set the stage for a better understanding of the target customer.

In Chapter 8, the focus shifts to men's furnishings, or accessories as they are sometimes called. (The term *furnishings* is used in this book.) The chapter draws upon the research and knowledge of the author to look at the various products that are included in a typical furnishings department. As important as the products are the merchandising techniques used to sell them. Without a properly executed merchandising strategy at the retail level, the furnishings department will not be profitable. One last item to be examined will be the specific design features that are important to the furnishings market.

KEY TERMS

American cut
Balmacaan
besom pocket

blazer
bluff stitch
British cut

British warmer

cut

double breasted

double-welt pocket

drape

drop

grade

half-top pocket

inset pocket

make

make 1, 2, 4, 4+, 6, 6+

modified American cut

natural shoulder

nested suit

notched lapel

on seam pocket

padded shoulder

patch pocket

peak lapel

pick stitch

pleat

polo coat

quarter-top pocket

reefer

rope shoulder

shawl collar

single breasted

slack time

slash pocket

soft shoulder

square shoulder

suited separates

tailored clothing

topstitching

trench coat

trim European cut

vest

western-style pocket

X-make

CHAPTER EXERCISE

1. Choose a men's dress or casual pant (not denim jeans). Your task will be to create a spec sheet and a make detail sheet. Using a word processing or spreadsheet program, create your own forms for both the spec sheet and the make detail sheet.

   a) The spec sheet is a listing of key measurements that are used to construct a pant. Use the six key measurements described below to create your own spec sheet based on the pant that you selected. All measurements should be made with the garment placed on a clean, flat surface.

   o Waist: With the pant zipped closed, measure from side to side on the inside of the waistband, and double the measurement. This should be the same as the size listed on the garment itself. If the actual measurement is different, what could account for the difference?

   o Seat: With the pant flat, measure 3 inches up from the crotch point, then measure across from side to side.

   o Knee: Fold the leg in half, bringing the bottom of the pant leg to the crotch point. Measure across at the folded point.

- o Inseam: As a finished garment measurement, this is done only on a hemmed or cuffed pant. Measure along the inseam from the hem to the crotch point.
- o Outseam: As a finished garment measurement, this is done only on a hemmed or a cuffed pant. Measure along the side seam from the hem or bottom of the cuff to the bottom of the waistband.
- o Rise: This is the difference between the outseam and the inseam. Just subtract the inseam measurement from the outseam measurement to arrive at the rise.

b) Once you have completed the spec sheet, it is time to complete a make detail sheet. The purpose of the make detail sheet is to describe the pant in detail so that you can prepare a package to be sent to your manufacturer, who will cost it and create a sample. You should also include the following information on the make detail sheet:

- o fabric content
- o recommended wash and care instructions
- o label placement

Remember that your instructor will not be able to see the pant you chose and will make judgments based on the details and measurements that you supply on your spec and make detail sheets.

REFERENCES

Boswell, Suzanne. (1993). *Menswear: Suiting the Customer*. Englewood Cliffs, NJ: Regents/Prentice Hall.

Gellers, Stan. (2006, December 11). Straight up with a twist. *DNR*, p. 16.

IntegrateIR. (2007, February 15). Kenneth Cole Productions and Lanier Clothes sign licensing agreement for men's tailored clothing. [online]. Available: http://www.ntegratir.com/newsrelease_demo.asp?news [April 22, 2007].

Lazarowitz, Elizabeth. (2004, September 1). More men suit up as jackets, ties make comeback. [online]. Available: http//www.usatoday.com/money/industries/retail/2004-09-01-suits_X.htm [February 21, 2007].

MBAStyle.com. (1996, October) *MBA Style Magazine's* tips on buying interview suits. [online]. Available: http://memebrs.aol.com/mbastyle/web/suits1.htm1 [February 21, 2007].

Menstyle.com. (2002, December). Style Guy: Suits and blazers. [online]. Available: http://men.style.com/gq/fashion/styleguy/suitsandblazers/577 [April 22, 2007].

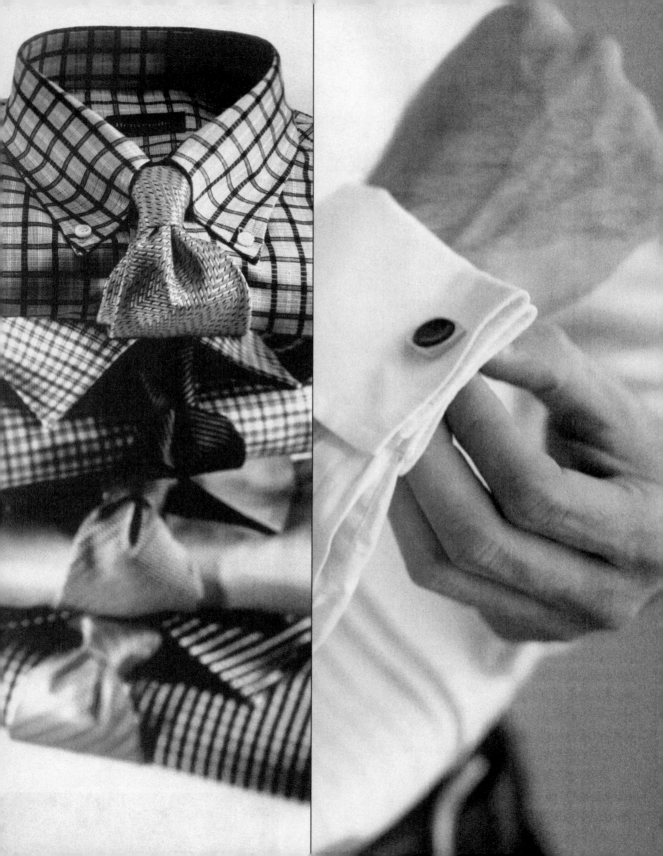

EIGHT

FURNISHINGS

IN THIS CHAPTER, YOU WILL LEARN
THE FOLLOWING:

- the range of products that are included in the menswear furnishings department
- merchandising techniques used in selling menswear furnishings
- specific design features of products that are classified as menswear furnishings

Peanut butter and jelly or ham and eggs go great together and seem to be missing something when they are on their own. The same can be said for suits and furnishings. A good suit is considered unfinished unless you have the proper furnishings to complement it. What constitutes men's furnishings? Several categories of furnishings will be examined in this chapter, including the following:

- dress shirts
- ties
- pocket squares
- socks
- suspenders (braces) and belts

Shoes are considered men's furnishings and are usually sold next to the furnishings department in better department stores. However, shoes as a category could fill several volumes on their own and will be left to the shoe experts of the industry.

Visiting the furnishings department can be an overwhelming experience, even for the savvy shopper. When a customer buys a new suit or sport coat and slacks, the shopping experience has just begun. The following questions face the customer in the furnishings department:

o   What color or pattern dress shirt will accent the suit or jacket and pants best?
o   Which tie will look best?
o   What color socks will complete the outfit?
o   Are suspenders an option? If so, should they be solid or patterned?
o   Is a new belt needed for the new outfit?
o   Is a pocket square needed to finish the look? (The answer to this question will depend on the customer's age. Anyone under the age of 35 should not consider a pocket square, as it portrays an older, more refined gentleman look.)

Many department stores and specialty stores pride themselves on customer service. Sales professionals in these stores are able to assist customers with selecting the furnishings that will best accent a new suit or sport coat.

DRESS SHIRTS

DRESS SHIRTS VERSUS SPORT SHIRTS

What makes a shirt a dress shirt and not a sport shirt? Some will argue that it is the fine fabric or the collar that signifies a dress shirt.

However, a nice sport shirt can be purchased with the same features. Some define a dress shirt by the fact that it only has one pocket, on the wearer's left; others say that a dress shirt is not decorative. However, in recent years, there has been a blurring of the two shirt types, based on changes in fashion. In fact, it is the sizing that dictates which is a dress shirt and which is a sport shirt. Most sport shirts are sized S, M, L, XL, or larger, while a dress shirt must be purchased by neck and sleeve lengths.

HOW TO OBTAIN THE PROPER FIT IN A DRESS SHIRT

If you are shopping for a dress shirt and you are not sure what size you need, most department and specialty stores have qualified sales personnel on the floor that can help. If not, you can use a tape measure and, with the help of a friend, do the measuring yourself. Two measurements are needed to purchase most dress shirts. You can obtain these measurements with the following steps:

○ Wrap a tape measure (a fabric tape measure works best) around your neck with the tape sitting on your Adam's apple. Take this measurement and add on 1/2 inch for comfort's sake.

○ Now, with the help of a friend, place the end of the tape measure on the center of your back at the base of your neck. Measure all the way down your arm to your wrist, where your cuff would be. This measurement is your sleeve length.

Figure 8.1 *Dress-shirt blues: fancy and solid dress shirts in a blue theme.*

With your neck and sleeve measurements, you are ready to select a dress shirt in the correct size. When shopping for a dress shirt, you will find that the neck size is always listed first on the packaging and on the woven label attached to the shirt, followed by the sleeve length. For example, if you have a 15-inch neck with a 32-inch sleeve, you would look for a size 15/32. If you are shopping for a short-sleeve dress shirt, only the neck measurement is needed. You would look for size 15, short sleeve.

A HISTORICAL LOOK AT DRESS SHIRTS

Throughout the 1800s and into the early 1900s, men's dress shirts were available predominantly in white. They were made from broadcloth and available in one sleeve length and several neck sizes. The neck sizes were 14, 15, and 16; if a man had an exceptionally large neck size, he had to have his shirts custom made. Prior to the Industrial Revolution, all shirts were hand sewn, but when they were delivered to the stores, they came only in the sizes mentioned. Given that men are not created in equal sizes, and that arm lengths vary from one individual to the next, it would seem that one sleeve length would prove to be problematic. However, men used **sleeve garters** to hold the sleeves in place. Think of a garter that women would use to hold up their stockings; men's sleeve garters were very similar. The garter had a fabric covering over an elastic-type material, and it was worn below the elbow to hold the sleeves up to the desired length.

The color of a man's shirt distinguished the type of work he did. White was the color of the day for dress shirts and was worn by men who worked in offices. Those who worked with their hands, performing manual labor, wore blue shirts with blue collars. The distinction is further drawn between the two groups of workers by the type of shirt. The so-called white-collar worker wore a woven dress shirt with long sleeves that was sized by neck and sleeve lengths. White-collar workers were paid on a weekly/monthly basis. The manual laborer was paid an hourly wage, and the blue-collar shirt he wore was typically a short-sleeve, woven sport shirt, sized S, M, L, or XL. His shirt was made from a much more rugged fabric that could withstand the wear and tear associated with manual labor. The short sleeves were a safety feature as well; men who worked with machines preferred the short-sleeve shirt because long sleeves tended to get caught in the machinery. Thus, the terms **white-collar worker** and **blue-collar worker** were born and are still a measure of one's place in the working world today. As dress becomes more casual for office work, this distinction is lessening.

SALES AND MERCHANDISING TECHNIQUES OF DRESS SHIRTS

Dress shirts constitute a multi-billion dollar business. Visit a department store and look at the tables, racks, and cubes filled with dress shirts. From a stock-keeping unit (SKU) standpoint, the investment is staggering. In recent years, in an effort to control SKUs, some manufacturers have gone to **split-sleeve measurements.** In order to cut down on inventory, these manufacturers have combined sleeve lengths. Instead of offering a size 15/32, they offer a size 15–32/33, thereby eliminating a sleeve length. This may seem like a good idea in theory, but in practice, the shirt will likely not fit properly. A 32/33-length sleeve is cut to measure 32 ½ inches, so if your sleeve measurement is 32 inches, this sleeve will be half an inch too long, and if your measurement is 33 inches, it will be half an inch too short. However, if your sleeve measurement happens to be 32 ½, then you are in luck!

You will obtain the best fit with exact sleeve lengths, or, if you can afford it, with custom-made dress shirts. Many tailor shops provide this service, and there are many custom shirt making shops throughout the world, as well as a growing number of online companies offering the same service. Many of these custom shops allow you to select your own fabric from their offerings and design the shirt based on collar model and sleeve treatment. Some will even allow you to choose your own buttons.

If you are interested in having a custom dress shirt or sport shirt made for you, the easiest way to find out where to go in your area is to do a Web search. Just search for "custom-made dress shirts" and the results will provide names of Web-based, custom dress shirt businesses, as well as local tailors. Examples include the following:

o   Best Custom Shirt (www.bestcustomshirt .com)
o   Mohan's Custom Tailors (www.mohantailors .com)
o   Bermini Custom Suits and Shirts, located in New York City
o   Delbert's Clothing Inc., located in Illinois

In addition, many department stores offer this service. In New York City, Bloomingdales and Saks offer custom-made dress shirts; they use a local production company to cut and sew the shirts.

Suppose you have the money (anywhere from $80 to $500), and you decide you want a custom-made dress shirt. You see an offer from Saks, so you go there. The tailor takes all the necessary measurements and asks you to choose the following:

- a fabric from their display
- a button from their collection
- collar stays, if you are selecting a straight-point collar
- the features you would like on the shirt

Then the tailor sends the package (fabric, buttons, collar stays, measurements, and instructions regarding the features you have chosen) out to the production company where the shirt will be made. The process will usually take 10 days from start to finish. For rush jobs, the process can take less time, but you may have to pay a premium over and above the cost of the shirt.

STYLE FEATURES OF DRESS SHIRTS

This section will examine the design features that make up the dress shirt. As you read, think about the features you would want on a custom-made dress shirt. In a construction project, various elements are added to complete the project; the same holds true for building a dress shirt. Why do some designers go for a straight-point collar and others a button-down collar? Why do some dress shirts have adjustable button cuffs but others do not? To be honest, there are no good answers to these questions, as how the shirt is built depends on the designer, private-label brand, and/or the manufacturer and what they think the target customer will want and buy.

COLLAR STYLES

The collar of a dress shirt is a key feature. In visual merchandising, focal points in a display are important, and displays are planned so that customers' eyes are drawn to these focal points first. With a dress shirt, the focal point is the collar. There are seven collar styles that have played, prominent roles in the men's dress shirt category. As in most areas of fashion, there are variations of each of these styles.

Designers have tried to improve upon the collar from time to time. Some have added different weights of fusible nonwoven material to give the collar more definition; others have removed all the fusible nonwoven material to give a very relaxed look. The construction of the collar varies by model, but most collars have some sort of nonwoven material sewn in between the top and bottom layers to give the collar body so that it lies properly when worn. One of the latest design features that seems to be taking hold among several designers and brands is a variation of the button-down collar. Instead of having the buttons visible and buttoning through the collar at the points, designers are affixing the buttons to the underside of the collar to achieve the same effect without the buttons being seen. Suffice to say, there is only so much that can be done to a dress shirt collar without changing the character of the look.

One of the key designs is the **straight-point collar.** As you can see in Figure 8.2, the name describes its appearance. What variations can be found in this style? Designers can change the length of the points as well as the width of the spread (measurement from one point to the other).

In order to keep the points from flapping in the breeze and exhibiting very little body, manufacturers have incorporated **stays** in the collars. In the early days of shirt making, stays were removable pieces of metal that were inserted in the underside of the collar points to give the collar shape. Today, designers and manufacturers prefer to use a medium-weight fusible lining in conjunction with a permanent stay. There are still dress shirts on the market today that have removable stays made from a hard plastic or lightweight metal. In some cases, brands and/or designers use the stays as marketing tools, engraving or printing their names or logos on them. Customers may even have their own names engraved on their stays; this service has been offered in catalogs as a gift idea. The engraved stays become marketing tools, as they are supposed to be removed during laundering or dry cleaning. When this occurs, the name is visible to the wearer and reinforces the brand identity.

ENGLISH-SPREAD COLLAR

The **English-spread collar** is similar to the straight-point collar, but it has a wider spread

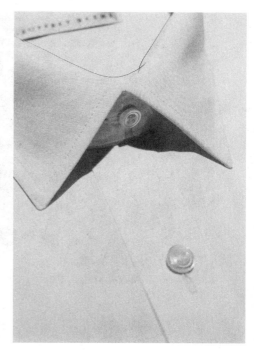

Figure 8.2 A crisp white dress shirt with a straight-point collar and a medium spread.

Figure 8.3 *Traditional English spread on two very English chaps.*

and narrower collar points (see Figure 8.3). Many of today's British designers use this as a signature feature.

WINDSOR COLLAR

During the 1930s, the Duke of Windsor had a collar style designed to accommodate the extremely large knots that were used to tie the Windsor knot on his tie. This style was called the **Windsor collar** (see Figure 8.4). The points of this collar look almost parallel to the waist of the dress pants. This style has endured over the years and is more popular in England than the United States.

ROUNDED COLLAR

The **rounded collar** originated in England and was popular with students at Eton College. Eton College was founded in 1440 by King Henry VI of Great Britain as a public school for boys. It is a very proper school with traditional

Figure 8.4 *The Duke of Windsor, pictured with his now famous Windsor collar pinned with a tie bar.*

roots. This collar style in the United States can sometimes be associated with the Ivy League set, which is made up of eight colleges: Brown, Columbia, Cornell, Dartmouth, Harvard, Princeton, Yale, and the University of Pennsylvania. Like Eton College in Great Britain, the Ivy League has historical roots dating back centuries, to 1636, when Harvard was founded. The rounded collar was worn by men attending these schools. This collar style can be accessorized with a collar pin (see Figure 8.5). In fact, several designers manufacture the rounded collar with eyelets in the collar to facilitate the wearing of the collar pin.

Figure 8.5 The Duke of Windsor in his younger days, sporting a rounded-collar dress shirt.

BUTTON-DOWN COLLAR

The **button-down collar** has become a mainstay in the wardrobe of today's man. It is a feature that can be found on both dress shirts and sport shirts (see Figure 8.6). This collar design has a functional origin; it was developed by polo players in England who were tired of getting slapped in the face with their collar points as they played. One player had the brilliant idea of buttoning down the collars so they stayed in place.

Today, this collar style is less formal, as it does not require stays and has a softer appearance that rolls over the tie. This collar style can be worn just as easily with the collar open. In recent years, a new twist on this old style has been to hide the buttons under the collar, giving the look of a straight-point collar with the functionality of the button-down collar. The actual buttons used on the collar are generally half the size of the buttons used on the front placket of the shirt.

Brooks Brothers was one of the first retailers to introduce the dress shirt with the button-down collar to the United States. Like the rounded collar, the button-down collar has been associated with the Ivy League and is sometimes considered a "preppy" look.

Figure 8.6 Neat tattersal patterns in button-down collar style.

TAB COLLAR

The **tab-collar** system uses two narrow strips of fabric sewn into the underside of the collar with a snap or button joining the two together (see Figure 8.7, shown here without the tie). This collar system was very popular in the 1950s. It was used like the pinned collar (see below) to emphasize the tie and make it a more prominent feature of the collar.

Figure 8.7 A tab collar.

The **pinned collar** is actually used in conjunction with the straight-collar model. An accessory known as a **collar bar** is used like the tab to make the tie stand out. The collar bar uses the following methods to attach to the shirt:

○ a clamplike structure that attaches itself to each side of the collar underneath the tie
○ the eyelet method, which requires the wearer to purchase a collar bar that has one end that screws off so that the bar can be inserted into the eyelets under the tie

The pinned-collar style is considered very stylish or dressy.

By far, the most popular collar styles in the market today are the button-down and straight-point collars, with the English-spread collar coming in a distant third. Oxford Industries, a maker of men's dress and sport shirts, has developed a new technique for manufacturing collars. They have even gone as far as naming the collar, calling it the The Lifetime Collar (TLC). This collar comes in the traditional spread and button-down models. It is a registered trademark of Oxford Industries. The company guarantees that the collar is manufactured for a consistent and comfortable fit—first time, every time for the life of the shirt. Through the use of new nonwoven technology, the fusible material that they use is guaranteed to stand up to wear and care for the life of the shirt. The actual collar style is not new, but the materials and methods of manufacture are giving Oxford a perceived advantage over their competition.

The overwhelming majority of dress shirts sold today are long-sleeve shirts. Visit a typical department store, and you will find that approximately 90 percent of the dress shirts on display are long sleeve for nine months of the year. There is a slight shift in the summer months, with perhaps 5 to 8 percent more short-sleeve shirts displayed. However, there may be a shift. David Colman wrote an article for *The New York Times* titled "Short-Sleeved Shirts, Nerdy but Nice, Are Back." In the article, Colman discussed the fact that it is hard for short-sleeve dress shirts to get any respect. "Unlike clothes that have rubbed elbows with super-cool characters, the short-sleeved shirt is the Dilbert of menswear, redolent of rocket scientists and substitute teachers. Think Ron Howard doing the right thing on *Happy Days*, Jack Webb of *Dragnet* barbecuing on his day off or, worse, Homer Simpson living the nuclear-family dream" (Colman, 2006). Colman uses these analogies to create a picture in the mind of the reader; think of the nerdy guy with the pocket protector you might have encountered in school or at the mall. The TV personas of Ron Howard and Jack Webb and cartoon characters Homer Simpson and Dilbert all wore short-sleeve dress shirts and typify the "nerd" look.

Designers Marc Jacobs, Thom Browne, Scott Sternberg, Alexander McQueen, and Michael Bastian see short-sleeved dress shirts as indispensable summer wear. These designers are well respected in the menswear industry and can and do set trends. If it is okay for them to promote and wear short-sleeve dress shirts, then it is okay for the average guy on the street to wear them as well. Who knows? If enough "cool" guys start wearing short sleeves, then maybe, just maybe, it will no longer be viewed as "nerdy."

CUFF STYLES

If a customer chooses a short-sleeve dress shirt, his choices are limited to the following sleeve finishes:

o   a hemmed sleeve
o   a cuffed sleeve (if available)

For the long-sleeve design, the customer can choose from the following:

o   **Barrel cuff:** The barrel cuff is the typical cuff found on most long-sleeve dress shirts. Designers create variations of the barrel cuff by altering the shape of the barrel to either a rounded cuff or a square cuff or by adding more than one button. If there is more than one button, it is said to be a two-button adjustable cuff. This type of cuff can be found on split-sleeve lengths or on single-sleeve lengths. With the two-button adjustable cuff, the customer can often get a much snugger fit at the wrist.
o   **French cuff:** The French cuff is elegant in styling and often associated with formal wear. The cuff folds back over itself and is held together by cuff links or studs. This styling is also referred to as **double cuffs.**

SLEEVE-PLACKET STYLING

Another facet of the long-sleeve dress shirt is the type of **sleeve placket** or vent that is

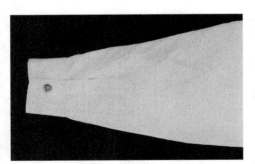

Figure 8.8 *Sleeve placket.*

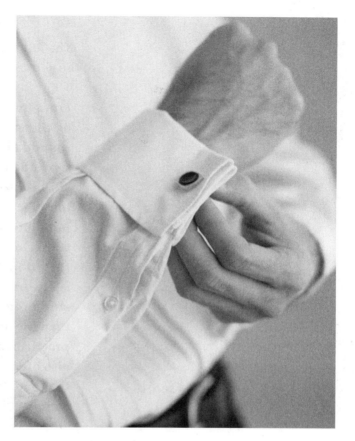

Figure 8.9 *Classic French cuffs.*

designed into the shirt. A plain slit for a sleeve vent is a sign of an inexpensive shirt make. With better-make shirts, the manufacturer incorporates a sleeve placket into the construction. The sleeve placket looks and acts like the front placket of a dress shirt. It will most likely have a button placed mid-span of the placket to keep the sleeve placket closed and looking neat. Remember the rule of thumb in this business: the more that is put into the construction of a garment, the more it will cost to produce and, therefore, the more it will cost to buy. Thus, a shirt with a simple sleeve vent will cost less than a shirt with a constructed placket.

The following features are found on the front of the shirt:

o Front pocket: The front pocket is generally on the wearer's left; many will have a rounded bottom with a V-stitch in the top hem. On a sport shirt or even dress shirts, a square-bottom pocket can also be found.

o Bottom: Most shirt bottoms are rounded with a longer tail in front and back to be tucked in. A square bottom can be found on some dress shirts, but not many. One type of shirt bottom does not signify a better make than the other, although the shirttail is more practical and does stay tucked in better. It also offers the wearer front and back tails that tend to hide underwear lines. In the early-2000s, a new way to wear the dress shirt was created. The dress shirt and the sport shirt with the rounded tail were worn out of the pants, creating a sloppy look and defeating the purpose of the tail bottom.

o Front closure, which can be styled in the following way:

o The plain front is achieved by turning back the face fabric of the garment, pressing it in place, and edge-stitching the underside.

o The placket model is achieved in the following way (see Figure 8.10):

o The continuous placket uses the front fabric and folds about 1 ½ inches of fabric before a row of stitches is run on the inner and outer edges of the placket.

Figure 8.10 White dress shirt with placket, also called top center.

Regardless of the method, dress shirt fronts will all have buttonholes and corresponding buttons on the opposite side of the shirt front.

As for the buttons, the choice is up to the designer to choose the button that will best complement the shirt. Buttons can be man-made (using plastics or other compounds), or they can be made out of natural shells, metal, stones, or horns. Buttons have even been made out of recycled cardboard. Once the choice of buttons is made, the next decision is whether to use two-hole or four-hole buttons. If four-hole buttons are chosen, the next decision is how the stitching will be done—parallel or cross stitch.

Most designers work with the following three areas on the back of the dress shirt to create a signature style:

○ yokes
○ pleats
○ locker loops

Figure 8.11 This shirt has a contrast-stripe yoke with an inverted box pleat.

Yokes are either single or split yokes, with more fashionable and more costly dress shirts sporting the split-yoke look. The yoke is on the upper part of the back of the dress shirt. Most yokes are single or one piece and run from side to side in the upper back, and some are split. If the yoke is split, it will be directly in the center of the upper back. This split is strictly a design feature, as it does not add or detract anything from the shirt itself. Inexpensive dress shirts can be found with one-piece backs, but this is uncommon. If a customer has decided on the split-yoke back, a **locker loop** can be added. When sporting a locker loop, it is common for the shirt to include a box-pleat feature as well, but it is not necessary. Two well-defined side pleats can be used as an alternative to the box-pleat, locker-loop look.

A true sign of quality in a dress shirt, regardless of the price, is single-needle, double-needle tailoring. Single-needle tailoring is used around the arm holes, and double-needle tailoring is used down the side seam. The use of single-needle tailoring around the armhole is evidenced by just a single row of stitches, which gives the armhole a clean, well-defined look, while adding strength to that area of the garment. Double-needle tailoring down the side seam also gives the shirt nice straight lines, and when done properly, allows the side seam to lie flat with no puckering of fabric, and gives stress points added strength.

Stitch count is also a sign of a well-tailored dress shirt, with the top makes achieving a consistent 16 stitches per inch. The more stitches per inch, the flatter the seams will lie and the better the shirt will look. Inexpensive dress shirts will just close all the seams with a serge stitch. The serge stitch is used in the production of less expensive dress shirts as it requires only one operation to close any seam, whereas the single-needle and double-needle operations have multiple steps in the sewing process.

DRESS SHIRT WEAVES AND FIBER CONTENT

Three main weave types in men's dress shirts include the following:

- **broadcloth**
- **oxford cloth**
- **pinpoint oxford**

These weave types are often used synonymously to describe a dress shirt fabric. You can determine which fabric is being used by a simple visual examination. Broadcloth is a flat weave with a smooth surface. An oxford cloth has a textured surface and looks like a bird's-eye pattern. The pinpoint is a variation of the oxford, but this weave uses much finer yarns. Therefore, it appears smoother while still giving the textured look of the oxford cloth. In terms of usage, the broadcloth shirt is number one, followed by the oxford-cloth shirt and then the pinpoint oxford.

Today, many variations in fiber content can be found, ranging from 100 percent cotton to cotton blends, as well as silks and man-made fibers. The 1970s and 1980s brought disco fever and the advent of the miracle fiber, polyester; during that period, many dress and sport shirts were produced in 100 percent polyester and polyester blends. Following those polyester years, the men's market went back to wearing mostly natural fibers. If a dress shirt is blended, it will usually have at least 55 percent cotton, which renders the shirt's chief value as cotton. Therefore, if the shirt is imported, as most are today, it will be able to enter the country under a cotton tariff, which costs less than importing synthetic fibers.

This chapter would not be complete without reference to wrinkle-free, wrinkle-resistant, and no-iron fabrics. Basically, they all exhibit similar qualities, and the terminology used to describe the dress shirt as wrinkle-free, wrinkle-resistant, or no-iron is based on manufacturers' claims about performance. Through the use of resin treatments, the fabrics and/or garments are treated so that the shirts retain their shape and need no ironing when laundered. Most treatments last the lifetime of the garment, although some do lose their crisp hand and feel soft and pliable after many launderings. Some dress shirts that are marketed as wrinkle-free may live up to that claim under ideal laundering conditions (i.e., appropriate water temperature, dryer temperature, and washer and dryer times). However, many need to be ironed to look their best.

SHIRT CUTS

Just as there are several different suit cuts, the same holds true for dress shirts. The key to finding the right cut is to know your body type and what looks good on you. The three cuts are as follows:

- **Full cut:** The full-cut shirt is also referred to as a box cut or regular cut and makes up the bulk of the dress shirts on the market today. The side seams on these models are straight, so most men can wear this cut, provided they have chosen the right size.
- **Tapered cut:** Those who consider themselves to be on the slimmer side will gain a better fit with a tapered cut, which angles down from under the armhole to the waist. The angling down has the effect of reducing the fullness in the shirt and making it more fitted to the body.
- **Fitted cut:** Men who consider themselves trim and fit might want to look for a fitted shirt. This model not only angles down the side but also introduces two darts in the back of the shirt to further reduce the fullness and provide a truly fitted silhouette.

Of all the categories in the furnishings department of any department store, the dress shirt area will occupy the most space. Consider the number of designers, brands, and private labels that can be offered in the dress shirt category. Now, multiply that number by the various colors, patterns, and sizes available. Think about how quickly your SKU control could get out of hand and your investment in inventory in this area could become overwhelming.

The primary method of presenting dress shirts at retail is folded and stacked in a cube. Some will display dress shirts on tables, but this becomes something of a housekeeping nightmare for the sales personnel. If you have purchased a dress shirt from a retailer, did you notice the packaging, polybag, stand-up collar, pins, plastic, and cardboard? If you have purchased one from a catalog retailer, you may have noticed a big difference in the packaging. The catalog version is flat-folded with a minimum of pins, plastic, and cardboard; presentation of each shirt within its packaging is not as important as in the retail store because you are buying the shirt based on how it looks in the catalog. Imagine what the shirts would look like if they were all stacked flat with no stand-up collar and no attractive packaging. The display would not be very inviting to customers.

Retailers vary on how they stock their dress shirt inventory. To help consumers find what they want, retailers display their merchandise in the following ways:

o   by size and color
o   by designer or brand

As far as colors go, several must be in the assortment. White and a shade of light blue will always be the top two sellers. Then pinks and greens, as well as the current fashion colors, will be stocked.

In addition to solid colors, consumers can choose from stripes, checks, and even plaids. Plaid shirts will most likely be large windowpane-type plaids with a minimum of color, so that they can coordinate easily with the suit. Designers of dress shirts follow the trends, and the width of the stripes and the size of the plaids and checks are all dictated by fashion.

New designs in the dress shirt market, with updated fabrics, colors, and features, will appear two to three times per year. Much of the stock will be replenished as needed throughout the season. Many of the manufacturers in the dress shirt industry use electronic data interchange (EDI) methods to replenish stock of key SKUs, so that they are always in stock when the consumer is ready to buy.

TIES

The tie is one of those seemingly unnecessary articles of clothing that men wear, but when it is not worn with a suit or sport coat, the impression given is that the wearer is not fully dressed. Why do men wear ties? What is the significance of the tie today?

In an article in *Psychology Today*, Jodi Balkan (2004) stated, "Dating back to around 1650, when the French, led by Louis XIV, followed the example of the Croatian mercenaries who donned neck apparel, the tie has flourished in various and elaborate incarnations. But in 1924, out of a need for a more practical, comfortable, and durable neckwear, Jesse Langsdorf developed the manufacturing system for the modern tie. And it has barely evolved since." Balkan further explained, "What has changed during the last 70 years, however, is why men wear them. No longer viewed today as a requirement or a sign of conformity and social regimentation outside of the business and political arenas, ties are now often seen as just what they are: simple ornamentation" (Balkan, 2004).

In her article, Balkan presented Jean-Claude Colban, director of Charvet, the distinguished tie shop in Paris, who stated, "As one of the few expressions of creativity and personality allowed to men, a tie has a lot of responsibility. It conveys a feeling, a situation, and above all the elegance of the wearer, since his choice of a tie is an expression of the inner self" (Balkan, 2004). Whether ties are an expression of the inner self or not is a personal opinion. However, ties do allow the wearer to show some creativity and personality.

TYPES OF TIES

To test your understanding of ties, venture into the furnishings department in your favorite department store and look at the assortment of ties from which you can choose. The assortment can be intimidating, and if you have any doubt about your ability to pick the right tie, you are not alone. When shopping for a tie, it is always a good idea to wear or bring the suit jacket or sport jacket that you will wear with the tie, as this will make the decision somewhat easier. When choosing a tie, you have a number of choices, which are broken down into the following categories:

- **Foulard ties** are represented by small shapes such as circles or diamonds in repeat patterns.
- **Repp stripe** or **regimental stripe ties** are the most traditional designs. These ties are found in varying widths and have their roots in the English army representing the various regiments.
- **Club ties** also have English roots, based on schools. In the United States, these ties are more closely associated with the Ivy League schools.
- **Paisley ties** have a classic pattern of a curved teardrop shape. These ties were popular in the 1960s and 1970s, and they occasionally surface as a fashion trend. However, this style has not been overly popular for quite some time.
- **Dotted ties** have more of a whimsical look.
- **Plaid ties** have been popular and can add color to one's wardrobe without making a bold statement.
- **Floral ties** made a brief foray into the men's market in the late 1980s and early 1990s. Although diminished in their offerings, floral patterns still maintain a place in the tie business.
- **Conversational ties** are those that have a theme, such as a sport or holiday. These are quite popular during specific times of the year and have become an acceptable wardrobe accessory.

Figure 8.12 *An assortment of ties—stripes, dots, updated paisleys, neats, geometrics and conversationals—all merchandised together.*

Two other types of neckwear that can be found in the men's furnishings department are the bow tie and the ascot. These two neck pieces make up a very small part of the market, and apart from Hugh Hefner and some actors in very old movies, few men wear the ascot. Outside of the formal-wear setting, bow ties are seldom worn.

TIE MATERIALS AND CARE

The most popular fabric for a tie is 100 percent silk. The fabric is cut on the bias so that it conforms to the wearer's neck and retains its shape after being worn repeatedly. The vast majority of ties today are woven, although some are knitted.

If knitted, the fabric of choice is wool or cotton. Several manufacturers have marketed ties made from polyester, but a polyester tie will not retain its shape or hold a knot as well as silk.

Ties should never be left knotted overnight, as the fabric will become creased due to the fact that ties are cut on the bias. Once this happens, the tie might as well be thrown out and a new one purchased.

Some men will wear a tie until it is soiled beyond repair, discard it, and buy a new one. They feel that it is easier and perhaps cheaper to throw it out than to take the tie to the dry cleaners. Dry cleaning is the only recommended method for cleaning a tie, and even this method can damage the tie due to the agitation involved. The practice of discarding soiled ties can be quite expensive, depending on one's choice of ties and retailers. Today, a good silk tie with a nice interlining, which is used to help retain shape, can be purchased for as little as $10 at your favorite off-price retailer (e.g., Century 21, Marshall's, TJX, Ross Stores, Burlington Coat Factory), or you can spend $125 or more at a better department store (e.g., Saks, Bloomingdales, Neiman Marcus) or specialty store (Barney's or the Men's Wearhouse).

THE FUTURE OF TIES

In a recent article on ties in the *International Herald Tribune*, Robert Galbraith (2007) noted that at a shareholder meeting the chief executive officer of Fiat appeared in an open-collared shirt, which caused much commotion. Galbraith went on to suggest that this act caused irreparable damage to the tie business. Luigi Turconi, CEO of the firm that produces ties for Valentino, stated that this action

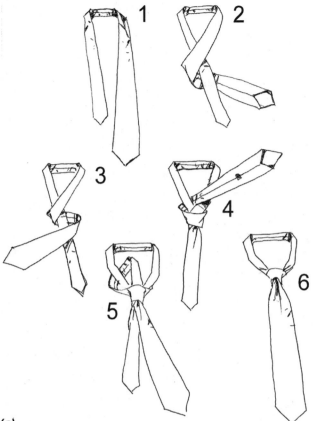

Figure 8.13 *How to Tie a Tie. The two basic knots are **(a)** the four-in-hand and **(b)** the half-Windsor.*

(a)

How to Tie a Tie

The Four-in-Hand Knot

The view is your image as seen in the mirror.

Step 1 Start with the wide end of your tie on the right, and extend it about one foot below the narrow end. This will vary based on the thickness of the tie and the desired length; it may take several tries to get it right.

Step 2 Cross the wide end over the narrow end, and then back underneath.

Step 3 Continue around while grasping the tie with your left thumb and forefinger, passing the wide end across the front of the narrow end once more.

Step 4 Pass the wide end up and through the loop you created.

Step 5 Grasping the front of the loose knot with the index finger, pass the wide end down through the loop in the front.

Step 6 Remove your finger and tighten the knot carefully. Draw up the knot to the collar by holding the narrow end now in the back of the wide end and sliding up the knot snug.

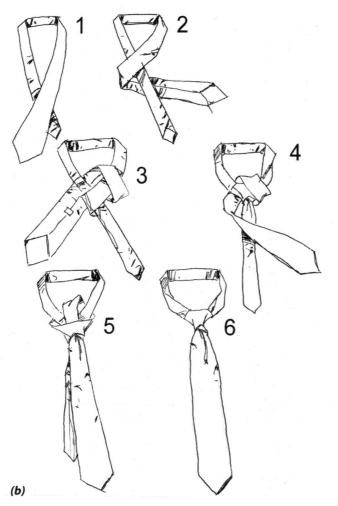

Figure 8.13 *How to Tie a Tie. The two basic knots are **(a)** the four-in-hand and **(b)** the half-Windsor. (continued)*

(b)

How to Tie a Tie *(continued)*

The Half-Windsor Knot

The view is your image as seen in the mirror.

Step 1 Start with the wide end of the tie on your right, and extend it about one foot below the narrow end. This will vary based on the thickness of the tie and the desired length. It may take several tries to get it right.

Step 2 Cross the wide end over the narrow end, and then turn it back underneath.

Step 3 Bring up the narrow end and turn it down through the loop.

Step 4 Pass the wide end around the front from left to right.

Step 5 Then bring it up and through the loop.

Step 6 Pass the wide end down through the loop you created in the front. Tighten carefully by sliding up the knot to the collar.

really reflected the greater freedom that executives have in their dress today. In Turconi's words, "Ties are coming back into fashion, but there is a different attitude than before. They are being worn more for pleasure" (Galbraith, 2007).

The article went on to say that the real trouble started in the 1990s with the casualization in America and elsewhere in the world. Once it became acceptable to dress down, not only on Fridays, but every day, worldwide sales of ties dropped by 50 percent. Roberto Cavalleri, sales and marketing director at Holliday and Brown, a London-based tie maker, said that the slump was most noticeable in the United States. "The tie was no longer seen as a mandatory part of the dress code amongst Americans. There was a dramatic fall in sales and attitudes changed around the globe" (Galbraith, 2007).

The news is not all that bad; Holliday & Brown, the London-based tie maker mentioned above, saw sales rise more than 10 percent in 2005 and 22 percent in 2006. The increases can be partially attributed to the backlash in response to all the dressing down and to the crash of the dot-com businesses. (The dot-com boom had spawned a more casual workplace, and some employees even worked from home, and so didn't need to dress up for work at all. As former dot-com workers began moving into different workplaces, they needed to add less casual pieces to their wardrobes.) In the business sector, there has been a resurgence in dressing up for work. This trend will continue for several more years, and with that increase, there will be a corresponding increase in the tie business. The tie business will probably never hit the peaks of the past, but the remaining tie makers and retailers should fare well.

Like the bow tie and the ascot, the pocket square is not a mainstay in the menswear wardrobe today. Worn during the 1940s and 1950s, this accessory did see a slight upturn during the 1990s, but it was relegated to a few fashionistas who had the confidence to pull off the look. Wearing a pocket square is not the norm in business attire, and only those who have a confident sense of style know how to use this accessory to their advantage.

The actual pocket square is made of silk, linen, or cotton. Silk gives the square a more flowing look and it can be tucked into the chest pocket of the suit jacket or sport coat. Whether the pocket square is in a solid color or a colored pattern, it should pick up at least one color from the wearer's tie. It is considered a fashion *faux pas* to buy one of those matched sets where the tie matches the pocket square. Linen and cotton squares will generally be white and give a more rigid look to the square.

Originally, pocket squares were functional and used for handkerchiefs. However, after they had been used once or twice to blow one's nose, these pocket squares were not very well suited for sitting in one's chest pocket for everyone to see.

DRY CLEANER'S INGENUITY

I remember, when I was growing up, having my suit returned from the cleaners with a faux pocket square in it, and wearing it on special occasions. The addition of the pocket square was really quite clever; it was used as a marketing tool for the dry cleaner. The square comprised only a small amount of material stapled or glued to a piece of cardboard, and the dry cleaner's information was on the cardboard. It slipped into the chest pocket of the suit jacket or sport coat with just the peaks of the fabric showing. It was quite ingenious.

SOCKS

"Socks are the most underrated item of clothing, since they're usually hidden and most people pay little attention to them. Yet, if you wear a brown pair of socks with black pants and black shoes, for example, people will almost certainly notice such a blunder" (Indiviglio, 2007). Given that fashion as a whole has many different opinions and options, there are different ideas about how best to wear your socks and what they should match. Choices include the following:

o   match your socks to your shoes
o   match your socks to your pants
o   match your socks to a color being worn above your waist

The consumer can decide for himself which of these three choices feels most comfortable to him.

SOCK LENGTHS AND SIZES

Socks can be purchased in the following lengths:

o   ankle
o   midcalf
o   over the calf

The sock length you choose is a personal choice. As a general rule of thumb for business attire, you should always go with an over-the-calf length so that if you cross your legs at a business meeting, your sock, and not your leg, is exposed.

Most socks today have size charts printed on the packaging, and some even have sizes on the socks themselves. Most socks fit many shoe sizes, thereby cutting down on SKUs. It is not uncommon to find a store stocking only two or three sizes that cover the majority of feet.

FIBER CONTENT

After determining the right size, the next choice to make is what fiber content to buy. Many socks today are made from the following:

o   man-made fibers
o   blends, which include man-made fibers blended with cotton or wool

Socks are also available in 100 percent cotton or 100 percent wool. One factor that will help in deciding what fiber content to buy is the weather. Consumers who live in colder climates will tend to wear a heavy wool sock, while consumers who live in warmer climates will tend to wear a lightweight cotton or blend. If you do happen to choose a synthetic fiber, your choices will be the following:

o nylon
o polyester
o acrylic
o blends of cotton or wool and the synthetic fiber

This chapter's focus is on socks as an accessory for dressing up. However, there are also many different types of socks used today for athletic purposes and casual wear. These socks are chosen according to end use; the true athlete will probably opt for one of the synthetic fibers available because of their **wicking properties**—their ability to pull moisture away from the skin and transport it outside of the fabric.

After navigating the treacherous waters of sockdom to find the right length, fiber, and size, the customer is faced with the challenge of choosing the right color and/or pattern. He should ask himself the following questions to help make the final choice:

o Am I bold enough to wear a bright color to match something above my waist?
o Am I conservative? If so, should I go with a basic black or brown to match the shoe or pant?
o Do I prefer patterns, stripes, dots, plaids, or argyles?

The last section of this chapter will present two functional items in a man's wardrobe. Both have the same end application—to hold up one's pants. The rule of thumb for wearing suspenders (also known as braces) or a belt is to choose one or the other to hold up your pants, but never to wear both together. For dress or formal wear, a pair of suspenders is a great way to top off an outfit.

The suspenders should button into the pants; the clip-on type should be avoided, as they are not very fashionable. A good pair of dress pants will come with three sets of buttons already sewn into the inside waistband—two sets in the front, one on the left and one on the right of the zipper opening, and one in the center back.

Depending on one's fashion point of view, suspenders can be worn in a color that accents or contrasts with the suit or sport jacket; the choice is up to the wearer. Some stores sell conversational suspenders with various motifs such as sports, cartoons, flowers, and movie stars. Generally speaking, suspenders such as these should be kept for the casual business meeting, not for formal occasions.

Every man should own one good brown belt and one good black belt for dress. Dress belts should be made of leather. They should have simple buckles; truck logos or beer labels are not acceptable. Business attire dictates simplicity as the best approach. As a rule of thumb, a black belt should be worn with black shoes, and a brown belt should be worn with brown shoes.

With the advent of casual dressing for the office, belt choices become somewhat more open.

If a man is wearing a pair of khakis, he might opt for a fabric belt, perhaps made of canvas or hemp, or a braided leather belt. These choices provide more of a casual look that complement the khaki pants.

CONCLUDING THOUGHTS

This chapter turned your attention to the area in the store in which men tend to feel the most uncomfortable: the furnishings department. The uncomfortable feeling stems from the myriad of choices the male consumer is confronted with in this department.

The goals of this chapter were to help you learn the following:

- o   the range of products that are included in the menswear furnishings department
- o   merchandising techniques used in selling menswear furnishings
- o   specific design features of products that are classified as menswear furnishings

This chapter broadened your understanding of the furnishings market by looking at key differences between dress shirts and sport shirts, as well as fabrics and cuts that are associated with the shirt market. Another key area in the furnishings department is the tie section. Various tie designs and fabrics important to this market were discussed. To a lesser degree, but important to many in the business are socks, suspenders, belts, and pocket squares; without them, no furnishings department would be complete.

Chapter 9 will focus on the formal wear market. As you learn about the origins of formal wear, you will discover that there are two competing theories. You will examine design features associated with the formal wear market and the differences in formal attire. The chapter will also look at the business of renting versus buying tuxedos.

KEY TERMS

barrel cuff	floral tie
blue-collar worker	foulard tie
broadcloth	four-in-hand knot
button-down collar	French cuff
club tie	full cut
collar bar	half-Windsor knot
conversational tie	locker loop
dotted tie	oxford cloth
double cuff	paisley tie
English-spread collar	pinned collar
fitted cut	pinpoint oxford

plaid tie

regimental stripe tie

repp tie

rounded collar

sleeve garter

sleeve placket

split-sleeve measurement

stay

straight-point collar

tab collar

tapered cut

white-collar worker

wicking properties

Windsor collar

Windsor knot

CLASS EXERCISES

1. Visit a department store, locate the men's dress shirt department, and make note of the different brands and private labels carried there. Answer the following questions:
   - Which brands are available?
   - How many private-label dress shirts are present?
   - How do style and design features differ between the brands and the private labels?
   - Which collar styles are available?
   - What choice is available in other dress shirt style features?
   - How do the different dress shirts compare in price?
   - What do you think makes up the price point differences?
   - Why is one brand more expensive than another?
   - What are the various countries of origin?

2. Find the area in the furnishings department that sells pocket squares. Note the various styles. Interview a salesperson to determine who the pocket-square customer is. Develop a picture in words of that customer.

REFERENCES

Balkan, Jodi. (2004). Tie me up, time me down: Men's ties as an expression of personality. *Psychology Today.* [online]. Available: http://findarticles.com [March 28, 2007].

Colman, David. (2006, June 15). Short-sleeved shirts, nerdy but nice, are back. *New York Times.* [online]. Available: http://www.nytimes.com/2006/06/15/fashion/thursdaystyles/15CODES.html [March 28, 2007].

Galbraith, Robert. (2007, January 16). A renaissance in men's ties. *International Herald Tribune.* [online]. Available: http://www.iht.com/articles/2007/01/16/news/rtie.php [March 28, 2007].

Indiviglio, Daniel J. (2007). Socks for every occasion. [online]. Available: http://ca.askmen.com/fashion/fashiontip_250/276_fashion_advice.html [March 29, 2007].

NINE

FORMAL WEAR

IN THIS CHAPTER, YOU WILL LEARN
THE FOLLOWING:

- o   the origins of the **tuxedo**
- o   the various design features that are incorporated into formal wear
- o   the differences in formal attire

White tie, black tie, semi-formal, should I rent, or should I buy? Formal wear can give rise to more questions than the average man on the street can answer. This chapter will present a brief history of the tuxedo and clarify some of the misconceptions about formal dress in today's society. The rules of formal dressing have changed for men, as well as for women. The easiest way to see the dramatic change in the way men and women dress for a dinner or evening party is to look at movies from the 1940s and 1950s and see how elegantly both men and women dressed for these occasions. In these movies, men attending dinner parties or formal affairs are usually wearing formal attire. Formal wear was *de rigueur* for members of society's upper classes who attended such affairs in the United States and in much of Europe.

THE HISTORY OF THE TUXEDO

Two theories prevail regarding the origins of the tuxedo. One theory credits Pierre Lorillard as the father of the tuxedo, while the other theory credits the Prince of Wales (who later became King Edward VII). Most information available supports the Lorillard theory. However, the British version tells the following story: James Brown Potter, who happened to hail from Tuxedo Park, New York, was vacationing in England in 1886. After meeting the Prince of Wales, Mr. Potter and his wife were invited to a formal ball. Not knowing the proper manner of dress for such an occasion, Mr. Potter asked the Prince for advice. The Prince sent Potter over to see his personal tailor. "Potter was fitted for a short black jacket and black tie, unlike the formal white tie that was worn in the United States for formal occasions" (Bellis, 2007). When Potter returned to the United States, he showed off his new formal wear at the Tuxedo Club in Tuxedo Park, New York. Pierre Lorillard was at the Club that evening and loved the new look. He modified it by increasing the length of the jacket and adding black trousers. He gave it the name *tuxedo* in honor of the Tuxedo Club.

The Lorillard family had made their fortune in tobacco, so Pierre had a bit more clout in the neighborhood than James Potter. It was natural for Lorillard to get the credit for naming the tuxedo. His son Griswold first wore the modified design to a formal ball in October 1886. The rest is history; the tuxedo caught on as the new formal wear for men and has not changed much since the original version.

As for the question of who really invented the tuxedo, it might be said that the idea originated with the Prince of Wales' tailor and was developed further by Pierre Lorillard.

Figure 9.1 *A classy guy, Mr. Fred Astaire, in a classic tuxedo.*

FORMAL WEAR ETIQUETTE

When should you wear a tuxedo? The following outlines the rules for men's formal wear:

"Black Tie" is not an unfamiliar term in today's party planning scene, so you may decide to add "Black Tie Optional," "Black Tie Preferred," "Black Tie Invited," or simply "Black Tie" to your invitation. Although the clothing industry is trendy, there are some definite rules. Bill Tzizik, President of Classic Tuxedo, suggests these guidelines: "If an invitation reads 'Black Tie Optional' or 'Black Tie Invited,' you can expect a nice affair and there will be people attending in tuxedos. Your host is leaving it up to you to dress formally or not. If your invitation reads 'Black Tie Preferred,' your host is suggesting that you dress formal and hoping you do, but you can make that decision and he won't be offended if you don't. Any invitation that has the words 'Black Tie' requires you to dress formal. 'White Tie' requires you to dress in evening tails. White Tie is the ultimate in formal dress for men." (Classic Tuxedo, 2003)

As Tzizik suggests, the choice is yours. It depends on the type of affair you are hosting and your expectations of your guests. Some of the answers can be determined by the venue you choose. Imagine you are celebrating a milestone anniversary. You are hosting a formal sit-down dinner in a five-star hotel with banquet accommodations. It would be appropriate to suggest "Black Tie Optional" or "Black Tie Preferred." If the event is in a banquet hall and you are having a buffet, any type of formal wear would not be appropriate. You might even suggest casual clothing, or not make mention of attire on the invitation at all.

TUXEDOS: RENTAL OR PURCHASE

In years past, a tuxedo was associated with wealth. The occasions for wearing tuxedos were usually such that any man attending them had the financial ability to buy his own tuxedo. The notion that every man could afford his own tuxedo began to change when it became fashionable to wear tuxedos to proms and weddings.

This fashion trend established the need for a rental market for tuxedos. Rental shops still dot the landscape throughout America and can be found in local tailor shops or dry cleaners.

If you live in or near a city and need to rent a tuxedo, your best bet is to find a Men's Wearhouse, an After Hours shop, or a Mr. Tux, or Squire Tux as they are sometimes called. Mr. Tux and Squire Tux are actually owned by After Hours and represent 511 stores in 35 states. These shops can be found in local malls or in downtown shopping districts. Prior to 2006, After Hours was a separate company; in November 2006, Men's Wearhouse acquired After Hours Formalwear. Men's Wearhouse now counts 1,165 combined locations for buying and/or renting formal wear. With their newfound strength in the formal wear market, Men's Wearhouse is positioned to offer men a much wider selection of products, as well as many more locations. Although Men's Wearhouse

Figure 9.2 *Tuxedo rental shops, like Men's Wearhouse, both rent and sell formal wear.*

acquired After Hours, all four entities have maintained their own identities and still trade under their original names. Each has added an e-commerce site to give consumers even more choices when looking to rent or buy formal wear.

At Men's Wearhouse, rentals start as low as $59.99. However, if you find yourself attending several occasions in one year, you might want to consider purchasing a tuxedo of your own. In today's global economy of mass production, you can find a basic tuxedo for under $200. Even JCPenney has entered the tuxedo sales business. Of course, by the time you buy the accessories, such as studs, cuff links, shirt, tie, and vest or cummerbund, the price rises somewhat. However, given a price of $200 for a tuxedo, so long as one is careful not to buy the most expensive accessories, it might be more affordable to buy than to rent several times a year. In any event, it is more affordable to own a tuxedo today than it was years ago, when it was a look reserved only for the rich and famous.

Figure 9.3 *After Hours Formalwear.*

Figure 9.4 *Wool and wool blends make great fabric choices for tuxedos. This shows wool in its natural state.*

The tuxedo itself will be made of 100 percent wool, with top-of-the-line tuxedos made from super 100s, 200s, or even higher count wool yarn. The terms *super 100s* and *200s* speak to the fineness of the wool yarn. The higher the number, the finer the yarn; the higher number indicates that more yarn is used in the weave, giving superior hand feel and drape to the garment.

A customer on a budget can also find a well-made tuxedo in a wool-polyester blend. It is important to keep wool as the chief value; the wool content should be a minimum of 55 percent of the garment as this will provide a reasonable fabric that will still exhibit the better qualities that wool has to offer, such as hand feel and garment drape.

The weight of the wool can vary, so be sure to select a wool tuxedo that you feel most comfortable in and one that you can wear to most occasions. Some wool and wool blends might be too heavy to wear year round and might be suitable only for fall or winter affairs. The tuxedo is mainly an indoor garment, so most manufacturers will use a light- to mid-weight wool. One exception to this rule would be tuxedos worn by those in the hotel and entertainment fields who might actually work outdoors, such as doormen. In these cases, a heavier-weight tuxedo might be a better option.

STYLING AND ACCESSORIES

The fashion-conscious man should be aware of the styling and accessories that are associated with both **black tie** and **white tie**.

BLACK TIE

TUXEDO JACKET

When the tuxedo was first introduced in 1886, the tuxedo jacket was the central focus. It was not until later that the addition of pants and accessories became part of what is known today as a full tuxedo. The jacket, or dinner jacket as it was called, was black or a midnight navy bordering on black. In low light, the midnight navy appeared black.

Main features of the jacket include the following:

o Collar: The collar traditionally has three versions: peaked, notched, and shawl. Peaked and shawl collars signify dressier models; the majority of the rentals choose the safe route—the notched lapel—as this is the most traditional of all collar styles. The lapels, which are extensions of the collars, are made with satin or grosgrain, and appear very shiny. Today, some Hollywood stars may be seen sporting collarless tuxedos on the red carpet. This style is considered very fashion-forward and will be very limited in its appeal. It has not been fully accepted in the mainstream of fashion and, therefore, not many are sold or rented. However, the

door for under $275. I still have that tuxedo, some 16 years later. It still fits quite well, and once I get into a room filled with men in similar dress, my $275 outfit cannot be distinguished from a $2,750 one.

Figure 9.5 The collarless tuxedo makes a fashion statement.

younger prom set may gravitate to the newer styles and, therefore, apply pressure to the rental shops to carry those looks.

- o Pocket treatments: The more elegant jackets feature besom pockets. The only variation would be the addition of flaps, which make the styling a little more casual.
- o Front closure: Traditionally, the jacket was styled in a one- or two-button single-breasted model. There is also a double-breasted version of the tuxedo. This style accounts for a small portion of the overall sales, as the wearer must have a slim body type to pull it off.
- o Back: Both single- and double-breasted models can have a center back vent or a double vent. The majority of the double-breasted models have a double vent.

Although styles and tastes vary greatly, the safe choice is to go conservative and not experiment, especially if you are making a rather large investment in a tuxedo that you will have for many years.

TUXEDO PANT

The significant styling that sets the tuxedo pant apart from a regular dress pant is the satin or grosgrain stripe running down the outseam of each leg. The stripe has its roots in military dress and was used by the military to cover and reinforce the outseams of the pants. Given the military origins of the stripe, there is no clear evidence as to why it was adopted for tuxedos. It certainly looked smart and gave the tuxedo pant a distinctly dressier look.

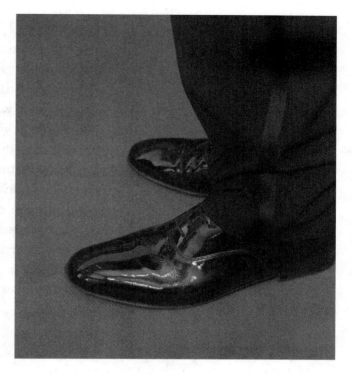

Figure 9.6 *Tuxedo pant with satin stripe running down the outseam of the pant leg.*

The fabric used in the stripe is generally 1 inch wide and is the same fabric used in the lapels of the jacket. The pockets are either on seam or quarter top. The tuxedo pant is always hemmed, it is never cuffed. There are no belt loops because the cummerbund or suspenders are worn as accessories to complete the outfit. The back of the pants can have one or two back besom pockets, with the wearer's right pocket having a button-through or button-loop closure. The front of the pant may also include an extended tab with a clasp closure or simply a button closure.

These styling features are dictated by fashion trends; they are also a function of cost. The more features there are, the higher the cost, since more labor is required to make the garment.

The tuxedo shirt is one part of the outfit with which a man can add a personal touch and create a somewhat distinctive look. The shirt is pleated in the front, with the pleats ending at the waist. The number, width, and style of the pleats are determined by the designer.

Most of the shirts are made in 100 percent cotton broadcloth, although some blends can be found. Some designers are experimenting with various weaves, such as oxford, pinpoint oxford, and even herringbone looks. One other option is a 100 percent silk tuxedo shirt. The silk is more difficult to care for than cotton, but it can give

Figure 9.7 *The traditional wing collar tuxedo shirt with wing tips positioned behind the tie.*

a look of elegance for the few times it would be worn.

As far as colors go, white is the safest choice, and it is the color that is worn the most. Some designers are trying to push the fashion envelope by introducing pastels and even bolder colors. As with the introduction of anything new and different, designers and retailers are betting that new colors will increase sales. It is generally those who consider themselves fashion-forward, regardless of age, who will experiment with new trends. In the end, the designers and retailers will generate the majority of their sales in white.

The two prominent collar styles for the tuxedo shirt are the wing collar and the straight-point

Figure 9.8 *Tuxedo shirt with straight point collar and stud closures.*

collar. The wing collar is the traditional style, as it is not seen in normal day wear. When wearing the wing collar, the collar tabs should be positioned behind the bow tie, not in front. The cuffs are generally French cuffs, or double cuffs, and they are worn with cuff links or studs. The straight point collar is the typical style found in many dress shirts.

ACCESSORIES

SHIRT CLOSURES

The front closure of the shirt can be fashioned with buttons, on the less expensive models, or with **studs**. Some shirts are actually sold with a strip of buttons to keep the shirt closed in the packaging. The strip of buttons can be removed on purchase and replaced with studs. When studs are used in place of buttons, the tuxedo shirt will have two sets of buttonholes, one on each side of the shirt. The studs are inserted into the holes to hold the front closed. If studs are chosen over buttons, simplicity should be used as a guide for making the best fashion choice. Studs can be made of gold, silver, onyx, and even silk. Studs can be used as cuff links; they function the same way at the cuff as they would on the front of the shirt.

CUFF LINKS

Choosing **cuff links** is purely a matter of personal taste, but the same rule applies: simple is better. Many jewelers and department stores carry a line of cuff links. Prices vary greatly, depending on the type of materials used and the workmanship incorporated into the cuff links. The materials can range from sterling silver to diamond-encrusted gold. Therefore, the prices will be commensurate with the cuff link that you select.

CUMMERBUND

The **cummerbund** is worn around the waist. It is pleated with wide pleats pointing upward. Some say the pleats are there to catch crumbs, but the real purpose of the pleats is to hold theater or opera tickets. The cummerbund has straps at each side and a clasp that closes in the back. It can be adjusted to fit most sizes. Besides catching crumbs or holding tickets, it also acts as a wide belt and hides the waistband of the pants. The cummerbund fabric generally matches the bow tie. Some designers have opted to add color or patterns to the cummerbund and the bow tie, rather than use the traditional black.

Figure 9.9 *The cummerbund with pleats up to catch crumbs.*

BOW TIE

When choosing a **bow tie,** you need to consider the following questions:

- Should the bow tie be colored or the traditional basic black?
- Should the bow tie be clip-on, pre-tied, or self-tied? The following points should be considered before making a purchase:
  - The clip-on can easily be detected and is reminiscent of children's bow ties.
  - The self-tied bow tie should be chosen only if you have mastered the technique of tying a bow tie the old-fashioned way.
  - The pre-tied version comes already tied with a strap that runs around your neck and clips to the back of the bow tie. With this choice, you always have a perfect-looking tie.

When selecting a tuxedo, the customer has the choice of wearing a vest instead of the cummerbund. In many instances, the designer of the tuxedo makes this choice, as most tuxedos come with one or the other. If a tuxedo with a vest is chosen, the vest will have the following features:

- It will generally have a shawl collar.
- The front will be cut low to show off the pleats on the tuxedo shirt.
- Studs or buttons can be used for closures.

Figure 9.10 *Vests are a great option to create a fashion flair.*

- In most instances the vest will not have a back; instead the tuxedo vest will have an adjustable strap in the back to keep the vest snug. The tuxedo jacket is meant to stay on, so the backless vest is not an issue.
- The vest can be made from the same material as the pants and jacket, while at other times it will be used as a fashion statement and the material, colors, patterns vary greatly.

FOOTWEAR

Two other accessories must be considered to complete a man's black-tie look: the shoe and **hosiery**. The shoe should be a classic pump or dress pump. This traditional style is meant for formal wear only and may appear feminine to some, as it has a grosgrain ribbon on the top front of the shoe and a low heel. Most men prefer to wear a good pair of black leather dress shoes, either slip-on or laced. When renting, the shoe of choice is the dress pump.

As for hosiery, a pair of lightweight, over-the-calf black socks will do. In this category, some prefer fine silk or lightweight wool, but a fine synthetic-fiber sock will do just as well.

WHITE TIE

White tie is the epitome of formal wear and is typically worn to affairs of state or formal balls. Occasionally, white tie is the formal wear of choice for a groom and his wedding party. The white tie can also be called full dress. The jacket style is different from that of the basic tuxedo. The style is in the tradition of the riding jacket, with its cutaway look and long split tails in the back. No cummerbund is worn with this style;

Figure 9.11 *White tie, reserved for the height of formality, diplomatic balls, receptions for heads of state or really fancy weddings.*

instead the backless vest is worn with a single- or double-breasted jacket. Traditionally, if a man was wearing white tie, he would also sport white gloves and a top hat. However, today, the choice is generally the wearer's. The invitation can always be used as a guide for what to wear.

CONCLUDING THOUGHTS

Chapter 9 turned your attention to the world of formal wear and the main element in this area, the tuxedo. The goals of this chapter were to help you learn the following:

o   the origins of the tuxedo
o   the various design features that are incorporated into formal wear

o   the differences in formal attire

These objectives were covered through discussions of the two prevailing theories of the origins of the tuxedo as well as research into the design features. The text also pointed out the pros and cons of renting versus buying a tuxedo outfit and discussed some of the key players in the tuxedo market. The following quotation sums up the chapter: "A tuxedo is by far the fashion mainstay of the sophisticated man who wants to stand apart from the crowd. You may not be loaded, but by wearing a tuxedo you can look and feel like a million dollars. Even if it is just for one night, make it the night of your life" (Men's Flair, 2007). When you wear a tuxedo, it does set you apart and make you feel special.

Chapter 10 will define men's sportswear by identifying the elements that make up this aspect of the business. You will study the differences in the men's sportswear classifications so that you can better understand how the market is segmented. While doing so, you will examine key silhouettes within the various sportswear classifications.

KEY TERMS

black tie
bow tie
cuff links
cummerbund

hosiery
studs
white tie

CLASS EXERCISE

1. a) Visit a Men's Wearhouse retail store and inquire about the various tuxedos they have for sale. Note the styles and prices. Why are some more expensive than the others? Next, ask to see their rental section, and compare the tuxedos that are for sale with those that are for rent. Note the differences.

   b) Visit a local tailor or dry cleaner that rents tuxedos. How do their prices and services compare with those of the Men's Wearhouse? How does the style selection vary?

   c) Which option would you choose if you needed a tuxedo? Would you buy or rent? Which establishment would you go to for your rental or purchase?

REFERENCES

Bellis, Mary. (2007). The history of men's tuxedos and male formal wear. [online]. Available: http://inventors.about.com/od/tstartinventions/a/tuxedo.htm [November 1, 2007].

Classic Tuxedo. (August 15, 2003). Become style savvy: Tuxedo terms for grooms. [online]. Available: http://www.classictuxedo.com/press/becomestylesavvy.htm [April 10, 2007].

Men's Flair. (2007, March 22). Tuxedo styles. [online]. Available: http://www.mensflair.com/style-advice/tuxedo-styles.php. [April 6, 2007].

TEN

SPORTSWEAR

- the elements that make up the men's sportswear industry
- differences in men's sportswear classifications
- key silhouettes that can be found in the men's sportswear industry

This chapter will shift gears to look at what the industry calls sportswear. This term can be misleading, as sportswear means different things to different people. What do you think of when you hear the term *sportswear*? Does your favorite sports team come to mind? Do you think of a sport that you have played? If this is your initial reaction, you are not alone. However, in the context of the menswear industry, you would not be completely correct. When you hear the term *sportswear* as it relates to the men's fashion industry, think casual. In terms of casual wear, sportswear includes the following:

- casual clothing
- khakis
- jeans
- T-shirts
- woven and knit sport shirts
- urban wear
- surf and skate wear

The sportswear market further defines itself beyond casual wear to include active sportswear,

Figure 10.1 *Casual sportswear can mean different things to different people. This man is wearing casual slacks and a long-sleeved woven shirt, fitting the profile for men's casual sportswear.*

and this is where ideas relating to sports teams and participation in sports come into play.

Sportswear can trace its roots to the 1920s. The idea for sportswear rose out of the leisure time that men found after World War I. Before the war, there was not much difference between what men wore for work and play. After the war, sports such as tennis and golf grew in popularity, and so did the need for clothes to participate in and to view these sports.

Today, health and fitness activities, along with professional sports, have an impact on active sportswear. Brands, designers, music, television, and movies continue to influence the casual sportswear market.

DRESS CASUAL

Over the past several years, the casual market has been further defined as a direct outgrowth of the casualization movement. The term **dress casual** has come into use, and this category has

Figure 10.2 Dress casual implies a step up from typical casual sportswear; it generally involves a sport coat and or dressier slacks.

become a thriving market. The look that best defines dress casual is a woven sport shirt that borders on a dress shirt, worn with a dress pant to give the wearer a look that is considered somewhere between casual (khakis and button-down collar sport shirts) and the suited look. More and more companies are allowing men to wear dress casual. This look is neat and clean. In a sense, it is akin to allowing men to take off the jacket and tie and just wear the dress shirt and trousers.

ACTIVE SPORTSWEAR

Within the active sportswear market, the industry is broken down into the following two broad groups:

- **spectator sportswear**
- **participatory sportswear**

The industry breaks active sportswear down in this manner for several reasons:

- At retail, the different categories are housed in different sections of the store.
- Some retailers carry only specific types of merchandise, such as running apparel or swimwear. These are considered specialty retailers.
- Brands and manufacturers often produce, sell, and market only one category of sportswear.

SPECTATOR SPORTSWEAR

Spectator sportswear includes items such as jerseys, logo T-shirts, jackets, and caps that are emblazoned with a team emblem, school logo, or athletic brand. Spectator sportswear can be seen every day on the street, in schools and work-places, and at the ball park. The overwhelming majority of these products are licensed by the teams, brands, or the colleges identified on the garments, or by the professional organizations that represent them.

Figure 10.3 *Although athletes do wear brands such as adidas and Reebok on the field, many people who purchase brands like these wear them just to hang out or watch a sporting event.*

PARTICIPATORY SPORTSWEAR

Participatory sportswear includes articles of clothing that are worn when actively participating in specific sports, such as run-ning, biking, mountain climbing, or swimming. Participatory sportswear is considered func-tional. Some companies develop products spe-cifically for sports enthusiasts. These products have technical qualities that the average casual and spectator sportswear will not have.

CLASSIFICATIONS OF THE SPORTSWEAR INDUSTRY

Within the sportswear industry, the market is further broken down into several classifica-tions, which can be described as large groups of merchandise that have related end uses. These classifications account for much of what people in the industry call sportswear. Note that these clas-sifications are loosely defined, and others might add or subtract from the list. However, the author has determined the following classifications to be the most useful for the purposes of this text:

o   men's and young men's casual sportswear
o   men's and young men's dress casual

- spectator sportswear
- participatory (functional) sportswear
- urban/street wear
- surf and skate wear

MEN'S AND YOUNG MEN'S CASUAL SPORTSWEAR

WOVEN PANTS

Men's casual sportswear includes woven pants made of fabrics such as cotton twill, cotton corduroy, cotton khakis, cotton denim, linen, hemp, canvas, polyester, and nylon. Each of these fabrics can be woven with spandex to

Figure 10.4 *Denim comes in many different washes and styles but still reigns as king of the casual bottom area.*

give a little stretch. Denim is by far the single largest category that dominates the men's casual wardrobe. The average man owns eight pairs of denim jeans.

From a design standpoint, the casual pant has a continuous waistband and any number of pockets. One style that was very popular in the early 2000s and refuses to die is the cargo pant, with its many pockets. This style even crossed over into the participatory arena with zip-off legs. Pockets are continuously used as design features. Most recently, several companies created garments with cell-phone pockets and even an iPod pocket.

KNIT AND WOVEN TOPS

Knit and woven tops are also part of the casual sportswear market. There is no end to the styles and designs created in this area. Fabrications run the gamut from natural fibers to synthetics. Styles include pullovers, button fronts, long sleeved, short sleeved, three-quarter sleeved, as well as sleeveless. This category includes virtually any top other than a dress shirt, including the sweater.

DIFFERENCES BETWEEN MEN'S AND YOUNG MEN'S CASUAL SPORTSWEAR

The difference between men's and young men's casual wear is not so much in the silhouettes but in the styling of these garments. In men's casual wear, the look is more conservative and classic. Think of the following designers and brands:

o   Polo
o   Calvin Klein

Figure 10.5 *The colorful woven striped sport shirt pictured here would be a welcome addition to any man's casual sportswear wardrobe.*

o   Perry Ellis
o   Tommy Hilfiger
o   IZOD
o   Brooks Brothers

The same categories exist for young men, but they have a much younger, edgier look. Think of the following brands:

o   Penguin
o   Ecko

- 7 Diamonds
- JNCO
- OTB
- Avirex
- Girbaud
- Cockpit

Many of today's retailers also do a very good job of developing these looks through private-label programs in their product development departments.

MEN'S AND YOUNG MEN'S DRESS CASUAL

Men's and young men's dress casual contains the elements in casual sportswear mentioned above, but the pants become more stylized, and the fabrics include wools, wool blends, finer cottons, and synthetics such as microfibers. The trousers have a split waistband so that they can be altered. Trousers in this category are available hemmed or cuffed, or they can be sold open bottomed, with no hem or cuff so that they can be tailored to fit the customer's exact inseam length. These pants can have a pleated or a plain front. The look can be dressed up even further with the introduction of British donegals, tweeds, plaids, and stripes. Donegals were originally a thick, homespun, tweed fabric woven by Irish peasants in Donegal, Ireland. Today, the term is used to represent wool tweed fabrics that have colorful, thick slubs of yarn woven into them. The use of the term *British donegals* has to do with the fact that many of the mills that specialize in this fabric are located in Great Britain.

Figure 10.6 *If you are looking to spruce up your dress casual wardrobe, you cannot go wrong by adding a nice Donegal tweed sport coat.*

Tops in this category are most often woven, as this fabrication makes for a dressier look than most knits.

People in the industry are always trying to invent or reinvent the wheel. Fashion is evolutionary, not revolutionary, and there is not a lot of newness—so when something truly new does happen, it makes a big splash. In a *DNR* article titled "Playing It Down the Middle," Stan Gellers stated, "America has jeans on its mind and the slacks industry is doing something about it for next fall with new hybrid, or bridge, models that cross over in an effort to combine the best of two worlds—casual and dress" (Gellers, 2006, p. 18). This so-called hybrid is taking the pocket treatment from jeans and applying it to dressier

Figure 10.7 *The cross-over between casual and dress casual is often defined by fabrics and make. Here is a nicely tailored pair of dress casual slacks in a polyester microfiber; notice the drape of the fabric.*

fabrics. In the same article, Geller cited Marshal Cohen of the NPD group as stating, "Most guys have more jeans in their wardrobe right now than they need, and the dressed-up jeans coming up for fall, as well as plain-front dress pants, give them something new that's actually needed. The bottom line is that premium jeans are helping the dress slacks business, and this is evidenced in the tremendous influence in jeans on dress slacks. I call them leaner and meaner" (Gellers, 2006, p. 18).

As mentioned above, men have more jeans than they know what to do with, so what is a designer to do? In this case, the designers have taken the popular look of the denim jean, which has two signature features—the fabric and the pocket treatment—and applied the pocket features to dressier fabrics. The hallmark of the denim jean is the five-pocket design with the following features:

o   three pockets on the front—two main pockets with the third being a small coin pocket on the wearer's right tucked into the main pocket
o   two back patch pockets

With the casual or dress pant, the pockets can have the following variations:

o   on the front: on-seam, quarter-top, or slash pockets
o   on the back: any variation of button-through, flap, or besom pockets

The idea behind these hybrid designs is to create another reason for the customer to go out and buy a new pair of pants.

SPECTATOR SPORTSWEAR

Spectator sportswear, or active sportswear as some in the industry call it, has seen a resurgence in recent years. Whether you are wearing a licensed product from your favorite team or heading out for the night in your branded product, the look is distinctly laid-back. Brenda Lloyd noted in an article for *DNR* that "consumers are buying the new, innovative designs and performance fabrics, and sports fans are acquiring all kinds of licensed team merchandise, including apparel" (Lloyd, 2006, p. 16). The article goes on to say that the licensed apparel will continue to be hot and will be fueled by local market teams that do well during the season.

Brands that have a presence in this market include powerhouses such as the following:

o   Nike
o   adidas Group
o   Reebok
o   Champion
o   Under Armour
o   Puma

In addition, there are many other companies that hold licensing agreements to produce apparel products under the watchful eye of organizations such as the following:

o   National Football League
o   Major League Baseball
o   National Hockey League
o   National Basketball Association
o   colleges and universities throughout the nation

The next time you pull on that New York Rangers jersey or that Mets T-shirt, you will be officially sporting what the industry likes to call spectator sportswear.

Spectator sportswear is a tops-driven business dominated by knits. There are some, but not many, woven tops that carry a team logo. Few woven bottoms are seen in the licensed apparel category. Knits, knits, and more knits predominate, from tanks and T-shirts to hoodies and beyond.

PARTICIPATORY (FUNCTIONAL) SPORTSWEAR

Many of the same names that have established themselves as powerhouses in the

Figure 10.8 *Today's athlete has many choices when it comes to functional sportswear, with new high-tech fibers and fabrics leading the way.*

spectator sportswear business hold an even more important role in the participatory, or functional, sportswear market. Nike, Reebok, adidas Group, Puma, Brooks, Saucony, Starter, Champion, Jantzen, Under Armour, and Gore-Tex, to name a few, are all names that are familiar to those who participate in sports. These companies, along with the chemical companies, have developed synthetic fibers and fabrics to use in products for performance. These garments can be worn as casual sportswear or spectator sportswear, but the main point of the products is to provide the athlete with superior performance.

Nike's mission statement is as follows: "To bring inspiration and innovation to every athlete in the world." In Nike's philosophy, the word *athlete* is not reserved for the elite few—in the words of company co-founder Bill Bowerman two decades ago, "If you have a body, you are an athlete" (Nike, 2007). True to their mission statement, Nike not only caters to the average person on the street, but the company goes beyond the normal range of products and continuously looks for fibers and fabrics that will help all customers reach their personal goals.

Under Armour's mission statement is "To provide the world with technically advanced products engineered with our superior fabric construction, exclusive moisture management, and proven innovation" (Under Armour, 2007).

As these mission statements imply, the products that these companies represent are used in the pursuit of an active lifestyle. They represent apparel that fits into the category of participatory sportswear and should not be confused with casual sportswear.

The products in this category cover the consumer from head to toe. Participatory sportswear comes in the form of socks, jocks, tights, shorts, tanks, tees, jackets, pants, and whatever else is needed to perform in a sport. In the past, runners wore cotton socks, nylon shorts, and cotton T-shirts or tank tops. Today, runners benefit from innovations that have resulted in fabrics made of synthetic fibers that wick away moisture, and clothing designed to keep them warm and dry when they run in rainy or cold conditions. Cotton does not cut it anymore, but the miracle fibers and fabrics that are on the market today do just what they are expected to do. These categories focus on function over fashion and distinguish participatory from spectator sportswear.

These products can be found in sporting goods specialty stores, big-box retailers (e.g., the Sports Authority, Dick's Sporting Goods, Eastern Mountain Sports, and Modell's Sporting Goods), and they can also be ordered online and through mail-order catalogs.

URBAN/STREET WEAR

Casual dressing can take on different meanings for different segments of the population. Since the 1920s, casual sportswear was geared toward the white male, with the exception of the **zoot suit**, which could arguably be considered the beginning of urban or street wear for black America. The zoot suit gained popularity during the Harlem jazz culture of the 1930s, and was originally called "drapes" (Just the Swing, 2007). The suit consisted of a low-waisted, wide-legged, tight-cuffed pant topped off with a long jacket with wide lapels and large padded shoulders (see Figure 10.9).

This oversized silhouette used a lot of fabric and even drew the attention of the War Production Board in March 1942. The Board banned the production of the zoot suit, reasoning that it was wasting valuable suiting material that could be put to better use for the war effort (Cosgrove, 1984). In spite of the ban, the suit continued to flourish. Was the zoot suit the forerunner of today's urban wear? That question will be left to interpretation, but certainly, the style was unique and worn predominantly in the black and Latino communities.

Today, there are many brands, designers, and manufacturers that count themselves part

Figure 10.9 Back in the day, the zoot suit was the epitome of urban wear. Many of today's urban/street styles can be traced back to the original zoot suit.

of the urban wear business. One that stands out as the first real commercially successful urban wear clothing company is FUBU (which stands for "for us, by us"). FUBU was started in 1992 by Daymond John, Alexander Martin, Cart Brown, and Keith Perrin. FUBU's rise to success is truly a rags-to-riches story. The company started in Daymond John's mother's house in Queens, New York. It was 1992; Daymond John was working in a Red Lobster restaurant and trying to get his apparel business off the ground by designing street-smart fashions that he thought were missing in the menswear industry. His mother taught him to sew, and he started his business with tietop hats. The hats were a rendition of the do-rag, which can be likened to any piece of fabric used to cover the head. The actual style can be traced back to the 1930s when women wore bandanalike fabric to hold their hairstyles in place as they set. From the 1930s to the 1960s, the do-rag was popular with African-American men, who used

Figure 10.10 Like today's casual sports-wear, urban wear takes on many different forms, with individuals creating their own style by mixing and matching fabrics, designers, and brands.

them to hold their chemically processed hairdos in place while they slept.

Daymond John's venture with tie-top hats started to grow, and he expanded the business to include T-shirts.

It was not until 1994 that success really struck. The group ventured to the Men's Apparel Guild in California (MAGIC) show in Las Vegas. They could not afford a booth in the actual show, so they invited members of the retail community to their hotel room, which doubled as a showroom. They wrote over $300,000 in orders! Faced with the daunting task of then having to deliver the goods, FUBU turned to an Asian conglomerate,

Samsung, to produce and distribute the line of clothing (Hoovers, 2007). From T-shirts and do-rags, they quickly expanded their line to include hip-hop style pants and bubble jackets, all with the FUBU label.

From its early beginnings, the company reached sales of over $350 million in the late 1990s. Today, FUBU has identified its target market as young men in the black and Latino communities. Along with apparel, the company is active in other areas, including entertainment, retail, and Y2G.com, a Web site that provides information on careers, personal success, and politics (FUBU, 2007).

As for the urban/street wear styles themselves, the garments, perhaps taking their cue from the zoot suit, remain oversized and use a lot of fabric. Baggy jeans and long T-shirts were once the uniform of the day, but they have evolved into much more. Labels such as the following all have their own version of what urban wear, street wear, or hip-hop is:

- ○ Enyce
- ○ Phat Farm
- ○ Pure Playaz
- ○ South Pole
- ○ Triple 5 Soul
- ○ Akademiks
- ○ Sean John

Each company brings its own unique perspective to the market, and many have used the urban wear platform to move their companies into tailored clothing.

One example is Sean John, a company that has successfully bridged the gap between urban wear

---

FUBU AND ME

I attended the MAGIC show at the same time as Daymond John, Alexander Martin, Cart Brown, and Keith Perrin. I can personally attest to the incredible buzz that this company was creating. It was electric and, in my mind, started the urban/street wear movement. The many players in the business today owe much to these four individuals.

I also had the opportunity in the mid-1990s to attend a *DNR* fashion summit at which Daymond John was a panel member. He discussed the rise of the company, and even he was amazed at the pent-up demand there was for their products.

FUBU established their offices in the Empire State Building, where I was working, and I have fond memories of seeing Daymond John pulling out of the parking garage on 33rd Street in his custom-painted, powder blue Bentley Rolls Royce … priceless.

Figure 10.11 Sean Combs, also known as Diddy, has created a mega-brand combining his street smarts with his business savvy.

and the clothing industry. Sean Combs, creator of the Sean John line, now has a complete line of tailored clothing, from suits to topcoats, in addition to his sportswear line. His tailored clothes can be found in Macy's and fine specialty stores in the United States. In addition, his line was recently featured on a DVD that was included in copies of *Esquire* magazine. For five straight years, Sean Combs has been nominated for his excellence in design by the Council of Fashion Designers of America (CFDA), and he was awarded Men's Designer of the year in 2004. In 2006, Sean John's flagship store opened on the corner of 41st Street and Fifth Avenue to showcase his designs.

As its name implies, the urban/street wear style emanated from the gritty city streets and depicted a lifestyle. This lifestyle quickly took on a life of its own and spread throughout the country and around the world. During the height of hip-hop fashion, you could go into any high school in middle America and find young males of all races decked out in baggy jeans and long T-shirts. The styles were sold by specialty retailers and quickly moved into mainstream department stores, which were eager to get in on this new and growing market. Suffice to say, urban/street wear is here to stay and has created a growing demand for fashion that appeals to various segments of the population.

SURF AND SKATE WEAR

All different styles and designs of denim jeans, T-shirts, hoodies, and boardshorts make up the nucleus of this industry. The United States is bordered by two very different oceans, and there is little surfing in between, yet the surf wear industry has spread across the entire country. Alan Green is credited by some as the father of the surf wear industry. He invented the **boardshort** in 1969 (Quiksilver, 2007), which was the genesis of the company Quiksilver. As far as surfing goes, the original boardshorts, with lengths reaching below the knee, were constructed from cotton or polyester-cotton blended fabrics. Since then, they have been updated to include nylon as one of the chief fabrics, because nylon dries faster.

One of the hallmarks of the surf wear industry can be traced to its use of all-over prints on the shorts and the use of logos on their printed T-shirts. Many of the original boardshorts carried Hawaiian-inspired prints. The T-shirts might have a logo or surf-inspired saying screen printed on the front, and some also carry a screen print on the back or sleeves. The T-shirts are made from 100 percent cotton and are generally fashioned in a crew-neck style.

Unlike surfing, skateboarding and inline skating required no particular apparel to participate in the sport. What these sports do require are tough knees, as skateboarders often land on them. This has inspired some jeans companies (e.g., JNCO) to create a tougher denim by weaving a tighter fabric. Some designers reinforced the knees of their jeans; others created canvas jeans strong enough to withstand the falls and spills that are part of these sports. In addition, they created a fuller fit for more maneuverability, which also happened to cross over into the hip-hop look.

The question is whether surf and skate wear garments are functional or fashionable. The answer is both—these garments perform double duty. Jeans, T-shirts, hoodies, and boardshorts can be worn outside of the sports themselves, giving the wearers a very casual sportswear look.

Some of the brands that have a major presence in the surf and skate wear industry include the following:

- Ocean Pacific
- Body Glove
- Quiksilver
- Billabong
- Hurley
- Vans
- O'Neill
- Zoo York
- OTB
- JNCO
- C1RCA
- Kr3w
- DC
- Special Blend
- Element
- Forum
- Foursquare

Figure 10.12 The surf wear market has grown over the years to include wet suits, knit tops, woven tops, board-shorts, and much more.

Figure 10.13 The skate market has emerged as a major force in the menswear industry. Here, a skater grinds a rail in style. Check out the camo pants.

As for shows, MAGIC and ASR (Action Sports Retailer Expo) are the places to go to find and buy brands that fuel this market. At a recent MAGIC show, the two areas that had the most action were the street wear section and the surf and skate section. As for the ASR, 20,000 attendees and 700 brands were present at the September 2007 show.

Even JCPenney has capitalized on the increased interest in this market. C7P . . . A Chip and Pepper Production was launched exclusively at JCPenney for the 2007 back-to-school shopping season (JCPenney, 2007). Chip and Pepper are identical twins from California who epitomize the surf lifestyle. This line of surf-inspired products centers around a fun, creative, young, and invigorating collection of affordable fashion to help JCPenney, as well as Chip and Pepper, connect with their younger customers.

CONCLUDING THOUGHTS

The goals of this chapter were to help you learn the following:

o the elements that make up the men's sportswear industry
o differences in men's sportswear classifications
o key silhouettes that can be found in the men's sportswear industry

In this chapter, you developed a working definition of how the market views the men's sportswear industry. You learned how the industry groups men's sportswear into different classifications, including casual wear, dress casual, spectator and participatory sportswear, urban/street wear, and surf and skate wear. You also took a quick look at knits and wovens.

The overall objective of this chapter was to convey that differences do exist in the men's sportswear market and to help you understand the terminology associated with those differences.

In the next chapter, you will look at various trends that affect the menswear industry and develop an understanding about how these trends are created and what significance they have in helping shape what you see and buy at the retail level.

KEY TERMS

boardshort

dress casual

participatory sportswear

spectator sportswear

zoot suit

CLASS EXERCISES

1. Choose a sportswear brand and determine which of the categories referenced in this chapter it belongs to. Why is this brand successful? Who is its target market? How does the company communicate with its target market?

2. Research a brand that provides both participatory (functional) sportswear and spectator sportswear. What are the main differences between the products for each market? How does the company deliver its marketing message so as not to confuse customers? What types of media are used by each segment of the company?

REFERENCES

Cosgrove, Stuart. (1984). The zoot-suit and style warfare, *History Workshop Journal*. Vol. 18 (Autumn) pp. 77–91.

FUBU. (2007). About Us. [Online]. Available: http://www. fubu.com [April 3, 2007].

Gellers, Stan. (2006, December 4). Playing it down the middle. *DNR*, pp. 18–20.

Hoovers. (2007). FUBU: Hoovers Profile. [online]. Available: http://www.answers.com/topic/fubu?cat=biz-fin [April 14, 2007].

JCPenney. (2007, March 22). C7P ... A Chip & Pepper Production launches exclusively at JCPenney for the back-to-school season. [online]. Available: http://ir.jcpenney.com/phoenix.zhtml?c=70528&p=irol-newsCompanyArticle&ID=976480&highlight= [April 14, 2007].

Just the Swing. (2007). A Hepster's Dictionary. [online]. Available: http://www.just-the-swing.com/liv/jive [February 9, 2007].

Lloyd, Brenda. (2006, December 18). An active year. *DNR*, pp. 16–20.

Nike. (2007). Mission. [online]. Available: http://www.nike.com/nikebiz/nikebiz.jhtml?page=4 [November 7, 2007].

Quiksilver. (2007). History of Quiksilver [online]. Available: www.historyofbranding.com/quicksilver.html [April 15, 2007].

Under Armour. (2007). About Under Armour. [online]. Available: http://www.fieldersonline.com/mailout/ua.htm [November 3, 2007].

ELEVEN

TRENDS IN THE MENSWEAR MARKET

- what a trend is
- current trends that are affecting the menswear industry
- that trends can and do come from all levels of the market

Trends are the lifeblood of the industry. Do you ever wonder how a new style comes about? It is difficult to report trends in a textbook given the very nature of what a trend is—the direction in which a fashion is heading during a specific time period. This chapter does not focus on specific color or style trends, as these are fleeting. Instead, you will examine the trends that are having an impact on the industry at the present time with the goal of predicting what you will see in the near future in the menswear market. The following list identifies some of the important trends influencing the menswear industry in 2007–2008:

- the influence of media
- the influence of technology
- changing buying habits
- licensing
- dressing for success
- man boutiques

- ○ men and bags
- ○ male grooming
- ○ nostalgia
- ○ Corporate Social Responsibility (CSR)
- ○ environmental awareness

THE INFLUENCE OF MEDIA

One current trend is the use of editorial fashion spreads in consumer magazines that transcend ethnic boundaries. *Vibe* magazine's September 2006 Fall fashion spread featured the following:

- ○ Rocawear
- ○ Polo Ralph Lauren
- ○ Phat Farm
- ○ Yohji Yamamoto
- ○ D&G
- ○ Lacoste
- ○ Live Mechanics

Vibe was founded by Quincy Jones in 1993. It was established with an urban/hip-hop consumer in mind and is billed as the pre-eminent brand in urban and music culture. When the magazine first appeared on the newsstands, it featured urban brands that were geared toward the magazine's urban customer. In the fashion spread that appeared in September 2006, it was clear that the magazine was attempting to broaden the appeal of the editorial space by including brands that had appealed to a non-urban demographic in the past. Over time, look for the lines of clothes to be less narrowly targeted to specific demographics.

Figure 11.1 *Trends in the media include a blending of culture. Here, urban meets Dior.*

Another example of this trend is Sean John's tailored clothing pictured in *DNR* alongside Polo Purple Label. This is also an example of a brand, Sean John, that started out catering to the urban population but has now achieved success in the tailored clothing market and now hangs with the likes of Polo. Conversely, the Polo brand has also been accepted in the urban market. Historically, in the menswear business, companies were established based on specific target markets, which, at times, were based on ethnicity. It was often difficult for these companies to move or attract a different and distinct audience for their products.

This trend creates an approach in which ethnic boundaries are broken and fashion is allowed to speak for itself across demographic groups. New opportunities will be created for you, the fashion student, to develop your business without having to overthink the target market.

THE INFLUENCE OF TECHNOLOGY

The growing use and development of technology is a much broader trend, which impacts the retail industry on a large scale. At the National Retail Federation convention in New York in January 2007, virtually every display booth involved some form of technology. Business journalist Mark Albright noted that "90 percent of the 550 trade show exhibitors were pitching some sort of technology package geared toward helping the retailer" (Albright, 2007).

Technology also affects how men shop. Microsoft's Chief Executive Officer Steve Ballmer, quoted in Albright's article, observed that "the young generation has grown up in a connected world which will continue to revolutionize how people shop." He further stated, "People will expect to research what they buy from home or a wireless device wherever they are. They want it in real time. Any time they walk in your store, they will expect you to be able to deal with all their gadgets. They will expect to be the center of attention of any business that tries to serve

Figure 11.2 *Technology continues to change how, when, and where we shop.*

them" (Albright, 2007). From the retailer's standpoint, this will mean that the consumers shopping in their stores will be better informed about the products they are looking to purchase. Consequently, the retailer will have to expend additional time and money to train the sales associates that work the floor in order to properly serve these educated consumers. Sales associates will need to be knowledgeable about their products, understand the consumers' needs, and offer superior service.

Online shopping has been around for only a decade or so, and men are driving the growth of Internet shopping. In November 2006, the *Financial Times* reported that men find it much more convenient and cost efficient to shop on the Internet, and this holds true for their apparel purchases. It is easier for men to purchase online than it is for women, as the sizing is relatively consistent from one brand to another, which is not the case with women's wear. If a man knows his waist size and inseam measurement, he can buy a pair of pants online. If the same man knows he takes a medium in a sport shirt, he can buy a knit or woven shirt and be confident that it will fit (Pickard, 2006).

Look for technology to continue to influence how consumers shop. Already, you can shop by using your remote control to order from Home Shopping Network or QVC, clicking the mouse on your computer, or tapping the keypad of your cell phone. During the rage of the dot-coms, people were making dire predictions that retailing, as we knew it, would disappear and the Internet would replace all those stores. That is far from the case, and it will not change anytime soon. Smart retailers are using the Web to supplement and support their physical store locations. They look to incorporate the Internet as one of the many tools they can use to reach the consumer.

CHANGING BUYING HABITS

Men of all ages are beginning to shop more, and they like it. As noted in Chapter 2, men's interest in shopping has increased. This trend will continue far into the future, as the younger demographic continues to become more comfortable with the shopping experience.

In an article in the *Contra Costa Times*, Blanca Torres noted that Jason Taylor, a seasoned shopper who was voted "Best Dressed" in his high school, likes to shop. Jason can be considered a trendsetter in his own right because he learned the importance of shopping and looking good. Jason provided some insight into how he developed his shopping habits, stating, "My mom was a really avid shopper and would kind of drag me with her. That's how I got to know Nordstrom on an intimate level" (Torres, 2006).

In the same article, Clarissa Nicosia, who teaches at the Art Institute of San Francisco, explains that men are more exposed to style and fashion at a much higher level than in previous decades due to exposure to more magazines, music videos, and, of course, the Internet (Torres, 2006).

Ken Hicks, president and chief merchandising officer of JCPenney, has also observed that men are doing more of their own shopping. "Five

Figure 11.3 *Choices abound for the menswear customer. One difference is that today's male is actually making his own purchase decisions.*

years ago, 70 percent of the menswear purchased at JCPenney's was bought by women, and today 70 percent of it is purchased by men," he said (Palmieri, 2006, p. 8).

These statistics show that there has been a monumental swing in purchasing power and decision making when it comes to menswear; men, not women, are leading the way. As a trend, it continues to point to the fact that there is a fundamental shift in *who* is making the purchase decisions and *what* is being purchased. It is clear that more and more men are using stores, catalogs, and the Internet to buy their own clothes. This trend bodes well for the industry. Men of all ages, and particularly younger men, continue to change the face of the customer. Designers and manufacturers are paying attention to these trend s and designing products that appeal to their sense of style.

LICENSING

Menswear companies, big and small, will continue to use licensing agreements to expand their markets. From a business standpoint, this makes perfect sense, as it is a proven method for companies to do the following:

o   expand their customer base
o   increase their brand awareness
o   make more money in a product category in which they do not have expertise in manufacturing

Many examples exist in the market. One such example is Sean John, which recently signed a licensing agreement with Americo Group Inc. to produce, market, and sell a line of underwear, sleepwear, and loungewear. As a company, Sean John wanted to expand its business, but it was limited by financial concerns and knowledge of particular markets. In this example, Sean John saw an opportunity to branch out and add underwear, sleepwear, and loungewear to its existing business by signing a licensing agreement. By signing such an agreement, the company can enter these new markets without needing to develop an entire infrastructure to support a new business. Instead, it can use the infrastructure already in place within the company with which the licensing agreement has been signed. The new product categories will increase the Sean John brand presence, and open new retail accounts for the brand.

Polo Ralph Lauren has signed licensing agreements with fragrance companies as well as eyewear companies. Polo is internationally renowned for its apparel, but it lacks expertise in designing and creating eyewear and fragrances. By signing licensing agreements, however, the company can venture into these new areas quickly and with confidence. Look for more brands, designers, manufacturers, and even retailers to get involved in licensing agreements.

DRESSING FOR SUCCESS

The days when you rolled out of bed and stayed in your pajamas to go to work are pretty much over. There are still those who telecommute and do not have to leave the house to go to work, but since the dot-com bust, many of those who

Figure 11.4 *Sometimes it is tough to figure out what to wear to the interview, but you can never go wrong with a good suit.*

enjoyed working from home in their favorite jeans and T-shirts are now back in the workforce, and that has changed the rules for dressing for success.

The job market is competitive, and if you want to get a particular job, you have to look the part. "'If you look sloppy, it says you don't care about yourself or your job,' says Italo Zucchelli, the head of menswear for Calvin Klein.... 'It's not that you can't wear jeans and blazers to work,' Zucchelli says. 'It just depends on *how* you do it. For example, today I'm wearing a button-down shirt, a blazer, jeans, and sneakers. But my jeans are not ripped, and my sneakers are clean'" (Souris, 2006). A word to the wise: wait until you have the job before wearing the jeans and sneakers. If you are going on an important interview, wear a conservative suit and tie, unless it is a creative position. In that case, you can express your creative side by wearing a fashionable tie. Many retailers and Web sites offer tips on dressing for success. If in doubt, seek the help of a professional.

As long as men are out in the job market interviewing for new positions, they will continue to need a proper wardrobe and help drive sales of tailored clothing, casual, and dress casual attire. It all depends on the job and the given situation, but the overall need to set the proper tone will be determined by that all-important first impression.

MAN BOUTIQUES

Forget Home Depot and Lowe's; there are new stores in town. All around the country, "man boutiques" are popping up. Man boutiques carry upscale products at designer price points. These are small, efficient shops with the guy in mind, and they are catering to men like never

Figure 11.5 Create the right atmosphere and you will own that customer for life.

before. Some have wine tasting, game rooms, and comfortable waiting areas for the significant other in their lives. These small, well-appointed boutiques offer the following:

o   a pleasant shopping experience with personalized service
o   new and exciting opportunities for designers to showcase their lines of apparel and to create new niche markets that cater to the discerning menswear customer

MEN AND BAGS

One article about men and bags features an interview with a 22-year-old university student named Chinmay Banchal. Chinmay considered himself a "real man." However, he did not mind carrying a leather shoulder tote. "I think it looks good. It's professional," he said. "My friends think it's a fashion statement" (Mason, 2006). Gone are those European man purses from the 1980s and 1990s. Today, men are carrying more shoulder-type totes and bags than ever before; they are more comfortable and fashionable than the handheld attaché case.

Sales of bags are up and the "man bag" is a growing category. These bags are not only comfortable; they are also practical. They have dividers so that work can be organized neatly, and they have places to hold all sorts of electronic gadgets, such as cell phones and iPods.

Alison Paster, academic director of fashion marketing at the Art Institute of Philadelphia, said the reason the man bag is becoming

Figure 11.6 *It is becoming more acceptable to be seen sporting a man-bag.*

popular among men might be aggressive marketing. "The trend is there's more acceptance of men's fashion. Now, you see beauty care for men, men's body sprays and a lot of other men's accessories." She further stated that the advertising campaigns targeting these products show confident, masculine men in salons and spas. "The message is it's OK," she said. "It's manly" (Mason, 2006).

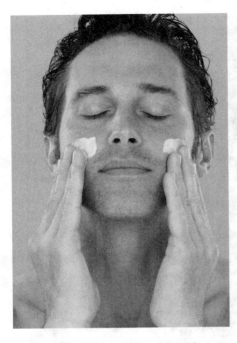

Figure 11.7 Grooming products for men have attracted the attention of the market, with many top cosmetic companies now offering products especially for males.

Not only is it manly, it is downright practical. As acceptance grows for the man bag, look for more retailers and manufacturers to get into this business, which will give the male consumer more choices at a variety of price points.

MALE GROOMING

The men's grooming market continues to grow with no sign of slowing. Recent sales for all outlets, from discounters to specialty stores, have been pegged at approximately $6 billion and is growing. Men today are more concerned than in the past with how they look and feel. The industry is targeting men in the following groups:

o Baby boomers (those born between 1946 and 1964): This group is looking in the mirror and not liking what they see.
o Generation X (those born between 1965 and 1976): This group is not embarrassed to spend money on looking good.

For the past 10 years, the growth has surpassed many of the industry predictions, with over 1,000 new products on the market aimed at the male demographic. New brands from traditional companies as well as upstarts continue to populate the shelves. Many products have been geared toward the hair care market, with additional emphasis focusing on skin care and bath and body washes.

The changing landscape for men's grooming products has also been a boon to the advertising industry. More new products creates more opportunities to advertise in consumer magazines, as well on TV, radio, and the Internet.

In a 2006 article in *The Independent,* Jonathan Thompson reported that the final taboo in men's grooming has been broken—makeup for men. "Even the most fashion conscious of men saw it as the final taboo. A spot of after-shave balm or moisturizer was one thing, but anything more was for women. Times, it seems, have changed. Gentlemen, brace yourselves and prepare to slap on the slap.... In upscale department stores, male concealer, eyeliner, and foundation are flying off the shelves. Leading luxury brands, such as Jean Paul Gaultier, Clinique, and Clarins, are scrambling to expand their lines to meet the boom in demand. Beauty for men is becoming big business" (Thompson, 2006).

How quickly and to what extent this trend will catch on with the average man on the street is uncertain, but it is happening and the market is responding.

In the same article, Thompson interviewed Julie Howard, Clinique's vice-president of product marketing, who said the company was test-marketing new products for men. "In the men's market, we've seen a move from basic skin care to an increase in eye care, wrinkle care and also lip care." She continued, "Make-up is now an eventuality in this category ... The demand is absolutely there ... Many men start borrowing products from their girlfriends or wives, and then go from there" (Thompson, 2006).

With an increase in disposable income coupled with the urge to look better, men are turning to cosmetic surgery to improve their appearance. Botox is just one example of recent procedures that men are willing to undergo to enhance their looks.

Figure 11.8 *Nostalgia sells—just look at the popularity of the rejuvenated VW Bug.*

NOSTALGIA

What is old is new again. For one reason or another, men go for the retro look. One prime example of this can be found not only in fashion, but in cars. The classic car industry is booming, and the big car companies are trying to cash in on this trend as well. For 2007, cars like the GTO and the Charger have been reintroduced. Let us not forget the PT Cruiser, Dodge 300, VW Bug, and the Magnum, which have also capitalized on the retro looks. At times, the retro trend in the automotive industry mirrors trends in the world of fashion. Men like to feel comfortable, and a way to achieve this is by appealing to objects from their past.

The interesting thing about this trend is that age does not matter. Guys of all ages understand and respect great cars and what they stand for. Thus, for car companies to play on that emotion makes sense. It is similar on the apparel side, where designers develop lines based on nostalgic themes. Take bowling shirts, western wear, denim jeans, polo shirts—all of these apparel products have gone through a nostalgic revival at some time in their history.

As we said at the start of this section, "what is old is new again." It is the designers, manufacturers, and retailers that pay attention to the fashion cycles and will continue to capitalize on this trend.

CORPORATE SOCIAL RESPONSIBILITY (CSR)

Corporate Social Responsibility (CSR) is a trend that is evident in the apparel industry, as well as in companies and organizations in general. Most manufacturing companies, brands, and retailers in the apparel industry have adopted codes of conduct under which they and their trading partners must operate. The codes address issues such as the following:

- workplace safety
- workers' rights, which include the following:
    - freedom of assembly
    - the right to unionize
    - the right to be paid a fair wage
    - the right to be paid overtime at pre-defined rates

Not-for-profit organizations, such as the Fair Labor Association and Social Accountability International, have sprung up in recent years. These organizations are trying to simplify the standards that exist and get everyone operating under the same codes. This trend is growing, and you will hear more about it as you move through your career. More and more companies have established positions within their organizations to handle compliance matters. As students going out into the workforce, do not be afraid to ask questions that relate to the social responsibility of the company that you would like to work for. If the company does not have a policy, seriously reconsider working there.

One might question whether prices will be affected with these additional expectations placed on the menswear industry. In the short run, the answer is yes, but the incremental increase that is imposed to properly adhere to these codes will be mitigated by improvements

Figure 11.9 The corporate world is paying more attention to how and where their products are manufactured. They are taking steps to ensure that the workers are treated fairly and are happy at their jobs.

in productivity. Therefore, the increased costs that are associated with compliant companies will be minimal at best, and in the long run, a fully compliant company could even see price reductions at the manufacturing level. Whether these cost increases or eventual decreases are passed on to the consumer is determined by the overall pricing strategy at two levels: manufacturing and retail. Each player in the market has an opportunity to bring about positive changes through the use of codes of conduct. Each player has to determine how much they are willing to pay for such changes, and whether, in the end, the consumer will bear an increase in prices to see those changes take place.

ENVIRONMENTAL AWARENESS: BECOMING ECO-FRIENDLY

With all the talk of global warming, people are looking at all aspects of their lives in an effort to help slow down and/or reverse the damage. This concern applies to what people wear, as well. Becoming eco-friendly is not only good for the environment, but in many cases, it makes good economic sense to be able to offer the consumer a choice. The buzzword in the industry is *sustainability*. There is great interest in the following:

○ crops that can be made into fibers
○ fabrics that are easily produced and do not put a strain on the earth and its natural resources

Fiber and textile companies have brought new products to the market in recent years, including fabrics made from soy, corn, seaweed, bamboo, and coconuts. Standbys like cotton, linen, hemp, jute, silk, and wool, which are all natural, cannot be forgotten. Although some of these fibers have come under attack from certain groups as contributing to environmental damage due to overuse of pesticides and water, they cannot compare to synthetic fibers and fabrics that are produced using nonrenewable resources such as oil.

Organic cotton has made a big splash in the industry recently. The production of organic cotton is currently equal to 1 percent of the total conventional cotton grown in the world. In fact, you could put all the organic cotton grown in one year worldwide into a single container ship (Cotton Incorporated, 2007a).

The issue with organic cotton is the supply and certification. As with most products sold, once demand begins to increase, people

Figure 11.10 Cotton is a renewable resource.

will look for ways to support those increases. That is where the certification issue comes in. Regrettably, there are unscrupulous people in the world, and if they see an opportunity to make some money by passing off conventionally grown cotton as organic, they will. Unfortunately for the consumer who wants to use organically grown products, the eco-friendliness comes at a price. Some of the newer sustainable fibers cost more to produce and process than conventional ones.

Where do men fit into the trend toward eco-friendliness? An article in Cotton Incorporated's publication *Life Monitor* concluded from a survey that men expend less energy than women when it comes to looking for eco-friendly apparel. According to the article, "only 2 percent of male respondents admitted to spending a lot of time on the quest, while 44 percent said they spent no time at all on the effort" (Cotton Incorporated,

Figure 11.11 *Bagir, a men's tailored clothing company, manufacturers suits from a fabric made of wool and post-consumer waste. Talk about being green!*

2007b). Given these figures, the marketing gurus need to find a way to change men's perception of eco-friendly products.

Several of the major fiber producers are getting back into the recycling business. In 1993, Malden Mills first introduced recycled fleece, which was made from recycled plastic soda bottles. The process proved costly and

Figure 11.12 This trend was spotted on the runway; it found its way into the market via trendsetters then made the leap into mainstream America.

difficult to market, but it was a great idea. Now, with all the emphasis on eco-friendly fibers and fabrics, the spinners are restarting the equipment that processes the soda bottles and turns them into fibers with some new modifications. Look for this trend to hit a few home runs; if the market does not embrace this now, it never will.

TREND SPOTTING

Have you ever wondered how a style or design gets started or how a trend becomes a trend? One answer to that question involves the use of trend spotters. What are trend spotters and what do they do?

In an article titled "Have an eye for fashion? Trend spotters are in demand," Vanessa O'Connell provided a glimpse of a day on the job with a trend spotter. "Standing near a cluster of bars at the corner of Red River and East 6th Streets in Austin, Texas, earlier this month, Helen Job grew anxious about denim. She had spent four days in the hip college town, trying to determine whether a new look was catching on" (O'Connell, 2007). Helen's job was to stand and watch people to try to discern if a trend that had been previously identified in other parts of the country was, in fact, a trend. This sounds easy, but in reality, it is not, and lots of money is at stake. Helen finally spotted a young woman with high-waisted jeans, proof to her that the trend she was looking for had taken root in this part of the country. Helen predicted that all the stores in New York would be carrying the style in about six weeks' time (O'Connell, 2007).

As a follow-up to this story, this trend did take hold throughout the country, and high-waisted jeans were marketed by Diesel, Abercrombie & Fitch, and J. Crew, to name a few.

"The role of a trend-spotter, sometimes also called cool hunters, has grown in importance as the fashion cycle has speeded up" (O'Connell, 2007). At present, two organizations that employ trend spotters are the Doneger Group and Worth Global Style Network. Over the past five years, the Doneger Group has doubled its trend-spotting staff to 120 people. If this catches on, as it seems it will, look for more trend-forecasting companies to follow suit by hiring more trend-spotters. You may even see some new companies opening up that specialize in trend spotting.

STUDENT CONFIRMATION

I shared this article with my students in one of our classes, and they confirmed that the high-waisted jean was, in fact, starting to appear in the stores a little less than five weeks after Ms. Job spotted the trend on the streets in of all places, Austin, Texas.

CONCLUDING THOUGHTS

The goals of this chapter were to help you learn the following:

o   what a trend is
o   current trends that are affecting the menswear industry
o   that trends can and do come from all levels of the market

In this chapter, you examined various trends that have had a recent impact on the menswear business. You looked at new and developing trends and examined how these trends will continue to affect the business of fashion for men. This chapter also set the stage for you to begin to understand that a trend in fashion can come from the bottom up (the street) or top down (key designers) in the marketplace.

In the next and final chapter, you will have an opportunity to study key organizations, companies, and associations that directly affect the menswear business. In Chapter 12 you will identify some key players in the menswear industry, and you will learn how those organizations work to support and help develop the industry.

CLASS EXERCISES

1. This chapter deals with trends, and trends are ever-changing. Research the market and identify three trends that are current. Analyze the trends to find answers to the following questions:
   o Why are they considered trends?
   o What is the driving force behind each of the trends you identified?
   o How was each trend established?
   o Who helped establish each trend?
   o Will these trends continue?
2. Review the trends examined in the chapter. Is each trend still valid? Have any of these trends grown stronger or weaker? Have you (or your friends or family) participated in any of these trends? If so, what was your (or their) experience?

REFERENCES

Albright, M. (2007, February 5). Future shop. *St. Petersburg Times*. [online]. Available: http://www.sptimes.com. [November 3, 2007].

Cotton Incorporated (2007a). Sustainability: U.S. cotton & the environment— A proven track record. [online]. Available: http://www.cottoninc .com/Sustainability [November 3, 2007].

Cotton Incorporated (2007b). Term limits: Green is apparel's gray area. *Lifestyle Monitor*. [online]. Available: http://www.cottoninc.com/ lsmarticles/?articleID=536 [November 3, 2007].

Mason W. (2006, August 10). Men have gotten a brand new bag. [online]. Available: http://www.phillyburbs.com [August 16, 2006].

O'Connell, Vanessa. (2007). Have an eye for fashion? Trendspotters are in demand. *The Wall Street Journal Executive Career Site*. [online]. Available: http://www.careerjournal .com [April 16, 2007].

Palmieri, Jean E. (2006, December 11). Men's a bright spot for YMA panel. *DNR*, p. 8.

Pickard, Jim. (2006, November 7). Men drive the growth of Internet shopping. *Financial Times*. [online].

Available: http://www.ft.com/cms/
s/0/c05d1b8e-6dbb-11db-8725-
0000779e2340.html?nclick_check=1
[November 7, 2006].

Souris, Evangelia. ((2006, August). How
to dress for success. [online]. Available: http://optimumimageic.com/
article.asp?id=195 [November 3, 2007].

Thompson, Jonathan. (2006, February
12). Male grooming: Suits you, sir.

The Independent. [online]. Available:
http://news.independent.co.uk/uk/
this_britain/article344943.ece
[November 3, 2007].

Torres, Blanca. (2006, October 12). More
and more, men like shopping.
Contra Costa Times. [online]. Available:
http://www.contracostatimes.com
[October 12, 2006].

TWELVE

SUPPORTING CAST

- important organizations in the menswear industry
- how various organizations interact within the menswear industry
- how these organizations conduct their business to support the menswear market

This chapter is dedicated to some of the organizations, companies, and groups that support the menswear industry by various means. This is by no means a definitive listing of all the important contributors, as that could take up an entire book. Instead, this chapter will present those organizations, companies, and groups that have influenced how the author has conducted business in the menswear industry.

TRADE AND FASHION SHOWS

MEN'S APPAREL GUILD IN CALIFORNIA (MAGIC)

Most people in the industry refer to the **Men's Apparel Guild in California** by its acronym, **MAGIC**. This is the biggest menswear show in the world, and it is held two times a year in Las Vegas, Nevada. The original shows were held in California, with Los Angeles hosting them for a number of years; it moved to a larger space in Las Vegas after

Figure 12.1 Twice a year the fashion industry flocks to Las Vegas for the MAGIC show to check out the new trends, designers, and apparel lines, and also to visit with longstanding vendors.

it had outgrown the California venue. Now, every February and August, the fashion industry converges on the gambling capital of the United States for four days of business.

MAGIC has grown; besides menswear it now includes children's wear and women's wear. Recently, a sourcing section was added to the show. This is an international show, and vendors and visitors come to it from around the world. In fact, the show boasts 3,600 manufacturers showcasing over 5,000 brands (MAGIConline, 2006). The author has personally attended and participated in the show over 25 times, starting in Los Angeles and continuing in Las Vegas.

MAGIC is a show that is greatly anticipated by vendors and buyers alike. It is also one that many vendors dread because they have to set up the show in August, when the heat in the building can top 100 degrees. This extreme temperature is due to the fact that all the bay doors are open to allow the crews to bring in all the booths and merchandise. Much of the set-up falls on the sales personnel attending the show. It is also a nervous time for sales personnel, as the managers or owners want to know how many appointments have been set up, who is being taken to dinner, and most of all, how much business is being written up. It is a great show to attend, and although stressful at times, it is usually a great experience.

For more information, visit the MAGIC Web site at www.magiconline.com.

OTHER TRADE AND FASHION SHOWS

In addition to MAGIC, many smaller regional trade and fashion shows are held throughout the country and around the world. Many of the regional fashion marts in the United States have their own shows to highlight local talent and to supplement the larger shows. Examples include the following:

o In Los Angeles, the California Mart hosts shows covering men's, women's, and children's wear, as well as textiles and accessories.
o The Dallas Market Center Complex is another destination for apparel buyers. It includes men's showrooms and has trade shows several times per year.
o The Chicago Apparel Center serves buyers from the northern and midwestern states.
o Atlanta opened the Merchandise Mart in 1961. It has seen its share of expansions and name changes. Today, Atlanta hosts the Americas Mart, which has the capacity to house 2,000 showrooms that can hold 11,000 lines of apparel and accessories.

Figure 12.2 On the west coast, the Los Angeles Mart is the place to be if you are in the fashion business.

○ Several smaller marts are located in Miami, San Francisco, and Seattle. Although smaller in scope, they still provide the same valuable services to the buyers as their larger counterparts.

Owners of local boutiques and small stores may not be able to afford the time away from their stores, or they may lack the funds needed to travel to Las Vegas to attend MAGIC for a couple of days. Regional trade and fashion shows provide opportunities for these retailers to shop key vendors under one roof, conveniently and cost effectively. Local and regional shows are valuable to the industry in the following ways:

o   they increase sales opportunities for manufacturers and designers
o   they provide valuable trend information to retailers

ACTION SPORTS RETAILER EXPO (ASR)

Action Sports Retail Expo (ASR) is the show for retailers to preview and buy products

Figure 12.3 *Anything goes at the ASR. Here, two guys test-market a new product.*

from leading manufacturers of surf, skate, snow, and directional apparel. This show started in 1981 and is held three times a year in San Diego, California. ASR is the largest show representing this segment of the market. A typical show will have 750 exhibitors and 17,500 attendees. The show represents the men's, women's, and children's markets and covers all price points.

For more information, visit the ASR Web site at www.asrbiz.com.

TEXTILE TRADE SHOWS

PREMIÈRE VISION

As textile trade shows go, **Première Vision** is the cream of the crop. Held in Paris twice a year, this show boasts the top textile mills from all over Europe. In addition, it holds a show in New York City twice a year called European Preview. This show is for those who do not have the chance to travel to Paris and who want to see many of the top European mills. Unfortunately,

Figure 12.4 Première Vision, the largest and most prestigious fabric show, is held in the fashion capital of Europe—Paris, France.

like much of the industry, the focus for textile production has shifted to the Far East, and the number of European mills is decreasing.

Première Vision has also witnessed the start-up of another show called Texworld, which competes with the European Preview for visitors. The main difference between the two shows is that Texworld features mills from all over the world and is more focused on commodity-priced fabrics, while European Preview focuses on the European mills. What the future holds for Première Vision is uncertain. The shift in production of finished garments continues to move toward the Far and Middle East, and with that, the textile mills are sure to follow.

For more information, visit the Première Vision Web site at www.premierevision.fr.

LOCAL AND REGIONAL TEXTILE TRADE SHOWS

Apart from Première Vision, people in the fashion industry can also attend the many

Figure 12.5 Texworld is another important fabric trade show. Here, buyers review and select fabrics to be incorporated into their lines.

smaller textile trade shows that cater to more local audiences. Although these shows are smaller, they are all important to the fashion industry. (See Chapter 3 for a list of textile trade shows.)

ORGANIZATIONS AND SERVICES DEDICATED TO THE FASHION INDUSTRY

COLOR ASSOCIATION OF THE UNITED STATES (CAUS)

The **Color Association of the United States (CAUS)** has been in existence since 1915 and has been issuing color reports since that time. The CAUS is a fee-based service that offers the latest color trends. CAUS experts will visit clients to make suggestions on their current color lines. They will even individualize a color trend for the client's company. Membership is required in order to receive these services.

The CAUS is made up of a panel of industry experts who meet to forecast colors as far as 18 to 24 months in advance of a season. How do they do this? They use a mix of history, trend analysis, and a bit of luck. Invariably, they are very accurate. Their accuracy rate may be due to self-fulfilling prophecy to some extent. The association identifies a certain group of colors as being important for a given season. The yarn spinners, textile companies, and chemical companies all buy into the announced trends and place their sample orders in these colors. The industry then presents the new colors in various trend forecasts, while the designers, manufacturers, and brands make their samples in these colors.

The buyers see the colors much closer to the season. Generally, these buyers will comment that the colors are great, and they will proceed to buy the garments that the designers have created using the new colors that were forecast 18 to 24 months earlier. Ultimately, the consumer has the final say in whether these colors are, in fact, saleable.

For more information, visit the CAUS Web site at www.colorassociation.com.

FAIRCHILD PUBLICATIONS

The Fairchild Group, a division of Condé Nast, has been a strong contributor to the fashion industry for many years. **Fairchild Publications** not only boasts a strong fashion industry textbook publishing division, it publishes fashion news daily in two mainstays of the industry: *Women's Wear Daily* and *DNR*. As mentioned in Chapter 6, these two publications are considered the bibles of the fashion industry. *DNR* serves the menswear industry, and *Women's Wear Daily* provides news on the women's wear market.

Figure 12.6 *Fairchild Publications (a division of Condé Nast) headquartered on Third Avenue in New York City.*

For more information, visit the Fairchild Publications Web site at www.fairchildpub.com.

INFOMAT

The search engine, www.infomat.com, boasts 350,000 entries specifically geared toward the fashion industry. These entries provide the following, all at the click of the mouse:

o guides on navigating the business of fashion
o research for the retail, apparel, accessories, and textile industries
o trade contacts and business directories
o marketplace features including a searchable trade event calendar
o looks at designer collections, trends, and publications

InfoMat offers a wide range of services about the fashion industry.

Figure 12.7 Screen capture from InfoMat.

AUSTRALIAN WOOL SERVICES

With over 60 years of experience in the wool industry, **Australian Wool Services** uses its expertise and innovations to perform technical research and development to improve the supply chain for wool and wool by-products. This organization owns the Woolmark and the Woolmark Wool Blend trademarks, which provide a quality endorsement of wool brands worldwide. Unlike some of the other fiber companies that represent different sectors of the market, Australian Wool Services charges a fee for the use of the Woolmark logo and tags on garments.

The mission of Australian Wool Services is to serve shareholders by being a financially sustainable company that provides the following:

○ quality certification from the fiber to finished garments
○ technological advancements that help producers improve any process

Figure 12.8 *There are more sheep in Australia than people.*

along the supply chain, including shearing, yarn spinning, finishing, weaving, and knitting

o products and services for the global wool industry

The company focuses on serving both customers and shareholders, seeking effective ways to improve and streamline the processes of textile production.

For more information, visit the Woolmark Company Web site at www.woolmark.com.

CASHMERE AND CAMEL HAIR MANUFACTURERS INSTITUTE (CCMI)

One of the lesser-known groups that support the industry is the **Cashmere and Camel Hair Manufacturers Institute (CCMI)**. It was founded in 1984 as the Cashmere and Camel Hair Manufacturers Institute of America. It changed its name in 1990 to reflect the international nature of the organization. This organization concentrates its efforts in the following areas:

Figure 12.9 *Cashmere is considered a luxury fiber thanks to the fine hair found on the underbelly of goats like these two.*

- international standards
- supply chain management issues
- market trends

The group provides product testing and has divisions that will help with government relations, public relations, and industry relations.

The fibers and fabrics represented by CCMI are luxury fibers; therefore, the market reach is limited to those able to afford to produce apparel and accessories out of such fibers, yarns, and fabrics.

For more information, visit the CCMI Web site at www.cashmere.org.

COTTON INCORPORATED

Founded in 1970 with a mission to ensure that cotton remains the first choice among consumers in apparel and home products, the organization has done a wonderful job with promoting cotton. **Cotton Incorporated** is a not-for-profit organization whose original charter was to represent the U.S. cotton farmer in the following ways:

- to see that they received a fair price for their product
- to help them grow cotton more effectively
- to see that the consumers were aware of the fiber
- to see that the mills were in a better position to run cotton on their machines

The Seal of Cotton, a registered trademark of Cotton Incorporated, was first introduced in 1973 and, today, boasts consumer recognition of over 80 percent. The main reason for the

Figure 12.10 *The world headquarters of Cotton Incorporated located in Cary, North Carolina. This facility is responsible for much of the research and development undertaken on behalf of the cotton industry.*

company's creation was to combat the marketing practices of chemical companies that were working to convince consumers to use synthetic fabrics in apparel and home textiles and experiencing growing success.

Today, the organization is worldwide, with offices in China, Mexico, Osaka, Singapore, and the United States. Cotton Incorporated is no longer funded solely by the cotton growers in the United States, but from cotton importers as well. In addition to providing support to the growers, Cotton Incorporated provides valuable color, design, and trend services to the industry here and abroad.

A shift in U.S. cotton imports and exports has occurred in recent years; for 2006–2007, the United States was predicted to grow 21.7 million bales of cotton. Each bale weighs 480 pounds. Of the 21.7 million bales, 14 million were to be exported, with China importing a large portion of U.S. exports and U.S. mill consumption sitting at around 5 million bales. In years past, U.S. mill use would have accounted for the lion's share of the crop. Check out Cotton Incorporated at www.cottoninc.com for much more information on how they serve the industry. Cotton Incorporated recognized in the mid-1990s the importance of the growing global market for U.S. cotton and opened an office in Shanghai, China, to better serve the needs of the Chinese market and help facilitate the imports by China of U.S. cotton. This proved to be an important move as evidenced by the numbers reported above. The United States continues to grow large quantities of cotton and while the demand for raw U.S. cotton in the States has fallen off dramatically

---

MY COTTON YEARS

One of my career stops was with Cotton Incorporated in the 1990s. I thoroughly enjoyed working there, and I might still be working there today if they had not decided that my services could be used to better advantage if I were to move to the headquarters in Cary, North Carolina, which I chose not to do. I served as managing director of U.S. marketing for over three years. One of my functions was presenting to the board of directors.

in the past several decades, the market for U.S. cotton around the world has increased. The increase in exports of U.S. cotton can be attributed to Cotton Incorporated's success in marketing the attributes of the U.S. cotton crop.

For more information, visit the Cotton Incorporated Web site at www.cottoninc.com.

Cotton Council International (CCI), the sister organization to Cotton Incorporated, serves as the export promotion arm of the National Cotton Council of America. The sole purpose of this organization is to increase exports of U.S. cotton, cotton seed, and U.S.-manufactured cotton products. CCI achieves its mission by examining every aspect of the supply chain and trying to influence the various stages of the supply chain to export U.S. cotton where possible. The council holds seminars around the world to promote the value of using U.S. cotton products.

For more information, visit the CCI Web site at www.cottonusa.org.

Figure 12.11 The COTTON USA hang tag is recognized around the world.

SYNTHETIC FIBER PRODUCERS

Synthetic fiber producers, also known as chemical companies, have played a major role in the apparel and textile business over the years, with DuPont leading the way. Other producers that have had an impact include Monsanto and Celanese. Synthetic (man-made) fibers have been around for many years. The following list shows when some of the more popular fibers came into use:

o   rayon (1910)
o   nylon (1939)
o   polyester (1953)
o   spandex (1959)

DuPont took its first step in the synthetic market back in 1920 when it produced artificial silk, better known as rayon (DuPont, 2007). Although rayon is considered a synthetic fiber, it does have its origins in wood pulp, which is a natural product. DuPont sold its textile and interior fabric divisions to Koch Industries in 2004 and renamed the company Invista.

The chemical companies held a dominant position in the market in the 1960s, 1970s, and into the 1980s, with the production of synthetic fibers. The mills loved these fibers because they ran so well on the machinery, and they enabled them to offer something new to consumers. These fibers were used to create wash-and-wear garments—easy care was a big selling feature, although the early products cannot compare with the microfibers that are available today.

One thing that the chemical companies had going for them was their ability to market the fibers, fabrics, and garments to consumers. These companies had very large advertising budgets and took market share from natural fibers, especially cotton. Eventually, however, synthetic apparel lost steam in the market, in part due to efforts by external forces such as Cotton Incorporated and also due to cultural shifts that saw a return to natural fibers. An example is the hippie movement and the associated popularity of jeans and T-shirts.

Today, there has been a resurgence in synthetic products as the technology to manufacture microfibers has given synthetic fibers a new lease on life. One other factor that has influenced the market is the "fiber unconscious" consumers who do not look at the fiber content in the garments. If they like the color, the silhouette, and the price, they buy it. Not everyone shops like this, but more and more consumers today leave out the fiber content when making buying decisions.

NOT-FOR-PROFIT ORGANIZATIONS

COUNCIL OF FASHION DESIGNERS OF AMERICA (CFDA)

The **Council of Fashion Designers of America (CFDA)** is a not-for-profit trade association that was founded in 1962. Its mission is as follows:

- to advance the status of fashion designers as a branch of American culture
- to raise the artistic and professional standards of the designers who are members of the CFDA

Figure 12.12 The CFDA represents the brightest and best talent in the design and art community.

- to define a code of conduct for CFDA members
- to promote appreciation of the fashion arts by providing a leadership role in setting quality standards and creating an atmosphere in which the aesthetic characteristics are valued

The association holds annual fundraisers and presents fashion awards, and it also offers scholarships and professional development programs. The association uses its clout in the market to raise funds for breast cancer and other worthy causes. Its presence in the industry has helped many aspiring designers achieve the status that they truly deserved.

For more information, visit the CFDA Web site at www.cfda.com.

The **Garment Industry Development Corporation (GIDC)** is a not-for-profit organization established in 1984 whose mandate is to find ways to strengthen New York City's apparel industry. GIDC connects buyers with producers, provides technical assistance and training, and generally responds to an ever-changing industry. In a demanding field such as apparel manufacturing, producing garments in New York City can be quite a challenge, one that GIDC members take on enthusiastically. The organization was founded by the following:

- the City of New York
- the Garment Workers' Union (now known as UNITE HERE)
- the New York Skirt & Sportswear Association

At present, little menswear is produced in New York City, although there is still some production available on specialized menswear products. The people at GIDC aspire to increase the availability of viable menswear resources in the New York City area.

For more information, visit the GIDC Web site at www.gidc.org.

TREND SERVICES

Trend services help the industry sift through information and discover new trends. Although companies and associations such as CAUS and Cotton Incorporated provide services (some fee free) to the industry, there is an entire group that makes their living as prognosticators of fashion. These trend resources include the following:

o the Doneger Group
o Here & There
o Tobe

THE DONEGER GROUP

The **Doneger Group** has been in business for over 60 years. It was started by Henry Doneger and is now run by his son, Abby Doneger. With offices in New York and Los Angeles, the company covers all markets and serves large and small clients. This fee-based company is the home of David Wolfe, who has created a reputation for spotting trends and disseminating them on a timely basis to the group's client base (Donegar Group, 2007). The company's services include the following:

o color forecasting
o design elements
o fashion forecasting
o live presentations, in which merchandise is shown and ideas are exchanged
o a full online service department

For more information, visit the Doneger Group Web site at www.doneger.com.

HERE & THERE

Here & There is a pioneer in the fashion intelligence industry with over 30 years of experience in trend forecasting, reporting, and consulting. In a recent development Here & There has joined forces with the Doneger

Group, combining years of experience to better serve their combined clients. Here & There will customize a presentation to suit their clients' needs and share the inspirational resources they have collected over the years. Fashion is evolutionary, not revolutionary, so historical collections are often a great source of information.

For more information, visit the Here & There Web site at www.hereandthere.net, or via the Doneger Web site.

TOBE

Tobe is an international fashion retail consulting service best known for the *Tobe Report*, which it has published for over 75 years. Tobe provides an in-depth analysis of the retail trends and delves into the business side of fashion to give their clients a better understanding of how well a retailer is performing from a financial perspective.

For more information, visit the Tobe Web site at www.tobereport.com.

CONCLUDING THOUGHTS

The goals of this chapter were to help you learn the following:

o important organizations in the menswear industry
o how various organizations interact within the menswear industry
o how these organizations conduct their business to support the menswear market

This final chapter has outlined some of the key supporting players in the menswear industry and how they contribute to the overall success of the industry. The organizations presented in this chapter were important ones that the author interacted with during his years in the industry.

KEY TERMS

Action Sports Retailer Expo (ASR)

Australian Wool Services

Cashmere and Camel Hair Manufacturers
    Institute (CCMI)

Color Association of the United States (CAUS)

Cotton Council International (CCI)

Cotton Incorporated

Council of Fashion Designers of America (CFDA)

Doneger Group

Fairchild Publications

Garment Industry Development
    Corporation (GIDC)

Here & There

InfoMat

Men's Apparel Guild in California (MAGIC)

Première Vision

synthetic fiber producers

Tobe

trend services

CLASS EXERCISE

1. Choose two of the supporting cast members described in the chapter and research them in more depth.

   a) Find answers to the following questions:
   - What is their mission statement?
   - Who are their core customers?
   - How do they add value to the market in which they work?

   b) Can you think of any additional industry groups that you feel should be listed? If so, identify them and explain why they should be included.

REFERENCES

Action Sports Retailer Expo (2007). Action Sports Retailer Expo [online]. Available: http://www.ASRBIZ.com [April 19, 2007].

Australian Wool Service (2007). Australian Wool Service [online]. Available: http://www.woolmark.com [April 19, 2007].

Cashmere and Camel Hair Manufacturers Institute (2006). Cashmere and Camel Hair Manufactures Institute [online]. Available: http://www.cashmere.org [September 5, 2006].

Color Association of the United States (2007). The Color Association of the

United States [online]. Available:
http://www.colorassociation.com
[April 19, 2007].

Cotton Council International (2007).
Cotton Council International [online].
Available: http://www.cottonUDA.org
[April 19, 2007].

Cotton Incorporated (2007). Cotton
Incorporated [online]. Available:
http://www.cottoninc.com
[April 21, 2007].

Council of Fashion Designers of America
(2007). Council of Fashion Designers
of America [online]. Available: http://
www.cfda.com [April 21, 2007].

Doneger Group (2007). The Doneger
Group [online]. Available: http://www
.doneger.com [April 18, 2007].

DuPont Corporation (2007). Dupont
Corporation [online]. Available: http://
www.heritage.dupont.com [April 21,
2007].

Fairchild (2007). Fairchild Publication Inc.
[online]. Available: http://www
.fairchildpub.com [April 17, 2007].

Garment Industry Development
Corporation (2007). Garment Industry
Development Corporation [online].
Available: http://www.GIDC.org
[April 20, 2007].

Here & There (2007). Here & There [online].
Available: http://www.hereandthere
.net [April 26, 2007].

InfoMat (2007). InfoMat [online]. Available:
http://www.infomat.com [April 19,
2007].

MAGIConline (2006). MAGIConline Home
Page [online]. Available: http://www
.MAGIConline.com [September 17, 2006].

Première Vision (2007). Première Vision
[online]. Available: http://www
.premierevision.fr [April 19, 2007].

Tobe (2007). TOBE Report Retrieved
[online]. Available: http://www
.TOBEreport.com [April 30, 2007].

807 production System introduced by the U.S. government in an effort to keep more apparel and textile jobs in the United States and as part of the Quick Response program.

A

Action Sports Retailer Expo (ASR) Trade show for retailers to preview and buy products from leading manufacturers of surf, skate, snow, and directional apparel. ASR is held three times per year.

advertising Any form of non-personal presentation and promotion of ideas, goods, or services by an identified sponsor.

American cut Describes the style of a suit coat or sport coat; it is geared toward comfort, and usually has a 6-inch drop, low armhole, soft-medium padding in the shoulders, and a fuller skirt, adding to the straighter lines of the silhouette.

Australian Wool Services Organization that specializes in the commercialization of wool technologies and innovations, technical consulting, business information, and testing of wool fabrics. Through the ownership and licensing of the Woolmark and Woolmark Wool Blend labels, the organization provides a unique worldwide quality endorsement of brands and symbols that are protected by rigorous and extensive checks and recognized as unrivalled signs of quality and performance.

B

Balmacaan A type of overcoat made of heavy fabric; it gets its name from an estate in Scotland, and is sometimes call "bal" for short. This coat features raglan sleeves, a standing collar, and a loose, full fit.

barrel cuff The most common form of cuff found on a woven dress or sport shirt; *barrel* refers to how the cuff is attached to the sleeve—it is sewn in a cylindrical form, so it resembles a barrel. This type of cuff can have one or two buttons.

besom pocket A pocket with a very narrow welt on the top and bottom sides of the opening. A besom pocket can be found on pants, suit coats, and sport coats. Also referred to as a slash, inset, or double-welt pocket. Often there is a flap inserted into the besom pocket on suits.

billboard A large outdoor advertising structure usually found in a high-traffic area.

black tie The semiformal level of formality; black tie is most often associated with the tuxedo, although dinner jackets and dinner suits can also be worn.

blazer A type of sport coat. Traditionally, the blazer is navy blue with brass buttons, and it may be single or double breasted. Today the term has been expanded to include any sport coat that comes in a solid color.

blended fabric Fabric constructed of one or more fibers with different origins (e.g., a 60 percent cotton and 40 percent polyester fabric would constitute a blended fabric).

blue-collar worker Describes a person who works with his or her hands (i.e., performs manual labor) and is generally paid an hourly wage.

bluff stitch Stitching on the edge of a lapel or flap that has no topstitching; also called a bluff edge.

boardshort A style of shorts most associated with water sports such as surfing or wakeboarding; this style is generally made from a smooth nylon or polyester, comes to the knee, is baggy in appearance, and is available in vibrant colors.

bow tie A type of necktie; it is generally worn with formal attire, but not exclusively, as men also don bow ties as a fashion statement. Bow ties come in clip-on, pre-tied, and self-tie models.

British cut Describes the style of a suit jacket; it is considered the most traditional of all cuts. Hallmarks of the British cut are its straight lines, virtually no shape, and only slight padding.

British warmer A traditional style that falls in the tailored outerwear category; it has set-in sleeves and generally comes in a double-breasted model.

broadcast media A means of disseminating information over a broad area; most often associated with radio and television.

broadcloth Tightly woven lustrous cotton cloth with fine embedded cross-wide ribs.

button-down collar A soft collar with no interlining that has a button on each point to secure the collar to the front of the shirt; the buttons are generally smaller than those on the placket and cuffs. This style was originally developed by polo players to keep the collar points from flapping in the breeze.

c

Cashmere and Camel Hair Manufacturers Institute (CCMI) An international trademark representing the interests of producers and manufacturers of camel hair and cashmere fabric garments throughout the world. The institute is the leader on domestic and international issues concerning these luxury fibers and advises on international standards, supply, and market trends.

casual years Term describing the years that the casual revolution took hold (mainly 1980s and 1990s).

casualization Term describing the change in the mode of dress from a formal style to a more relaxed, casual style.

catalog A marketing tool to present products to consumers; includes print catalogs mailed directly to consumers; video catalogs presented in store; and electronic catalogs, which are available online.

chain store Two or more outlets that are owned and controlled in common; they have a central buying and merchandising system and sell similar lines of merchandise.

chesterfield coat A classic coat found in the tailored outerwear department; features a long, slim cut with set-in sleeves and a black velvet collar. The classic color for the chesterfield is gray.

chiton A garment made of two sheets of light drapery fabric worn directly over the body and held in place by a belt.

cloak A loose-fitting garment worn over clothing to protect the wearer from the elements; it fastened at the neck or over the shoulder and sometimes had a hood.

clothing A classification of apparel in menswear that typically includes suits, sport coats, dress slacks, and tailored outerwear.

club tie A type of necktie with a small repeated pattern woven into it. Originally, the tie represented membership in a particular club.

CMT Cut, make, and trim; this term is associated with the manufacturing process and denotes that a company performs a cutting service (cutting fabric into garment parts), make or sewing service (actual sewing together of the cut parts), and trim service (affixing the labels, tags, and packaging of the finished garments).

code of conduct Set of rules outlining the responsibilities of or proper practices for an individual or organization.

collar bar An accessory used to accentuate the tie by raising the knot to a more prominent position; it is worn under the tie and fastened to the collar on both sides.

collection A group of styles designed for a particular selling season; often the premier line offered by a designer or manufacturer.

Color Association of the United States (CAUS) The oldest color forecasting service in the United States. Since 1915, CAUS has been issuing color reports in an elegant fabric-swatched booklet form. It is the only forecasting service that selects its colors through a committee panel of eight to twelve industry professionals.

contractor A firm that provides sewing or specialty services.

conversational tie Type of necktie that has an unusual pattern (e.g., bold, large-scale) or represents a theme (e.g., holiday, sport, art).

cost The value given up in order to receive goods or services; the total dollar amount invested in a product.

Cost, Insurance, Freight (CIF) A term used in importing specifying who bears which costs. The party accepting the goods after shipping is responsible for paying for the goods, insurance on the shipment, freight, and duty.

cote Term used to describe a basic tunic in the Medieval period.

cote-hardie A short tight-fitting men's over-gown with a button front.

Cotton Council International (CCI) The export-promotion arm of the National Cotton Council of America. CCI's mission is to increase exports of U.S. cotton, cottonseed, and U.S.-manufactured cotton products through activities that affect every phase of the marketing chain, from the initial purchase of cotton fiber from the mill, or of U.S. cotton-rich yarns and fabrics, on through to the final consumer.

Cotton Incorporated The marketing arm of the U.S. cotton industry whose mission is to ensure that cotton remains the first choice among consumers for apparel and home products. This is accomplished through agricultural, fiber, and textile research, market information, and technical services, as well as advertising, public relations, fashion forecasting, and retail promotions.

Council of Fashion Designers of America (CFDA) A not-for-profit trade association of 273 of America's foremost fashion and accessory designers. Founded in 1962, the CFDA continues to advance the status of fashion designers as a branch of American art and culture, to raise its artistic and professional standards, to define a code of ethical practices of mutual benefit in public and trade regulations, and to promote appreciation of the fashion arts through leadership in quality and aesthetic discernment.

cuff links Decorative mechanisms used to close the cuffs on a French cuff shirt. They link the two sides of the cuff opening to keep them in place.

cummerbund Wide, pleated belt-like garment worn with formal wear; when worn, the pleats always face up.

cut A term used to describe the shape of a garment; most often associated with a suit or tailored outerwear.

D

Daily newspaper Local newspaper that is published on a daily basis.

dalmatica A long tunic with loose sleeves.

demographics Information developed by the study of human populations in terms of size, density, location, age, gender, race, occupation, and other statistics.

department store A retail organization that carries a wide variety of product lines, typically clothing, home furnishings, and household goods; each line is operated as a separate department managed by specialist buyers or merchandisers.

designer An individual who creates the concept of a style and, either individually or through others, implements its production.

direct mail A form of marketing that uses the post to send offers, announcements, reminders, and other information to people.

discount retailer A self-service store offering merchandise at greatly reduced prices.

domestic production A term associated with the production of apparel or other items that are made within the U.S. borders.

Doneger Group The leading source of global market trends and merchandising strategies for the retail and fashion industry. The Doneger Group has been in business for 60 years and is privately owned.

dotted tie Necktie with a dotted pattern.

double breasted A style of coat opening that is asymmetrical, overlaps itself, and has a double row of buttons.

double cuff The British term for a French cuff. See *French cuff.*

double-welt pocket Another term for besom pocket. See *besom pocket.*

doublet A form fitting button front jacket worn during the fourteenth through the seventeenth centuries.

drape A term used to describe how the garment lies against the body.

dress casual Describes a cross between casual dress and wearing a suit; dress causal takes elements from both looks and blends them to give the wearer a polished look.

drop The difference in inches between the waist and chest as measured on a suit. For example, if a men's suit is a 38 regular with a 6-inch drop, the pants sold with that suit would be a 32-inch waist.

duty A tariff or fee imposed on goods brought into a country.

E

Electronic Data Interchange (EDI) Computerized, two-way exchange of information to facilitate ordering, manufacturing, and/or distribution of goods.

English-spread collar A collar style made popular by the Duke of Kent, brother of the Duke of Windsor. The collar spread falls between a straight point and a Windsor collar.

F

Factory outlet store A retail outlet, usually manufacturer-owned, that sells company merchandise at reduced prices. The original factory outlets were attached to or housed in the factory where the merchandise was produced, and opened one or two days per week to sell excess inventory or seconds to the factory workers.

Fairchild Publications A division of Condé Nast; a leading publisher of trade, consumer magazines, books, it is considered the authority on fashion.

farthingale sleeve In menswear, the style derives from a sleeve fixed to the doublet with wire or bone.

fibulae A pin used during the ancient Greek period to hold the himation closed at the shoulder.

findings Parts of a garment other than fabric, such as buttons and zippers.

fitted cut Describes a garment cut to be close-fitting to the body.

floral tie Necktie with a floral pattern.

foulard tie Necktie with a small shapes (e.g., circles, diamonds) in a repeating pattern.

four-in-hand knot One of the most traditional knots used to tie a necktie. The name is derived from the necktie style popular with English coachmen, who held the reins of four horses; their mode of transportation was called "four in hand."

Freight on Board (FOB) A shipping term used in contracts that determines who bears the cost of the freight. Generally, it means that the person receiving the goods owns them as soon as they are loaded onto whichever means of transport has been arranged—most often a ship. Also called free on board.

French cuff A shirt cuff that folds back over itself and is held together by cuff links or studs. Also called a double cuff.

frock coat A coat worn during the eighteenth century; it was loose fitting with a turned-down collar.

full cut Describes the style of a suit; synonymous with the regular-cut suit with a 6-inch drop.

full package Describes the purchase of apparel or accessories whereby the manufacturer of record provides all the necessary components, including fabric and trims, needed to cut, make, assemble, and ship the finished products.

Furnishings A classification in menswear that includes shirts, ties, underwear, socks, pajamas, and accessories.

G

Garment Industry Development Corporation (GIDC) A not-for-profit organization established in 1984 by the City of New York, the Garment Workers' Union (now UNITE Here), and the New York Skirt & Sportswear Association to strengthen New York City's apparel industry. This is accomplished by providing business consulting, sourcing referrals, training, and technical support to New York apparel manufacturers and workers.

General Agreement on Tariffs and Trade (GATT) Multinational trade agreement whose fundamental purpose was to promote free trade and equalize trade among all countries; it has been replaced by the World Trade Organization (WTO).

gipon A tunic worn under armor during the fourteenth century; it was later adapted for civilian use.

goods A term used in the apparel and textile industry to describe products that have been, or will be, purchased.

grade An indicator of quality; increase or decrease in a single size of a pattern.

greatcoat A large overcoat typically made of wool, designed for warmth and protection against the elements.

H

half-top pocket A type of pocket found on dress pants and casual slacks that is less conservative than the two-sided pocket style.

half-Windsor knot A triangular shaped necktie knot; it uses one less wrap than the full Windsor knot.

Harmonized Tariff Schedule of the United States (HTSUS) A system for assessing tariffs on imports and exports based on the metric system.

Here & There A division of the Doneger Group that provides the industry with the most comprehensive offering of color, trend, and forecast information.

himation A long garment resembling a cloak that was joined at the shoulder by a type of pin, called a fibulae.

hosiery A traditional term for men's socks.

houpplelande A flowing gown that falls in folds from the shoulder to the ground with very wide sleeves.

I

import To bring raw or finished goods into one country (e.g., the United States) from a foreign country.

InfoMat Fashion industry search engine; with over 350,000 entries, it enables researchers to find information about fashion designers, showrooms, retailers, global manufacturers, textiles, apparel, and accessories.

inset pocket See *besom pocket*.

inspiration Something that provides a creative idea; for example, designers and others may draw inspiration from their surroundings to create products for the fashion industry.

Internet A vast public web of computer networks connecting users all around the world to each other and to a large information repository.

Internet/e-commerce Buying and selling activities supported by electronic means, primarily the Internet.

J

jacket A short outerwear garment.

jerkin Short, close-fitting jacket worn over the doublet with wide sleeves.

K

Kaledo Design Management A collection of software programs linked together to offer the fashion industry state-of-the-art computer applications in apparel and textile design.

L

Landed Duty Paid (LDP) A mechanism to purchase goods from an overseas supplier, who takes on the responsibility of shipping the merchandise and paying the duty once it arrives in the United States.

letter of credit (L/C) A financial instrument used in the purchase of merchandise that guarantees payment providing terms of the agreement are met. The letter of credit is negotiated between banks.

licensing Involves creation of a contract in which one party, the licensee, agrees to pay another party, the licensor, a royalty or fee for the use of an intellectual property, such as a name, trademark, or symbol.

line A grouping of related merchandise designed for a specific target market.

locker loop A small piece of fabric fashioned in a loop that is attached to the center back of a shirt where the yoke is joined.

M

mail order/catalog retailer Retailer that uses catalogs, mailed directly to consumers, as a means of marketing and selling products.

make Designation that indicates the number of hand-sewing operations involved in the construction of a garment.

make 1, 2, 4, 4+, 6, 6+ Various levels of make associated with men's suits; the level is determined by the number of hand-sewing operations, with 1 designating very few if any hand operations, and 6+ designating a garment that has the greatest number of hand-sewing operations.

make detail sheet A mechanism used to convey the construction details of a particular garment.

mantle An open garment similar to a cloak, sometimes with a hood attached.

marker A diagram or arrangement of the pattern pieces for styles and sizes that are to be cut.

matrix buying A system used by retailers whereby vendors are pre-approved, allowing buyers to work with the approved vendor and buy merchandise from them.

Men's Apparel Guild of California (MAGIC) An organization established in 1933; it hosts two major trade shows per year, connecting a global audience of buyers and sellers. The MAGIC show is the premier menswear show in the world, and has expanded to include women's and children's apparel and accessories. The show originated in California and is now held in Las Vegas, Nevada.

modified American cut A cross between the American full cut and the European trim cut; this style gives the comfort of the American cut and the fashionable look of the trim European cut.

Mods A term, derived from *modernist*, attributed to a subculture that originated in London in the 1950s and 1960s; it was a source of fashion inspiration during that period.

morning coat A formal coat that is usually double breasted with a high collar in the back and low in the front forming a V shape.

N

natural shoulder A very lightly padded shoulder of a coat with a rounded appearance at the shoulder-to-armhole seam. Also called a soft shoulder.

nested suit A suit coat and pant of the same fabric sold on the same hanger.

net terms Condition of sale in which a cash discount is neither offered nor permitted.

nonstore retailer Refers to selling that occurs outside traditional brick-and-mortar retail establishments (e.g., via television or the Internet).

North American Free Trade Agreement (NAFTA) An agreement between Canada, the United States, and Mexico that allows for the free flow of goods among the three countries.

notched lapel The most common collar/lapel treatment; the notch usually forms a 45-degree angle.

O

off-price retailer A retailer that buys goods at a reduced cost and offers them for sale to the consumer at a special price; an example is TJ Maxx.

on-seam pocket Type of pocket located directly on the seam of the pants.

outdoor wear Any type of outerwear garment that is worn outdoors.

overcoat A heavyweight outerwear garment sold in the tailored clothing department.

oxford cloth A soft, somewhat porous fabric usually made from cotton or cotton blends; generally used for men's shirts, either dress or casual.

P

padded shoulder On suit coats and sport coats, where extra padding is added to the shoulder area to provide shape and height to the garments.

paisley tie Necktie with a classic curved teardrop (or ameba-like) pattern.

participatory sportswear Apparel used in the performance of a particular sport, such as shorts and singlet used for running.

patch pocket Pocket sewn to the outside of a garment; resembles a patch with an open top.

pattern Two-dimensional template or guide used for cutting fabric to form a garment.

peak lapel Lapel that forms a sharp, angled point on the coat front; more often found on double-breasted models.

Petersham coat A type of greatcoat with a velvet collar, known for its form-fitting appearance; named after Lord Petersham (circa 1812).

petticoat Waist-length coat-like garment worn between the doublet and the shirt for warmth.

pick stitch A form of topstitching originally done by hand; stitches are small and placed wide apart to give an elegant look. Today the appearance of pick stitching can be created by special machines.

piece goods Fabrics/textiles that are cut and then assembled into garments.

pinned collar A straight-point collar with holes at the points into which a collar pin (small rod-like accessory) is inserted to raise the tie up to a more prominent position.

pinpoint oxford A less porous variation on the basic oxford weave, where the fabric is more tightly constructed using finer yarns; this fabric is also more expensive than the basic oxford cloth.

plackard See *placket*.

placket A finished opening edge of a garment that usually buttons. The front opening edge of a woven shirt has a placket as well as sleeve vents. On the woven shirt, this opening edge is sometimes referred to as the plackard.

plaid tie Necktie with a pattern consisting of colored bars or stripes crossing at right angles. Plaid implies a multi-colored motif.

planning analyst A position in the retail industry that has been created to assist the buyer in developing and executing buy plans. This position relies greatly on computer skills and deals with budgets and numbers; the planning analyst does not usually get involved in selection of merchandise.

pleat A fold in a garment created as a design feature.

polo coat A long dress coat traditionally made from camel hair to give it a distinctive camel color, although it is available in a variety of colors; it features a belted back, patch pockets, and a double-breasted front.

polo shirt A knit shirt with a two- or three-button placket front, and knitted collar and cuffs. It may include various features, such as hemmed cuffs on the sleeves, a long tail, split vents, and a soft collar. This style was originally created by René Lacoste as a tennis shirt.

Première Vision A fabric trade show held in Paris, France, two times per year, exhibiting textiles from European mills. It is considered one of the top shows in the world for textiles.

price zone A retail strategy of pricing merchandise to fall between set prices; prices are based on the approximate wholesale cost of the merchandise.

PrimaVision Print A computer program created by Lectra to help designers/merchandisers develop print patterns.

PrimaVision Weave A computer program created by Lectra to help designers/merchandisers develop woven patterns.

print media In the menswear business, the three key types are consumer publications, trade journals, and daily newspapers.

product developer A member of a team that (1) works from the concept stage through making the new styles ready for production, (2) develops the product after the designer and merchandiser have approved a new style for development, (3) searches the market for items to be included in a retailer's lines, usually looking to stores of higher stature to find unique items that they then can adapt for their target market.

psychographics The collection of information about consumer traits, such as personality, values, and lifestyle, with a view to understanding why consumers buy what they buy; the information is used to divide a market into groups based on these traits.

public relations (PR) Building good relations with a company's various publics by obtaining favorable publicity, building a good corporate image, and/or heading off unfavorable rumors, stories, or events. Public relations can be a form of unpaid advertising.

Q

quality control (QC) Effort applied to assure that the end product/services meet the intended requirements and achieve customer satisfaction.

quarter-top pocket Type of pocket found on men's pants that slants slightly away from the side seam; originally designed to slant one-quarter of the way across the front pant panel.

Quick Response (QR) A comprehensive business strategy incorporating time-based competition, agility, and partnering to optimize the supply and distribution systems, and to improve customer service. Originally developed as a U.S. strategy to combat imports.

quota Amount of goods that a government allows to be imported into the country. As part of the GATT Uruguay Rounds of 1995, all quotas were to be phased out in 2005.

R

radio frequency identification (RFID) Automated identification method using computer technology to track products, people, or animals by attaching a transponder and using radio waves.

reefer A single-breasted version of the British warmer.

regimental stripe tie A traditional striped necktie with bold stripes representing different British army regiments.

repp tie Necktie made of a closely woven fabric with a ribbed surface. ("Repp" is also spelled "rep," which is an old word for "rib.")

retailer Business whose sales come primarily from retailing.

retailing All activities involved in selling goods or services directly to the final consumers for their personal, non-business use.

rope shoulder Style with heavy shoulder padding, with additional material in the armhole that gives the appearance of roping, elevating the sleeve slightly higher than the shoulder-pad area.

rounded collar A dress shirt style in which the collar points are rounded off.

S

safeguard In a fashion-industry context, a limit on imports into a specific country. In the WTO articles there is a mechanism whereby a country can petition for safeguards if it feels that too many imports are flooding its market and disrupting business; this mecha-

nism is to offset the removal of quotas, which had limited amounts of products imported.

shawl collar A softly rounded lapel.

single breasted Coat style that has a single row of buttons along the center of the front opening.

skirted coat A nineteenth-century coat style with tails in the back divided by a vent and pleated tops with buttons on the hips.

slack time A term that became popular after World War II; it referred to spare or extra time when one was not working; the word *slacks* derives from this expression.

slash pocket See *besom pocket*.

sleeve garter Elastic covered in fabric used to keep men's long sleeves in place when there was only one sleeve size available.

sleeve placket See *placket*.

soft shoulder A very lightly padded shoulder of a coat; the padding gives the effect of softness. Also called a natural shoulder.

spec sheet A brief written description of a product's measurements, which are used as a guide in manufacturing of that product. Also called a specification sheet.

specialty store A retail store that carries a narrow product line with a deep assortment within that line.

spectator sportswear Men's casual apparel that is sport-related but not used as functional apparel (e.g., a sweatshirt that bears a team or college logo).

split-sleeve measurement Combined sleeve lengths in men's long-sleeve dress shirts, so that instead of stocking a style in two different sleeve lengths (e.g., 32 and 33), a retailer can stock the style with a sleeve length of 32/33. This was developed to cut down on the number of SKUs sold at retail.

sportswear A classification of men's apparel that embodies the casual aspect of the menswear business; contrary to its name, it does not represent a sports theme.

square shoulder Shoulder treatment on men's coats that creates a square shape.

stay A slim rectangular plastic or metallic insert used to keep collar points straight; usually found on dress shirts and some sport shirts.

Stock-Keeping Unit (SKU) Designation of a product at the unit level for merchandise planning or inventory control purposes; usually represents a combination of style, size, and color.

stomacher Garment added to the doublet as a front chest piece to cover the low-fronted garment.

straight-point collar The most popular of all collar styles; it uses stays to keep the points sharp.

studs Decorative closures for formal shirts; they are inserted into buttonholes on both sides of the shirt.

suited separates Suit jackets and pants of the same fabric that are designed to be worn together but merchandised separately.

super-tunic Short garment to be worn over another tunic; its sleeves end in a bell shape with turned-back cuffs.

surcote Another term for the super tunic.

swatch A small fabric sample.

synthetic fiber producers Companies that specialize in the production of man-made fibers.

T

tab collar A dress shirt collar that is held in place by small fabric tabs on the underside of the collar to keep the tie neatly in place.

tabard Sleeveless garment reaching the calves and open at the sides, fastened at the waist by clasps; forerunner to today's poncho.

Taglioni coat Comfortable greatcoat named after a celebrated Italian family of professional dancers.

tailcoat A formal evening coat with tails that start at the waist and taper toward the back of the knee and are vented. The coat is short in the front and does not button; it is the full dress coat worn for white tie occasions.

tailored clothing Men's apparel category that includes suits, sport coats, dress slacks, and tailored outerwear such as topcoats, overcoats, and trench coats.

tapered cut Describes a garment that is styled to create a slim, form-fitting appearance.

target market A set of buyers that share common needs or characteristics and that a company decides to serve.

television retailer A seller that uses television to conduct sales, for example on shopping channels such as QVC or HSN.

Tobe An international fashion retail consulting service. It is best known for the *Tobe Report*, a leading publication for retailers.

toga A garment worn in ancient Roman times; it was made up of many yards of fabric draped around the body in folds, with the left arm covered to the wrist and the right arm exposed by a short sleeve.

tolerance The stated range of acceptable measurements expressed in a plus or minus; part of the spec sheet.

topstitching Decorative stitching along the edge of various parts of menswear, such as lapels, collars, and pocket flaps.

trench coat A classic coat, first designed for British troops during World War I as a rain/topcoat; its name is derived from the trench warfare during that time.

trend services Part of the industry that focuses on gathering information about future directions of consumer behavior, color, fabrics, and fashion styles, and sharing that information with relevant industry members.

trim European cut Describes the style of a coat with trim lines and a narrow silhouette.

tuxedo A semi-formal suit with satin lapels and a satin stripe running down the side of each pant leg.

U

ulster A greatcoat with a detachable hood and button closure.

Universal Product Code (UPC) One of several bar code systems used to identify merchandise. A UPC is a 12-digit number that identifies the manufacturer and the merchandise item by stock-keeping unit (SKU).

Uruguay Rounds A series of meetings held by member countries of the General Agreement on Tariffs and Trade (GATT) to determine trade policy. During these rounds, in 1995, it was decided that all forms of quota would be phased out over a 10-year period; the 1995 round also established the World Trade Organization to replace GATT.

V

vest A sleeveless garment with a button front. Styling varies by the number of buttons and types of pockets.

video catalog A video produced to resemble a catalog offering; it can be viewed in the home for selection of merchandise, or used as an in-store marketing tool.

W

waistcoat Another term for a vest.

western-style pocket Pocket that has western details, such as a scalloped top.

white-collar worker A term used to describe a person who works in an office setting.

white tie The highest level of formality in evening dress; for men, it requires a tailcoat or full dress.

wicking properties The ability of a fabric to pull moisture away from the body and allow it to pass through the fabric and evaporate into the air.

Windsor collar A dress shirt collar with a wide point spread.

Windsor knot A large triangular knot on a necktie.

World Trade Organization (WTO) Primary body regulating world trade; it replaced the General Agreement on Tariffs and Trade (GATT) in 1995.

X

X-make Describes the make of a men's suit that has virtually no hand-sewing operations.

Z

Zoot suit Style popularized by African-Americans, Mexican-Americans, and Italian-Americans during the 1920s and 1930s. The garment was characterized by high-waisted, wide-legged, tight-cuffed pants topped with a long coat with wide lapels and wide padded shoulders.

CREDITS